Artists and Writers in Paris
The Bohemian Idea, 1803–1867

To my wife
in love and gratitude

FRONTISPIECE. Octave Tassaert (1800–1874): 'The Studio', 1845. *Louvre.*

A picture exactly contemporary with the earliest of Murger's stories of 'Bohemian' life. The red jacket of the young painter could have belonged to Chintreuil; or, in fiction, to the Marcel of *Un Envoyé de la providence*, a tale whose comic situation arises from the need to find a more respectable substitute for this garment.

Artists and Writers in Paris

The Bohemian Idea, 1803-1867

BY
MALCOLM EASTON

New York
St Martin's Press
1964

First published 1964

Library of Congress Catalog Card Number 64–24268

Printed in Great Britain by
Butler & Tanner Ltd, Frome and London

Foreword

The older studies of 'Bohemia', greatly as I am indebted to them, were histories of literature. Even modern investigators in this and related fields spare themselves only an occasional, incurious glance at the painter and sculptor: why should they do more?* It seems to me, however, that something ought to be added to redress the balance. While Bohemia is primarily a literary conception, it had—perhaps still has—considerable influence upon the artist. What part did he play in the evolution of the Bohemian Idea?

Since the global extravagance had hardly begun when my own inquiry ends, I have been able to keep within narrow geographical limits, confining myself indeed to Paris. A comprehensive survey of Bohemia would have taken us to America, where Whistler discovered the *Scènes de la Bohème* in 1854, and to George Du Maurier's home in Hampstead, where the Never-Never-Land of *Trilby* was actually invoked forty years later. Of 'tourist' Bohemia nothing will be found here. The topic (not to me a particularly attractive one) would require at least a volume to itself. I ought to add: the terminal points printed in the sub-title represent the publication-dates of Charles Nodier's *Peintre de Salzbourg* and Edmond and Jules de Goncourt's *Manette Salomon*, works which set convenient bounds in time to Bohemia's initial phase.

*

My debts are many. In the first place, I could have done nothing without the generous help of Professor G. T. Clapton, who supervised my doctoral thesis submitted to the University of Leeds some years ago. For a long period, Professor E. H. Gombrich

* Two recent works, both useful in their presentation of the literary aspect, are Robert Baldick's *The First Bohemian. The Life of Henry Murger*, 1961, and Maurice Z. Shroder's *Icarus; the Image of the Artist in French Romanticism*, 1962.

has watched over my struggles: I am lucky to have had his wise counsel and wish the result did him greater credit. I was able to profit, also at an earlier stage, from some detailed criticisms made by Professors H. J. Hunt and Jean Seznec. Professor Stephen Ullmann was good enough to assist in elucidating the word 'bohème'. An old and candid friend, the late Gerard Hopkins, urged me to make drastic alterations to this original version: now that they have been carried out, I see how wise his insistence was. I am indebted to the French Government for having made possible an extension of my travels on one occasion.

Lately, I have had the good fortune to be able to call upon Professor Donald Charlton for advice. He brought a number of errors to light and suggested improvements which I was very glad to put into effect: I should like to take this opportunity of saying how much his encouragement has meant to me. Finally, I wish to thank Mrs Kay Austin for her admirable typing of the manuscript; and the staffs of two university libraries, those of Leeds and Hull, for their willing help at every stage.

M. E.

Hull, 1964.

Contents

List of Plates

Introduction

i

The Revolution in France profoundly changed the life of her artists. From tranquil insignificance, it raised them to uneasy glory, bringing them at the same time into the world of the writer. Yet this does not mean that all pre-Revolutionary painters and sculptors accepted their humble rating without protest—nor that all literary men scorned or ignored them. Watteau, whom the Goncourts were to regard as the prototype of the temperamental practitioner of their own day, the first *modern artist* 'disinterestedly idealistic' and 'careless of the morrow', won the warm affection of critics and connoisseurs alike.

Later in the century, a close friendship sprang up between Falconet and Diderot. The sculptor of the equestrian monument to Peter the Great was quite aware of the respect due to his talent; while Diderot never tired of analysing the mysteries of artistic creation. All the same, as Falconet himself admitted, Diderot must be looked on as exceptional. It was almost unheard of for a writer to seek out the artist, consult his opinions in the picture-gallery, and learn by watching him at work. And the truth is, even the enlightened Diderot could not help regarding Falconet as his inferior. A document exists in which he describes how, in Falconet's presence, he inspected the celebrated monument just alluded to.[1] Despite the sculptor's anxiety, it pleased Diderot to reserve judgment for three hours. When at last he condescended to praise the work, the joy and relief of his friend made him chuckle. Roslin, a painter and an acknowledged authority, had all the while been available to give his opinion; why then, mischievously asks Diderot, did Falconet, expostulating at 'three cruel hours of delay', await a mere layman's verdict with such apprehension? The questioner supplies his own answer. Falconet valued Diderot's opinion above that of a fellow-artist, however gifted, because, in order to grasp the significance of the composition as a whole and recognize its 'côté poétique', it was necessary to possess the superior understanding of the literary man.

In the earlier eighteenth century, the artist's position fell sadly short of all that had been urged on his behalf in the sixteenth and seventeenth. Societies existed for his improvement—the Academy proper, for instance, and the Academy of St Luke—and benevolent persons wished to see him make the best use of his time and talents. Such persons often put their views in writing; but, when they did so, it was with a discouragingly protective or pedagogic air. Till the Revolution set him free, the artist filled a place somewhere between the upper-domestic, and lower-civil, servant, and in his apprenticeship suffered worse indignities, of course, than well-meant advice from *amateurs*. For years after his arrival in Paris he might still be potboiling for the Pont Notre-Dame emporium or at the Cars's engraving-shop, where it was not unusual for him to sleep on the premises. His world was a narrow one, his education strictly technical. And he had to be uncommonly lucky, as well as uncommonly clever, to achieve independence or attract a clientèle of his own. Sometimes, it is true, the unexpected happened and he did succeed in catching the eye of a rich man. Then his future was to some degree assured. But whoever his patron, whatever the rewards of his skill, a ready servility was still expected of him. In 1767, the painter Doyen made a name for himself with a sacred picture called the 'Miracle of the Fire-Stricken'. Critics compared him with Rubens, and he was discussed at length by Diderot in the *Salon* for that year. Not long afterwards, Doyen received a request from a gentleman attached to the Court: would he turn his talents to a subject less elevated? And the painter was presented with the programme for the 'Swing', a commission he indignantly refused—leaving it to Fragonard, whose wholly delightful piece of naughtiness is now in the Wallace Collection.[2]

Perhaps the courtier was not altogether to blame for what he had assumed. Those artists at the very top of their profession, and welcomed, therefore, to Mme Geoffrin's dinners, showed little sign of delicacy. Marmontel says: 'I had no difficulty in perceiving that, despite some natural wit, almost all of them lacked education and taste.' Carle van Loo and Joseph Vernet were thorough-going vulgarians; Soufflot was deplorably narrow-minded, Lemoine a mere lout; Boucher's conversation echoed that of the sluts who posed for him; La Tour bored one to death with his pretensions.[3] And Diderot himself, in spite of his affection for Falconet, held that sculptors came into a special category of surliness: 'If you happen to meet a sculptor who is polite, gentle, well-mannered, and modest, you can say he is, and always will be, *second-rate*.' [4]

This 'smell of the shop' was very natural at a time when art throve as a trade. Most painters and engravers expected to keep their business in the family. Cochin, a distinguished and important person in the art world of his day, tells us that it would be folly to take on a wife who could not make herself useful about the studio.

The Goncourts, by emphasizing their pleasure in the graceful school, the Bouchers, La Tours, and Fragonards, tend to give the impression that, for a whole century, the 'Joli' triumphed over the 'Beau'. But painters dependent on the Court and the whims of the pleasure-loving rich were in a minority. For nine artists out of ten, recognition by the Academy was the goal to aim at. Founded in 1648, this powerful organization was controlled by successive Directors-General of the Royal Buildings. In spite of frequent financial crises, it had many rewards to offer: commissions, pensions, grace-and-favour studios and accommodation, as well as several Chairs and Directorships. While a few gifted painters were monopolized by the Pompadour and her successors, the Academy impressed upon the great majority the importance of being serious; and it was within this organization that the artist came into contact with the *littérateur*.

A joint campaign to improve the status of the artist led Lenormant de Tournehem, Director-General in 1745, and Charles Coypel, First Painter to the King from 1746, to revive the official lecture-programme. Here was an opportunity for the class of 'free associates' to play a significant part in Academy affairs. Coypel, a ready collaborator, welcomed this opportunity to 'fraternize with select persons who, emulating the example of M. le comte de Caylus, will let us take part in their profound and learned debates and be ever ready to support us in our academic tasks. To give the public a true and noble idea of the Arts we profess, what fitter method could one conceive than to bring these

Arts into the closest possible contact with erudition, refined taste, and the philosophic spirit?' [5]

His 'select persons' were not only ready to assist the artist on points of historical accuracy, they were determined to alter the whole moral tone of his work. From the closing years of the previous century up till about 1750, the French artist had sought to please rather than to edify, but the Academy now urged him to become conscious of a mission in life. Joined together to forward this purpose were a number of busy publicists and critics of art: J.-P. Mariette, Watelet, the Abbé Leblanc, Estève, etc. As literary men, they made no bones about their preference for history-painting; and in this they had the support of the *encyclopédistes* outside the Academy, particularly of Diderot, who often reminded artists of the need to follow Poussin and Le Sueur. From bedroom allegories and quasi-domestic service, the painter was dragged into the library and lecture-theatre. At first it required the united efforts of Directors-General, free associates, and those who ran the Academies in Paris and Rome to keep him there. Certain artists resisted or were too old to change. Against these the critic waged ceaseless war, as Diderot never missed an opportunity of attacking Boucher. But it cannot be denied that, on the whole, the social advantages of this 'moral rehabilitation' outweighed its annoyances: it gave to what was still essentially a trade something of the solemnity required of a profession, and to the Academician who minded his ps and qs a new aura of respectability.

As the century neared its close, reports of J. J. Winckelmann's activities in Rome were constantly circulating in France, and in 1781 appeared the first French translation of his *History of Ancient Art*. In this famous work, the author spoke of the high esteem which painters and sculptors had enjoyed in Antiquity: 'The fame and fortune of an artist did not [in Greece] depend upon the whims of proud or ignorant patrons. Works of art, far from reflecting the mean taste and narrow mind of one man set up as judge by slaves and sycophants, were appreciated and rewarded by the cream of the nation's intelligentsia in the general assemblies of their country.' [6]

But these claims for a complete readjustment of the artist's standing were not satisfied all at once. Referring to a landscape by Joseph Vernet, Diderot might say, in lighthearted vein, 'The painter has humiliated the philosopher',[7] but the generally schoolmasterish attitude of the writer to the artist remained unchanged.

The truth is that the ambitious machine-pictures which the Director of the Buildings and the free associates encouraged the artist to produce—whether inspired by Poussin or by a later revival of interest in the Greeks and Romans—increased the artist's standing at the cost of stifling his powers of self-expression. The paintings of those who enjoyed continuous private patronage often appear trivial, yet delight us by remaining personal: and in the eighteenth century, indeed, only the rarest conjunction of fashion and good fortune permitted that.

How little the artist was disposed to dramatize himself may be seen in the portraits and self-portraits of the period. With few exceptions, these are content to draw attention to the *métier* or emphasize the sitter's respectability. Backed by a cast or two, surrounded by the tools of his trade, he puts forward no claim to individual distinction. Thus do Coypel, Largillierre, and Boucher introduce themselves to us. Only La Tour, with his impudent smile, and Liotard, in a Turkish costume, thrust their personalities beyond the frame.[8] A certain *débraillé* may be observed, but it is that of the artisan: a loose neckerchief, or bands buttoned into the waistcoat to prevent their becoming soiled. Clothes and wigs are usually as conventional as the wearers' expressions. Like the writer and musician, the artist sometimes dons a gown rich in pattern and texture, but this was the customary fatigue-dress of the man who worked at home; and in one of his two self-portraits in the Louvre, Chardin does not scruple to show us eyeshade, mob-cap, and spectacles. Examples like this abound to prove what an ordinary fellow the eighteenth-century artist was held, and held himself, to be. The new character of the self-portraits of the turn of the century is therefore all the more striking: the ill-boding one of Girodet as an Italian bandit, at Grenoble, for instance, or of the eighteen-year-old Rude, in a mass of Byronic curls and a poet's collar carelessly joined by a flowing ribbon, at Dijon.

We might perhaps have met with such self-consciousness earlier, had a real intimacy existed between writer and artist before the Revolution; a real intimacy (and this is most important) *at a formative stage in the lives of both*. It is common to use the term 'bohème' when referring to the period of Diderot's obscurity, echoes of which recur throughout the dialogue of the *Neveu de Rameau.* Yet among the young poets, actors, musicians, and pamphleteers of this Bohemia there is no mention of a painter or a sculptor. We can only presume that, for the artist still a practical tradesman with his nose to the grindstone—philandering at the Café de la Régence was a luxury he simply could not allow himself.

And what had been true of the fourth decade of the century remained true of its last years. In the picaresque tales of Restif de la Bretonne, published between 1767 and 1802, references to artists are scanty and unimportant. Only in passing does the author mention the stipend of a male model or the presence of an artists' colony in the Rue des Poulies. But there were no artists to compete for the attentions of Edmée and Reine Girard, *grisettes*, or of Zéphire, prostitute. In Nougaret's house in the Rue de la Harpe, the pains and pleasures of debauch were reserved for penniless writers and students from the School of Medicine.

It was when he had achieved success at Court, or high office in the Academy, that the artist met his literary colleagues on something like equal terms. But even at the parties of Mme Geoffrin and M. de la Popelinière the relationship must have been a little uneasy. For the literary man who undertook Salon-criticism was beginning to enjoy the power which this activity brought with it. Some artists, like Cochin and Falconet, themselves took to writing about art in order to hold their own against a flood of intruders from the world of letters.[9] The greatest number, however, accepted the writer's domination, if only for fear of the harm that any other attitude might do them.

Thus, at some sacrifice of his independence as a craftsman, the artist had achieved respectability. When the Revolution finally severed his ancient bonds of servitude, the time was ripe for the complete parity of esteem which Winckelmann had demanded and Quatremère de Quincy urged with redoubled zeal; and there appeared, in the painter Jacques-Louis David, just the stern, ambitious reformer necessary. But of course we cannot expect to find the temper of the nineteenth-century artist in those who sat on Revolutionary tribunals—in an actual Topino-Lebrun, or an imaginary Évariste Gamelin.[10] For by the time that temper came into being, the artist was no longer an active politician burning to make his art, and himself, of service to the Party.

We must move forward to the Directory, when David had retired from the political arena. His victory over the Academy was short-lived. In a few years, his own reputation would be as odious as that of the reactionaries against whom he had led the revolt. From the clash, however, and the triumph—so slight, when measured in time—there emerges an artist who has thrown off the flunkey's coat. It is exchanged for nobler liveries: first, the sash and plumes of the *conventionnel*, then the military splendour of the war-artist. And when these rôles have passed from the repertory (to glance for a moment into the future), the artist invents his own uniform, neat and formal for the Classicist, carelessly distinctive for the Romantic; but both designed to stress that condition of independence which, whether a matter of comfort or discomfort, would never again be seriously disputed.

Meanwhile, under the Directory, David's pupils, neglected during their master's term of imprisonment, welcomed him back to his teaching-studio in the Louvre.

I

The Meditator

i

Initiated under the Monarchy, the granting of free accommodation to certain privileged artists continued uninterrupted by the Revolution. David benefited under both régimes, first as artist, then as artist and teacher, retaining studios in the Louvre even during a period of imprisonment, from which the amnesty of 1795 finally set him free.

In the following year, Étienne Delécluze, our sole authority at first hand on these matters, began his studies under Charles Moreau and found himself a neighbour of David's pupils.[1] He gives us a picture of the shabby cantonment of the artists in the 'Old Louvre'. David's quarters consisted of his own personal studio; another, lent by him to Moreau; and a third, devoted to the instruction of between twenty and thirty students. Latrines, improvised in the Colonnade near by, contaminated the air of this otherwise rather lordly domain, as squalor so often clipped the wings of grandeur for the artist under the Directory. This was the period when Prud'hon drew vignettes for commercial brochures, and when many of those recently hailed as the 'most ardent supporters of a system which gives man back his dignity' faced actual starvation. Waiting impotently for the manufacture in Antwerp of the canvas destined for the 'Sabine Women', David spent the greater part of his time with the students; occasionally, no doubt, glancing up above the classic lamps and curule-chairs (designed for him by Jacob) at a once-applauded 'Brutus' or a now-forgotten 'Oath of the Horatii', pictures which must have been bitter reminders of past triumph and present eclipse.

On the surface, the events of the 9th Thermidor—when Robespierre fell, and David, a fervent admirer, barely escaped with his head—had done little damage to the artist's professional reputation: 'As for David's talent,' M.-J. Chénier had reminded those who were to pronounce sentence, 'no one will dispute *that*';[2] and there was no reason why persistent attempts on the part of the Academy and Museum cliques to belittle him should succeed. Above all, in spite of every kind of interference from the same quarter, he was still the most highly-regarded teacher of his day.

The man himself was not the savage that political enemies liked to pretend. Delécluze, who had watched him briskly marshalling the pageant of June 8th, 1794, and later, ashen-faced, protesting his innocence before the Convention, saw nothing that suggested the Jacobin now beyond a certain sternness of demeanour and the little cockade sewn to his hat. David, in fact, was tolerant of his students' politics, of whatever colour, and they in turn respected his. An observer could wonder at the tactful behaviour on both sides, when it fell to the master's lot to instruct young Mme de Noailles, whose father, M. de Laborde, had been executed during David's term of office on the Committee of Public Safety.

From the day of his release till the arrival of the canvas for the 'Sabine Women', itself a symbol of peace and reconciliation—for six months, in effect—painter and pupils lived together on equal terms. Every Monday, they drew lots for places round the model, and when the common purse would not run to the expense of a professional, a volunteer would step on to the throne instead. At the end of the week, a vote was taken to decide whose had been the most successful study—a vote that, on one occasion certainly, went against the great man himself. And, on Sunday, David always entertained the students at his own house, or joined them on picnic-parties. The intimate relationship thus established was further strengthened by his outspoken contempt for the newly-reconstituted Academy schools. David's pupils were taught to consider themselves vastly superior to the official recruits, and were encouraged to cultivate a neatness and cleanliness which really did distinguish them physically from the common herd. This was his way of insisting on the new dignity of the profession as he saw it, and the story, Romantic in origin no doubt, that he exercised a brutal tyranny over his students is quite apocryphal.

In any case, these pupils of his would have been no mere

cyphers: brought up amidst the play of violent and contradictory opinion, they were hardly likely to give unquestioning allegiance to any superior. David, as they very well knew (he never ceased to remind them of it), was an unrepentant enemy of 'systems' himself. Mature students and beginners alike must have been always ready to be tempted away from the path laid down for them; and his sarcastic warnings against the style of Girodet—'here we just teach painting!'—show that David, too, recognized the danger.[3] But, by demanding a higher standard of education in his pupils, he had unwittingly encouraged heresy. The more intelligent the student, the greater would be his impatience with the drudgery inevitable even in the most enlightened apprenticeship to art. And this is without taking into account the literary revolution which had occurred since Virgil and Tacitus were dinned into the heads of students at the École royale and Cochin, its Secretary and Historiographer, recited to an Academy audience, drowsy but resigned, the first thirteen books of the *Iliad*. Literary influences which would play a major part in disrupting discipline during the Romantic period were already in covert existence in David's studio in the Louvre.

ii

We don't know just when or how the rebellion in this studio actually broke out, but its instigator, Maurice Quaï, had begun to air his theories by the year 1797.

Seen in the perspective of history, this young man amounts to little more than a firebrand; yet he would not have been able to attract the attention of his fellow-students by word of mouth alone. Was he perhaps a better artist than the solitary surviving example of his skill, a portrait at Aix, suggests? He certainly had a mind of his own, and was not afraid to voice an unpopular opinion. On one occasion, we are told, he interrupted some criticism of the Bible by announcing: 'You can take it from me, the Gospel is even finer than Homer or Ossian!' [4] a remark which conveniently summarizes his belief that art could prosper only if its practitioners set about returning to the most ancient—or *primitive*—sources of inspiration. In Ossian they would find a poetry uncorrupted (!) by civilization; in Homer, heroic subject-matter at its purest; but in the New Testament, something that included both and was more splendid than either: a complete pattern of the primitive *way of life*.

What, then, was the substance of his disagreement with David? That the old *montagnard* had betrayed the cause of art by frittering away his energies on politics. The arduous task of reform remained unaccomplished. Insipidity and the Rococo still ruled French painting. David himself might suppose he had introduced the 'masculine style', but to Quaï it reeked of a general effeminacy. Nor had he any confidence in David as a teacher. What hope was there for a school which still displayed casts in the worst Graeco-Roman manner? One day these bogus masterpieces would have to be consigned to the scrapheap.

'And let there be no mistake about it,' he declared: '*that day is coming*!' [5]

Back to the purer forms of the fifth century B.C., back to Phidias, back—at least—to the Quattrocento! To hasten the arrival of this millennium, Quaï and his friend Perrier strolled through the streets of Paris dressed as Homeric chieftains. And when they had done so, Quaï himself continued to wear the long hair and beard he had grown specially for the occasion.

Every art school has its *enfants terribles*, who raise a smile or two and are thereafter paid little attention. Yet we know that Maurice Quaï was very generally liked and respected—and that now he displayed a gift for persuasion. Even the older students found themselves admitting that there was logic in this extension of David's oft-reiterated 'Emulate the Greeks!'; while among the class of juniors, beginners like Colson, Duqueylar, Pierre and Joseph Franque, there was wild enthusiasm. The movement did not, as might have been expected, turn out to be a mere passing infatuation. On the contrary, this little escapade of 1797 broke the bounds of its nursery, and we find Primitivism, or Etruscanism, as it was sometimes called, arousing disquiet in official reports as late as 1813.[6] In time, the movement became respectable, and boasted pamphleteers like Artaud, Keeper of the Musée at Lyons, and Paillot de Montabert, whose treatise on painting dates from 1799. Broc, Granger, and Heim, artists distinguished in their day, modelled their style not only on the Periclean Greeks, but cultivated also—as Quaï had advised—the Italian painters before Raphael; and we are not likely to forget this 'pre-Raphaelite' phase, since its master-works survive in exquisite early portraits by Ingres.

There are no details of any immediate stand taken by David against Quaï and his growing body of supporters, the *Primitives*, as they were now called. At this time, probably, their master's thoughts were all upon his painting, and when the 'Sabine Women' was at last completed and received its ovation, it would have been strange indeed if so pleasant a return to favour had not led him to temper justice with mercy. All the same, we know that Pierre Franque got his marching-orders (but still, presumably, retained his *lodging* in the Louvre)—and no sooner do we learn this than the same informant speaks of another sect's coming into being.[7] Between the new group, called the Meditators, and the earlier one some differences are said to have existed: unlike the Primitives, the Meditators were a wild lot who disgraced themselves by adopting a 'tenue cynique' and terrorizing women-visitors in the dark corridors of the Louvre. At this, David is supposed to have taken drastic action, yet the biographer's phrase, 'mass dismissal', is not particularly illuminating, for we do not know who, or how many, were involved. What is clear is that, despite the distinction between Primitives and Meditators just noted, the same names crop up in the leadership of both: Maurice Quaï, Perrier, Pierre and Joseph Franque.

It was through a friend of Lucile Franque (the wife of Pierre) that Charles Nodier, a young writer from her own Franche-Comté, appeared on the scene. His brief lifetime had been spent in almost continuous skirmishing against authority. Like the Franque twins (solemnly entrusted to David's care by order of the Convention), he had first attracted notice as an infant prodigy, and was commissioned to hymn the Revolution's martyrs while a boy at school. Though no artist, this veteran 'clubiste' was an obvious candidate for admission to the secret councils of the Meditators.

Once elected to the society, he attended its meetings with fervour, both in the entresol above Moreau's studio and in a deserted monastery at Passy, where he and his companions squatted in a circle, smoking Oriental tobacco and listening to readings from *Ecclesiastes* and the *Apocalypse*, or to the improvisations of Quaï.[8] The ultra-Classicist revolt already showed a Romantic, 'Gothick' character. Its devotees had been encouraged by David himself to disregard the narrow limits imposed by any lingering conception of art as a 'trade', and urged instead to cultivate their minds and interpret the mood of the moment. Here was the result. In place of the time-honoured studio thesaurus, a Rollin's *Ancient History* or a Ribadeneira's *Flower of the Saints*, they carried very different aids to inspiration, works of an exotic or 'foreign' flavour, such as would help them navigate the new and bewildering cross-currents of the world they lived in.

Of these works, one was more potent than all the rest put together.

iii

In the *Proscrits*, a story of 1802, Nodier describes the library of Franz: first, in order of importance, came the Bible; then Klopstock's *Messiah*; then the works of Montaigne, Shakespeare, Richardson, Rousseau, and Sterne. But these were by way of preliminaries—the decisive book had yet to come: 'Franz gently pressed my hand, glanced at me mysteriously, and took from its shelf an ebony box, which he opened with caution, drawing out a volume wrapped in crape. "Another friend", he said, passing it to me. It was *Werther*.' [9]

Goethe's *Die Leiden des jungen Werthers*, first translated into French nearly thirty years earlier, was still the most effective agent of German Romanticism west of the Rhine. These *sorrows of young Werther* owed much, of course, to a strain of melancholy in English, and earlier French, literature of the eighteenth century, and the *Peintre de Salzbourg*, the story Nodier published in 1803, reveals his debts to both. But the author, who was given to apostrophizing his 'divine' Klopstock, was above all Germanophil. His friend Weiss had no difficulty in deciding that the principal character of the *Dernier Chapitre de mon roman* must be Nodier himself, since he wore the blue coat and yellow waistcoat of Werther. As we read in a late preface to the *Peintre de Salzbourg*: 'My hero is twenty; he is a painter; he is a poet; he is GERMAN. He is precisely how I saw myself at that age. . . .' [10]

It is true, then, that in Charles Munster, painter of Salzburg, Werther is created over again. Werther was no monopoly of Nodier's, however, but equally the hero of those young artists I have just been discussing. Delécluze tells us of a tragedy that took place in 1804, when a member of the sect of the *Meditators* threw himself to his death from one of the towers of Notre-Dame, 'as a result of some private unhappiness and a *too uncritical admiration of Werther*'.[11]

And how fitting a model was Werther for an artist secessionist: Goethe's hero himself painted—and turned his back on the letter of instruction! In one of those reveries he shared with the Meditator, Werther early laid it down that:

Only the treasures of Nature are inexhaustible, and only she forms the great artist. It is possible to make out a strong case for rules that can provide foolproof arguments in favour of bourgeois society. A man who models himself on them will never create anything cheap and shoddy, just as a stickler for etiquette will never grow into an unendurable neighbour or an out-and-out blackguard. *Yet, all the same, and say what you like, without exception rules destroy a true understanding of Nature and its true expression.*[12]

Werther echoes here a dislike of academic training that was already a powerful conviction in Germany, as the explosive correspondence between Carstens and Heinitz and the picturesque outbursts of Heinse, Friedrich, and Kleist make abundantly plain. But he might be questioning the discipline of any teaching-studio, David's, for example, just as pertinently. With Werther, in fact, a new kind of artist emerges from the literary chrysalis—one who will walk by himself, interpreting his melancholy as genius and seeing in suicide the inevitable (and glorious) solution to all his problems.

Though Nodier had no need to be introduced to Goethe by his friends in Paris, they may well have influenced him in his decision to imitate Goethe's choice of an artist as hero. Quaï, Nodier's dearest friend and leader of the group, was a painter; Lucile, for whom the young author felt a deep admiration, also painted. Thus, though the *Peintre de Salzbourg* follows Goethe's conception of the artist-dreamer very closely, it adds something too; for, stimulated by the ideas of this particular group of youthful artists in Paris, Nodier's book helped to scatter the seeds of Romanticism in soil where the stern ideals of David alone seemed capable of flourishing.

Once more, the hero is a *proscrit*, a political refugee.[13] With much still of Werther, he combines the religiosity of the Meditators themselves, a Rousseau-istic pietism, it must be admitted, pretty generally in vogue at that epoch. Dogged by misfortune, Charles Munster has staked everything on the love of his gentle Eulalie; but by the time the story begins she has already rejected him. The painter revisits a ruined monastery, once the scene of their courtship, to steep himself in its melancholy associations. He has quite lost the power to create. His old ideas have a habit of swelling into monstrosities or dwindling away to nothing: he is aware of one picture only—Eulalie's, and while this obsesses him he can never paint another.

A chance meeting with the girl herself, in the monk's burial-ground, confirms his worst fears: for the last time, Eulalie refuses to alter her decision to marry his rival. Munster knows now that death alone can end his misery. Sometimes he seeks consolation in the 'naïve story' of Ruth or the *Song of Solomon*; sometimes he listens to the wind echoing, it seems, the lamentations of Daniel and Jeremiah through the desolate arches of a Gothic ruin. He finds a last satisfaction in helping a friend, Guillaume, whose hopes have been similarly blighted, to enter a religious order; and the conclusion of the tale is 'written by another hand'.

Though his rival conveniently dies and, before he does so, expresses a wish that the lovers be reunited, Eulalie takes the veil and Charles Munster prepares to join Guillaume in the monastery at Donnawert. Nodier gives a picture of the artist on this fateful journey, a picture which might be a portrait of Maurice Quaï himself at some inspired moment, his hair untended, his beard long, and wearing, instead of the conventional dress of the day, a 'sort of coarse tunic'. Then the threatening skies break and the waters of the Danube flood the surrounding countryside. When Guillaume is able to venture out in search of Charles, he finds a corpse; and this, since his fellow-monks suspect suicide, he is forced to bury with his own hands.

An essay entitled the *Méditations du cloître*, published with, and forming an epilogue to, the *Peintre de Salzbourg*, strikes more directly at those features of the age to which the Meditators took particular exception. In it, one seems to catch the accents, aggrieved and angry, of the whole group of young rebels.

Nodier bewails the sad fate of his generation: victims of crisis after crisis, they have tasted blood from the cradle. Now a dictatorial government seeks to clap fetters on them. The blindness of Authority! Can it not understand that these young people, deprived of all initiative, weary and cynical before their time, will still discover an outlet for their energies—in violence? They have already done so! 'In bitterness and horror,' he continues, 'I say that, at this very moment, we are being decimated by the pistol of Werther and the executioner's axe!', and he concludes on a note of despair: 'CETTE GÉNÉRATION SE LÈVE ET VOUS DEMANDE DES CLOÎTRES!' [14]

iv

The *Peintre de Salzbourg* had ended with the line: 'Eulalie exists; she is now eighteen years old.' But when Nodier arrived back in Paris from Besançon, early in 1803, with the story to dispose of, there was no Lucile Franque to greet him. At twenty-two, she had died suddenly of consumption. This tragedy and a serious brush with the police seem to have decided him to patch up his quarrel with the régime. An apology for his *Napoléone*, under the title of *Prophétie contre Albion*, soon appeared in print, and on the strength of it, Lefebvre secured him a pardon from Bonaparte. The young man was allowed to return to Besançon, where he remained under good-natured surveillance.

His next publication, the *Essais d'un jeune barde* of 1804, has therefore no political message. Its short pieces—translations, adaptations, 'imitations'—follow each other incoherently like pictures in a scrapbook. Though its dedication is not without significance (Nodier addresses his work to Nicolas Bonneville, whom Sainte-Beuve was later to regard as first instigator of the 'proud and starveling clamour of neglected genius'), the real interest of this little book lies in a curious obituary notice on Maurice Quaï and Lucile Franque: for, shortly before the *Essais*' appearance, Quaï, barely three years older than Lucile, had died as suddenly of the same disease.

Nodier tells us of his ambition to offer 'THEM' a really splendid monument; and if, for the moment at any rate, he can do no more than compose this brief memoir, at least it will serve to record his close association with the two young people, and make the world realize how proud they have made him feel.

Maurice Quaï, he would have it known, was a man who,

'beneath the form of Antinous and Hercules, concealed the soul of Moses, Homer, and Pythagoras, and combined the courage of the strong with the simplicity of the child, the wisdom of the sages with the enthusiasm of the poets. About the head of this personage, whose beauty was indefinable, unchanging, and eternal, like that of the gods, who combined in his lofty character something of the Almighty, of Raphael, and of the Jupiter of Myron,* might play at any moment, it seemed, the lightning of Olympus and Sinai', etc., etc.[15]

Lucile, too, comes in for a similarly high-flown, if shorter, citation: had she wished, she could have been the 'Michelangelo of poetry or the Ossian of painting';[16] and the author laid down his pen only when he had exhausted the superlatives of admiration and regret.

It is impossible to think of an eighteenth-century author—even allowing for the exuberance of youth—speaking of his artist-friends as Nodier here speaks of Maurice Quaï and Lucile Franque. One may, I believe, see in this rather more than an extravagant personal statement. The artist's social equality with writers being established, what follows now is a general heightening of interest on the part of his new comrades in the character of the artist *as a man.* The magic of a work of art is transferred to its creator, whose 'spirit-resonance' (as the Chinese called it, centuries before) can be limited no longer to the four walls of the exhibition-room or the dealer's shop. An artisan-painter of the eighteenth century owed any reputation he acquired to performance: Charles Munster, *who produces not a single sketch*, bases his claim to be accepted as an artist of genius on sensibility alone. Herein lay the danger of 'Meditation', of dreaming instead of doing, as Delécluze, a trifle wise after the event, did not forget to point out: such a cult might very well end in a total paralysis of the creative function, and render the artist a burden to himself and society. This cult, furthermore, was likely to expand with a growing comradeship between artists and writers, particularly when both were immature and always on the point of being carried away by their enthusiasm.

But to return to Nodier: the obituary notices on Quaï and Lucile seem to have been his farewell to this kind of frenzied aesthetics. From about 1804, having abandoned the political

* There is no Jupiter of Myron!

scene, he found his enthusiasm for Ossian and Werther cooling. In 1808 (now married to Lucile's half-sister), he was drawn into another kind of society, of which his celebrated salon at the Arsenal—the 'vraie boutique romantique'—became the centre. At the same time, the drums of war rolling louder and louder, many of David's former students must have been rudely awakened from their *meditations* to be pressed into the Emperor's propaganda service, when not into the Army itself.

Though he had a private infatuation for the vaporous warriors of Macpherson, in public Napoleon preferred to bask in the reflected glory of Alexander and Augustus, praising the Classical style, among other things, for the healthy discipline it imposed on students: 'The heads of our young men must be doused in the Greeks and Romans', he said on one occasion.[17] In fact, battle-pieces and ceremonial subjects, in flavour anything but Classical, enjoyed undisputed vogue. David, titular First Painter, who (in spite of Quaï's protests to the contrary) had always striven to reproduce the austerer ideals of ancient sculpture, was more often twiddling his thumbs than carrying out the ambitious projects he constantly put up to his master. The Emperor would scold the Institut for denigrating this artist's work, then himself forget David's existence for months together. David nevertheless worshipped Napoleon and, when this second idol of his disappeared finally from the scene, he preferred exile in Brussels to any truce with the Bourbons.

For the moment, then, it seemed that Nodier had justly inveighed against a government which turned out to have so little regard for art. French painting, its more embittered critics would assert, had been reduced to a school of epaulettes and top-boots!

The last glimpse we have of Maurice Quaï's successors in Meditation belongs to 1808. In that year, another pupil of David, a young man called Monrose, decided to grow his hair and beard. Prevented by lack of funds from adopting Greek dress, he made up for it by inviting his friends to picnic naked in the Bois de Boulogne. The company recited Ossian to the music of a guitar and, feeling cold as night approached, set light to a tree. The flames were seen by keepers, who called the police; and the youths regained their freedom only after giving solemn assurances that for the future they would dress, shave, and cut their hair like ordinary, decent citizens.[18]

Yet, in spite of the dissolution of the Quaï-Nodier group and of this painful little comedy to remind us of it, something remarkable had happened. For the first time, the drab ranks of artists *in statu pupillari* were broken by the flamboyant rebel with flowing locks and beard who, in slightly different garb, still haunts us to-day. Were it not for our knowledge (slight as it is) of this Primitive or Meditator, we might make the mistake of supposing that the picturesque artist of the 1830's sprang fully equipped from Dandyism. As with these initial antics, so always, I believe, admiration for a particular school of the past did more than mere fashion to determine the artist's style of dress. Thus we can trace the famous beret to self-portraits by Rembrandt and Gerard Dou; and the cut of waistcoat and frockcoat, at times, to a vogue for certain enigmatic sitters from the studio of Titian.

All future rebels of the art world—and how many there would be!—owe something, therefore, to the Meditator, whose epitaph is less well rendered in the *Essais d'un jeune barde* than in the *Peintre de Salzbourg* itself:

> Sa jeunesse fut rapide;
> Le feu qui l'animait n'a brillé qu'un moment,
> Et voici que l'onde avide
> Roule sur son monument. . . .*

* 'His youth passed swiftly to its close; the vital spark burned for a moment only, and, behold, the hungry wave rolls over his monument.'

II

Balzac's Artists

i

The Empire may have degraded art, but it raised the artist himself to a position more splendid than he had ever known before—the new rich and the newly ennobled having no grounds on which to disdain the parvenus of painting and sculpture.

In the houses of Hainguerlot, the banker, and Séguin, the contractor, and in many others, the artist was received with open arms. And this hospitality could often be returned in surroundings as luxurious. From the Consulate onwards, studios began to be elegantly furnished, hung with tapestries and trophies, or, like Isabey's, decorated throughout by Percier and Fontaine, the fashionable masters in that field. Artists entertained men and women of the highest rank: Gros, the élite of the Army; Gérard and Isabey, the leaders of civil Society. Very soon they acquired the habits of the new aristocracy with whom they mixed, and displayed a passion for sport and horsemanship, affecting at the same time a quasi-military dress and bearing. Gros and Horace Vernet belonged to this school, together with the youthful Géricault, devotee of Epsom and Newmarket. For the sporting artist, closely connected with the dandy, was a conception borrowed from England, at a time when Frenchmen were curiously convinced of the superiority of almost everything British.

From the portraits and self-portraits of the first twenty-five years or so of the nineteenth century, we get the impression of a general bid for dignity on the part of the artist. Significant is the series of small portraits, painted in 1800 by Louis Boilly, for the group picture of Isabey's studio.[1] Here Girodet, Vernet, Gérard, Serangeli, Isabey, and Boilly himself give no inkling of the rigours and labour-stains of their calling. Elsewhere, when, as in Advinent's portrait of Jean Bestieu (Montpellier), the artist is shown, palette and brushes in hand, his cropped hair and impeccable white stock give him the look of a Leicestershire squire. And though there must have been a number of older painters—and sculptors (Attiret and Marlet, for instance)[2]—little concerned with fashion, the rising generation was more fastidious. At the outset of his career, Géricault had ample means to indulge his tastes as a dandy. Vain yet bashful, he was mortified at being discovered by Lebrun, on the eve of a ball, in curlpapers. Other artist-dandies of the period can be seen in a portrait by Léopold Robert at Avignon, and at Toulouse in one by Gérard. The future baron Gros appears in this latter as a dashing young swell, whose chestnut locks are crowned by a 'tip-top castor of the aristocratic price'.

Antoine Duclaux's painting of a group of Lyons artists, preserved in that city and dated 1824, offers a useful illustration of art modes in the provinces. When Vigny was brought into contact with an intellectual circle at Lyons, some twenty years later, Laprade told him of the foundation in 1826 of an academy with the device *Lyon contre Paris.* Such is the brave independence of Duclaux's group. The young painters (one a guitarist) have settled for an afternoon's sketching on the banks of the Rhône, sporting here and there a poetic cloak and coiffure, and varying the tasselled cap and steeple with a scarlet tarboosh. But there are no moustaches and no beards. Neither in the sky of the Rhône Department nor on the faces of the young artists themselves can there as yet be observed any Romantic *clouds.*

It is not till we reach Géricault, and a Géricault dissatisfied with the smart, Vernet set, that the dandy becomes melancholy and passes into the Romantic. There is more than a hint of this in the 'Portrait of an Artist' in the Louvre, which may indeed be an early Géricault self-portrait, where the young sitter seems haunted by premonitions of tragedy; and in another self-portrait of his 'school' at Montauban, the likeness of some youth bowed under the storm-wrack, wearing just that expression of anxiety with which we are to become familiar in the Romantic portraits of later times.

In 1813, the skies were still clear. Géricault had received a gold medal for his 'Officer of Chasseurs', and had been highly praised in the fashionable world of Gros, Guérin, and Heim. His dandyism, his shy but charming personality, and musical accomplishments would have made him welcome in any society; and with Horace Vernet's military and sporting friends he was especially popular. A lover of horses from childhood (even aping the jockey's gait), delighted by the colour and ideographs of military uniform, to the casual onlooker he must have seemed destined to win for himself at last all the stars, and more, that glitter on Vernet's breast in that curious photograph by Nadar.

But appearances are deceptive. The wealth and fame enjoyed, or soon to be enjoyed, by the few artists I have mentioned give a quite false impression of the art world in general, either then or at any time during the course of the century. Though his friends were Liberals, Géricault suddenly took it into his head to follow the King to Béthune, during the Hundred Days, in the uniform of the Musketeers. As a painter, he was equally unpredictable, and paid dearly for it. The impecunious Triégler in Champfleury's *Les Noirau*, a story set in 1827, remarks: 'So much for the gay life of the artist! M. Géricault, my *patron*, though in the front rank, earns less than 600 francs a year from his pictures.' [3] Champfleury's error over the date (Géricault died in 1824) is in itself a comment on the neglect into which the most brilliant and original painter of the age had sunk. But Géricault received his secondary medals and State commissions, and there were many totally-ignored performers who must have envied him even the abuse hurled at the 'Raft of the Medusa'.

Behind the imposing façade, in fact, swarmed a host of indigent and despairing artists. They had been encouraged in their choice of career by official promises of fame and financial security since the outbreak of the Revolution. Yet now everywhere was heard the complaint that the profession had become overcrowded. Established painters viewed the multiplication of free places in State art schools with alarm. And while the new aristocracy was prepared to accept artists already illustrious—who were, in any case, quite capable of looking after themselves—it had no such traditional generosity to extend to beginners. Between 1791 and 1812, the number of exhibitors at the Salon increased from 166 to 430 and, under the Empire, the annual number of pictures refused rose to an average of 850.[4] Clearly, the class of balked exhibitor and *refusé* was growing to proportions that would one day create a social problem. And this was happening at a time, as we have seen, when young enthusiasts like Quaï were moving

PLATE I. Théodore Géricault (1791–1824): 'Portrait of an Artist'. *Louvre.*

Romanticism is in the wind; the artist seeks escape from the commonplace in his profession; *Werther* and the Meditators have contributed to the introspective character of this portrait, or self-portrait. The attribution has been questioned, though the signature is plain enough on the rail of the chair; but the mood, if not the picture, is undoubtedly Géricault's.

PLATE II. Eugène Delacroix (1798–1863): 'Self-Portrait as Hamlet', 1824. *Société des Amis d'Eugène Delacroix, France.*

The title of this early work (its brief dimensions, 15¾ by 12¼ inches, give it an added intimacy) is traditional: Delacroix could equally well have been identifying himself with some hero from the poems of Byron—or the novels of Scott, though the inscription on the back, which reads 'Raveswood', does not refer to the subject of the picture. All the same, it serves to remind us (and Delacroix returned again and again to the Hamlet theme) of one of the favourite sources of Romantic painting. Demonstrated, in any case, is a new attitude towards society on the part of the artist. Delacroix's haughty, sallow features express all Hamlet's—or Childe Harold's—pessimism and contempt for the world. The principle of mourning, appropriate in the picture if the old title is correct, Delacroix carried, consciously or unconsciously, into real life, where his dandy's wardrobe was stocked almost exclusively with 'suits of solemn black'.

towards a conception of painting diametrically opposed to the modified Neo-classic embraced by the Academy, and now the popular style of art in France.

We can watch this conception develop. How easily the cult of the Primitive slips into the cult of the Gothic! The deserted monastery, so dear to Nodier and the actual scene of meetings staged by his friends, turns up next in the sketchbooks of Ingres. There followed a craze for the bizarre; then a new superexaltation of colour. The special part played by Gros in this is well known, but the banner was not raised solely on the battlefield. In the locked studio where Girodet invented mysterious harmonies by lamplight, in the Louvre, and wherever the works of the early Italians, and of Correggio and Rubens, were eagerly examined and discussed, colour began to assert its authority. Géricault's 'Raft', of 1819, had still been conceived in black-and-white; already, in 1822, with 'Dante and Virgil', Delacroix hinted at what lay in store; but not till two years later were the full implications of the revolt disclosed in the same painter's 'Massacre of Scio'.

The subject of this picture by Delacroix—scenes from the Greek war of independence—would have recommended itself, in part at least, as a tribute to Lord Byron. It was the era when Byron and Walter Scott shared an astonishing popularity in France and had begun to supply her artists with a whole new range of subject-matter, exotic or picturesque. For a while, between 1820 and 1830, Scott eclipsed all rivals: but the vogue for Byron proved more enduring. Géricault it was who, not long before his death, actually initiated the endless stream of Laras, Giaours, Mazeppas, and Brides of Abydos. Louis Boulanger, Horace Vernet, the Devéria brothers, Nanteuil, Ary Scheffer, and others who will appear again in these pages, repeat, untiring, the same themes till we reach the threshold of the 1840's. If, pretty generally about that date, interest in the English writers begins to flag, Delacroix provided the exception. Though as literary critic he viewed Byron and Scott with less indulgence than formerly, as artist he seems more than ever their devoted slave. Second only to Shakespeare, Scott, in fact, rather than Byron, became Delacroix's preferred source late in life. Thirty years after the earliest translations of *Ivanhoe*, the artist was still pondering fresh versions of *L'Hermite de Copmanhurst* or *Rebecca enlevée par les Africains* (*Journal*, December 29th, 1860). Matching this free confession of debt on the part of a great painter to a great novelist are the generous acknowledgments to Scott in the foreword to one of the most ambitious literary projects of the age.

ii

If to deal with the Balzac of the *Comédie humaine* before the Hugo of the 'grand cénacle' (the subject of my next chapter) suggests some disregard for historical order, it has also in this particular context certain advantages. First, whereas Hugo's interest in painting and sculpture (if not in architecture) was focused almost exclusively upon the work of a small circle of personal friends, at the peak of their form—the majority of them—during the short reign of Charles X, Balzac's ranged with the greatest freedom over the whole period of the Empire and the Restoration. His stories, therefore, provide a natural transition from the events already described in Section I to the account of the Hugo 'cénacle' to be given in Section III. The same arrangement serves to emphasize the fact that, though separated by more than twenty years, Balzac's *La Maison du chat qui pelote*, of 1830 (originally published in 1829 under the title of *Gloire et malheur*), still stands next in succession to Nodier's *Peintre de Salzbourg*, in the annals of French fiction, as a serious study of the artistic temperament.

Typical of its barren treatment during the interval is a play by Scribe and others, *La Mansarde des artistes*, which was produced at the Gymnase in 1824, its final chorus trotting out a philosophy which must have struck even a musical-comedy audience as somewhat superficial: 'A beginner in the Fine Arts finds himself overwhelmed by poverty and suffering, then the storm abates and the sky clears, and he finishes up wealthy and respected by all.'[5]

In 1830, it would have been ludicrously wide of the mark. Balzac expressed no such easy optimism, either when studying his contemporaries' prospects or, as happened frequently, when reviewing the fortunes of painters and sculptors during the Empire and Restoration. Like Nodier, he was able to base his conception of the artist on his friends; but Balzac, of course, composed on the grand scale, and for every one reader who had skipped through a slim *Peintre de Salzbourg*, thousands were to devour the ever-multiplying chronicles of the *Comédie humaine.* Balzac's gifts as a storyteller ensured that his delineation of the artist reached a Philistine public that would never have tolerated the precious Charles Munster. While his interest in the whole field of human activity did not often permit him to entrust the artist with a leading rôle, what he then made of the character could not but leave its mark on the minds of the general public over a period of composition lasting some sixteen years. Without question, it impressed a number of his fellow-writers, and coloured their interpretations. If popular ideas about the artist spring largely, as I believe they do, from the works of some favoured storyteller, then the image created, or popularized, by Balzac deserves a more than passing scrutiny.

By upbringing he would not have been one to sympathize outright with the revolution in painting initiated by Gros, in 1804, and culminating in the work of Delacroix, twenty to twenty-three years later. He would have been aware that changes in the character of art are as inevitable as any others, that a new attitude as well as a new style had marked the modern artist since the turn of the century. But he had grown up with the standards of taste accepted by the petty bourgeoisie from which he sprang, and never altogether departed from them. This is apparent in his rather mechanical references to Raphael as the final canon in visual judgments, as also in a bourgeois fondness for the Dutch school. Among moderns, he preferred Guérin and Girodet, whose 'Endymion' inspired the tale, *Sarrasine*, and whose 'Deluge' is often alluded to.

It was from 1829 that his work for Émile de Girardin's paper, *La Silhouette*, brought him into personal contact with artists, in particular with Charlet, Achille Devéria, the brothers Johannot, Henry Monnier, and Gavarni. The same band of artists went on to provide drawings for *La Mode*, a paper to which Balzac himself also contributed. Illustrators and writers were in touch with one another almost daily in these editorial offices. Their intimacy became more than a happy accident, for the aim of both was identical: to provide a searching comment on the world of their time.

At least two of the artists just mentioned had talent above

the ordinary. In Gavarni and Monnier, Balzac met two acute observers who were capable of something more than charming fashion-plates and topical cartoons. Monnier made the deeper impression on first acquaintance, for the other's drawings revealed little as yet of wonders to come; and the possibilities opened up by Monnier's *Scènes populaires* and character-sketch of 'Mossieu' Prudhomme must soon have been appreciated by Balzac at a time when he was beginning to see the new direction his own work would take.

If, hitherto, Balzac had been somewhat inclined to accept a bourgeois view of the artist as one fit for nothing but to carry out the ideas of his employers, then it may well be that acquaintance with the spirited personalities of Gavarni and Monnier did much to modify this attitude. Indeed, the doctrines of Saint-Simon had already developed arguments in favour of the loftier view, and Balzac had given them serious attention: endowed with special gifts, the artist had also special responsibilities. He alone was spiritually equipped to guide his brothers along the straight and narrow path.

By 'artist', Saint-Simon had meant not only the painter and the sculptor, but the musician, the poet—and the novelist. Balzac certainly used the word in that wider and (for the painter and the sculptor) more flattering sense; frequently in his letters, as in his other writings, actually identifying himself with the visual artist. But, for him, the mission was social rather than religious. The artist must reconcile man to his destiny here on earth, and give him, not so much faith in God, as belief in himself. Out of the conflict between pursuit of this ideal of service to the community and the cool reception offered to such dedicated persons by the community itself, Balzac arrived at the sobering conclusion that to be an artist meant, also, to be unhappy. By the Saint-Simonians, this martyrdom of the artist had been accepted as a temporary misfortune: Balzac believed that no Utopia dreamed of by man could ever alter it. The most noticeable results of his thinking on the subject are the demand that the artist should set himself the austerest standards, and his severity towards those of his characters who, having taken upon themselves the responsibilities of the profession, fail to rise to the challenge.

iii

Balzac presents us with fourteen painters and sculptors. Though eight of these play insignificant, or comparatively insignificant parts, what is left is still a remarkable total, if one recalls that in the combined output of three slightly younger contemporaries on the other side of the Channel, Dickens, Thackeray (despite his early experiences), and George Eliot, there is not a single serious study of the kind. In the *Comédie humaine*, then, we have the pleasure of encountering at least six clearly-drawn members of the profession: Sommervieux, Frenhofer, Joseph Bridau, Dubourdieu, Grassou, and Steinbock.

In *César Birotteau* (1837), Joseph Lebas refers with horror to the disastrous marriage between his sister-in-law and the first-mentioned, the painter Sommervieux. When artists become a topic of discussion among the perfumier's friends, it is agreed that at all costs such blackguards must be kept out of respectable, middle-class households.

The events of the *Maison du chat qui pelote* (1830) provide, it is true, some excuse for this sweeping condemnation, though Sommervieux, born an aristocrat and advanced to the peerage, like Gérard, *en plein Salon*, was never in any respect a suitable husband for the cloth-merchant's daughter. Since Balzac was better acquainted with the Rue Saint-Denis, scene of the shop called the 'Cat and Racquet', than with the Faubourg Saint-Germain, there is a certain vagueness surrounding Sommervieux. At the same time, the author clearly intends here a dashing Romantic figure. *La Maison du chat qui pelote* is set early in the period of the Empire, and though Sommervieux has just spent three years in Rome, he is going to be as much of a disappointment to his Academic supervisors as to those concerned for the happiness of his wife, Augustine. In spite of his engaging air of sincerity, he is a born philanderer, and in spite of the 'antique' cut of his cloak and a head of curls *à la Caracalla*, he is a heretic after Girodet's own heart.

Sommervieux woos Augustine with tempestuous enthusiasm, but their marriage soon breaks up. When, in discussing the causes which have led to this state of affairs, Balzac makes use of the word 'artiste', he seems to weight the scales a little unfairly; as, for instance, in the generalization that *artists*, if crossed, are quite merciless. Artists, too, it seems, are habitually irreligious, and sensualists who do not understand the true meaning of love. We cannot help feeling, however, that Augustine, quite unable to adapt herself to a different mode of life, would have fared as ill had she married a successful soldier or man of business.

Yet such reservations do not alter the fact that Balzac made Sommervieux an artist, and the drama one that arises, at least in part, from Augustine's inability to share his admiration for Raphael—and Carlo Dolci! Sommervieux is mature only in the practice of his art: where human relationships are involved, he is as wilful as a child, pursuing in general the erratic course noted by Augustine's mother, when she caught a glimpse of him on horseback, careering down the Champs Élysées. 'There goes a man completely lacking in judgment!' complains the shopkeeper's wife; and if one feels that she assumed too much, it is interesting to recall the passage in Delacroix's *Journal* where he uses precisely the same analogy to sum up the character of Géricault.[6] A successful artist, Balzac is saying, may very well prove a complete failure as a man. The duchesse de Carigliano, half-pitying, half-condescending to, the wretched Augustine, whose husband she has enticed away for her own amusement, points the moral: 'We women ought to admire men of genius as one enjoys a play, but *live with them*—never!'; [7] and 'a friend' (who can only be the author) revisits the grave of the unhappy girl every year, to remind himself of the truth that a modest, humble flower, which has grown up in the shelter of the valley, will die if transplanted to the mountain-heights, where storms may break at any moment and the sun scorches.[8]

iv

About a year later, probably in 1831, Balzac wrote his *Chef-d'œuvre inconnu*, of which a second, enlarged, version appeared in 1837. This story, which brought tears to the eyes of Cézanne, offers an astonishing contrast in subject and treatment. For it is not a romance—the relationship between Poussin and Gilette providing a very minor theme—nor yet an exercise in the historical *genre*. It is perhaps the first story ever written which discusses convincingly the deeper problems of painting. How did Balzac, who had neither the time nor the opportunity to specialize in connoisseurship, come to weigh the pros and cons with such authority?

He must have had the help of someone who was an expert. Could this have been Eugène Delacroix? The two had met for the first time about 1823, and became better known to each other in the 1830's. While Delacroix the dandy shuddered at Balzac's horrific *ensembles* and was often at pains to dissociate himself from the novelist's ideas on more important matters, we know that he read everything Balzac wrote with the closest attention.[9] This was perhaps unfortunate, for he was bound to discover that in *La Rabouilleuse*, of 1842, the author had based the characters of Joseph and Philippe Bridau quite unashamedly on Eugène and his brother, General Delacroix. The friendship between painter and writer, always one-sided, did not long survive this appalling indiscretion.[10]

Delacroix distrusted literary men—yet could not resist the temptation to discuss his work with them. We hear of a famous conversation with Musset, when the two walked back and forth between their respective apartments for many hours. There was, too, a long, starlit promenade with Maxime Du Camp, during which the painter complained of the incompetence of laymen who wrote about art. But would he have talked freely with Balzac, who was notoriously indiscreet? For answer, we have to take into account Balzac's well-attested skill in 'pumping' those whose experience he wished to make use of, and admit that there are some curious parallels between ideas expressed by Delacroix and words put into the mouth of Frenhofer.

In the *Chef-d'œuvre inconnu*, the young Poussin, having steeled himself to call upon a famous contemporary, Pourbus, finds at the last moment that his courage fails him. Happily, his visit coincides with the arrival of Frenhofer, an almost legendary master, in whose wake, most conveniently, he gains admittance. Frenhofer has come to see a work by Pourbus, but on learning that Poussin, too, has ambitions as a painter, puts him to the test and is sufficiently pleased with the result to invite the boy to his own studio.

There, Poussin is overwhelmed by the suberb skill displayed on the walls, and is eager to discover the old man's professional secrets. An opportunity presents itself. Frenhofer requires a particularly beautiful model in order to complete his masterpiece, the 'Belle Noisette'; and Poussin, in return for the privilege of seeing this picture, agrees that his mistress Gilette shall undertake the sittings. The girl's beauty so delights Frenhofer that he is impelled to draw back the curtain from his painting there and then, and to set about expounding its merits. To their consternation, Pourbus and Poussin see nothing but a meaningless blur of form and colour. When Frenhofer at last discovers the terrible truth, he dismisses his visitors and, that same night, burns his work and kills himself.

We can only be astonished at the masterly, not to say 'modern', criticism offered by Frenhofer on the subject of Pourbus's 'St Mary of Egypt', and at the grandeur of his own theories, when he comes to put these forward too. It is now, as I have just suggested, that we think we catch distinct echoes of Delacroix. The latter writes in his *Journal*, while staying at Champrosay: 'Here I am at my window, looking out upon the loveliest of landscapes, *and the idea of a line never enters my thoughts*'; '*In nature*,' says Frenhofer, '*there are no lines*.'[11] Delacroix, discussing with Jean Gigoux the authenticity of an 'antique' bust, remarks: 'Whereas the artists of the Renaissance concentrated on outline, those of Antiquity *started from the centre*'; '*One ought*', observes Frenhofer, '*to capture form from the centre and work outwards*.'[12] Whether the similarity is conclusive or not, to what view of the artist do such opinions lead? To that, briefly, of a man who, attempting the impossible, loses his reason. While interested in Delacroix's ideas and an admirer of his work, Balzac seems to have had strong reservations of his own, expressed in the criticisms of Frenhofer advanced by Pourbus and in the tragic outcome. The final impression one gets is that any attempt to sacrifice line to colour, or to draw *par les boules*, must result in disaster—or produce a riddle, conveying meaning only to the artist himself. There is nothing in Balzac's story which can be construed as a plea for daring experiment.

But Frenhofer's tragic mistake does not make him less representative of the mysteries of his profession: 'As he gazed at this ethereal being, the fertile imagination of Nicolas Poussin grasped clearly and distinctly that what he saw before him was a complete picture of the nature of the artist, that lunatic nature so generously endowed with powers, which, too often, it abuses . . .'; and, again: 'Thus, for the enthusiastic Poussin, the old man was suddenly transformed into Art itself, Art with its secrets, its passions, and its dreams.' [13] Frenhofer is a great dreamer and spends long hours chewing the cud of his reflections. Pourbus advises Poussin not to imitate him in this: 'Get down to work! If painters *must* meditate, then let it be brush-in-hand.' [14] It is improbable that Balzac alludes here to the historical cult of Meditation; after all, Dürer had given his apprentices the same warning, centuries before. More likely, he had in mind a general failing of Romantic artists. But it would have been difficult for any painter to please him. Through the lips of Pourbus, he seems to demand the impossible: that the loftiest vision be accompanied by the labour of a navvy and the routine of a counting-house clerk.

No wonder that, when Joseph Bridau, the hero (though by no means the most vividly-realized character) of *La Rabouilleuse*, lays claim to all these qualities at once, he strikes us as an insufferable prig. Alas, for the best-behaved artist in fiction—who never really comes alive! He is a dutiful and affectionate son, a loyal brother to Philippe in very difficult circumstances. Though he has his love-affairs, these are never sordid, nor do they divert him from his purpose as artist. He is an honest fellow who knows exactly what he wants, from the moment when he strays, as a small child, into Chaudet's studio. The obstacles to his progress seem insurmountable to the reader, but they do not halt Joseph. Like Delacroix (legally at all events), he is the son of a solid public servant in the confidence of the Emperor, and experiences the same financial embarrassments after the Restoration. Again like Delacroix, he is embarrassed by the foolish behaviour of a soldier-brother retired on half-pay. But the resemblance is most marked in the pictures he paints and their reception by the public: soon quite as powerful a colourist as his master, Gros, he discusses art with him on equal terms; though, unlike Gros, he contemplates openly breaking with the conventions of the Classicist school. He girds himself for the struggle, which will continue without ceasing from the day when he first appears before the public at the Salon of 1823—just twelve months after Delacroix's own début with his 'Dante and Virgil'.

To tide himself over this period, he obtains humdrum commissions and (through Gros's help) credit at the colourman's. Though he has firm belief in his own powers, he is much encouraged by the 'cénacle' ('club', or 'society') of the Rue des Quatre-Vents; and Schinner finds decorative work for him at the Château de Presles while the great picture for the Salon of 1823 is in preparation. In addition, Balzac tells us: 'He read widely, acquiring that deep and serious education a man can get only through his own efforts, and to which all artists of talent between the ages of twenty and thirty submit themselves.'[15] When finished, the picture is accepted as one of the masterpieces of the modern school. A courtesan is shown standing before a Venetian senator, to whom she has been brought by an old procuress. It was a truly co-operative affair: Mme Descoings sat for the procuress, Lucien's mistress, Coralie, for the girl, and Michel Chrestien, founder-member of the Cénacle, for the senator. Joseph's enforced toil as copyist stood him in good stead on this occasion, for Gros himself mistook the work for a Titian!

Small wonder that the picture exhibited at the Salon of 1823 aroused envy as well as admiration. From remarks made by Balzac, we assume that an element of fantasy gave more positive offence, and that the author had in his mind's eye some work by Eugène Devéria, Boulanger, or the young Delacroix; or an amalgam of all three. But Delacroix, revolutionary yet student too of the old masters, best fills the bill.

And Joseph's subsequent career continues to follow Delacroix's very closely. By 1828, though acknowledged leader of the younger school, and moving in the best society, Balzac's hero can only just keep his head above water—as Delacroix, addressing an urgent request to Motte for payment during the winter of that same year, once said: 'C'est comme du temps de Dagobert pour les arts!'[16] Bourgeois patrons shrink from a talent that arouses so much hostility in the Institut and among the critics; but the deserving artist is saved in the nick of time by marriage to the daughter of a millionaire. About the same period, the death of Philippe secures him the title of comte de Brambourg and a small estate. Yet the author takes care to tell us that, even in 1842, after so much fine work and loyal service to his fellow-painters, Joseph Bridau had not yet been elected to the Academy.

In the search for Balzac's conception of the artist, we are naturally more interested in those whose work or character he admires. However, the *Comédie humaine* presents us with two bad painters, Pierre Grassou, to whom a whole story is devoted, and Dubourdieu, who appears for a moment only in *Les Comédiens sans le savoir*.

Pierre Grassou produced 'daubs' to suit the bourgeois, but in earlier years was a close friend of Joseph Bridau and belonged originally to the same group in the Rue des Quatre-Vents. Tiring of its severe standards and aware that, if his modest talents were to achieve worldly success, he must follow a very different programme, Grassou sells his soul to Élias Magus, a dealer, for whom he produces copies of the old masters, later to be passed off as genuine. His own work is a mosaic of borrowings, yet assembled with sufficient patience and cleverness to score some early triumphs. Thus at the Salon of 1829, where a number of painters from the d'Arthez circle are represented, it is Grassou's 'Toilet of a Chouan', a ludicrous plagiarism of Gerard Dou's 'Woman with the Dropsy', that is bought by Madame and earns for the artist the Cross of the Legion of Honour. As time passes, the painter's success grows. The bourgeois public is delighted to find a man who can satisfy its taste and at the same time display the virtues of industry, thrift, and good citizenship which it admires. Grassou, no doubt, was the exact type of a certain class of painter of this period favoured by the Liberal bourgeoisie, a Benjamin de Rolland or Pierre Duval Le Camus. Balzac makes it quite clear that he owed his fame to the dislike of the public for real genius, and to its weakness for a 'hard worker', whatever the quality of his work. But in the studios Grassou came in for the harshest ridicule.

Dubourdieu, one of the curiosities of Paris exhibited to his country cousin by the successful landscape-painter Léon de Lora, represents a less usual type, the wrong-headed artist. In *La Rabouilleuse*, Balzac had reminded the reader on several occasions that one sign of genius was its independence of social and political theories. A 'madman' is the impression made by Dubourdieu on the country cousin. Léon de Lora attempts no defence, but explains:

He's got flair and intelligence . . . but Fourierism has cooked his goose. You've just seen there, Cousin, one of the effects of ambition upon artists. In Paris, it happens only too often that, with the idea of taking a short cut to that kind of celebrity which, for them, spells fortune, they borrow wings from circumstance, and suppose they can rise in the world by attaching themselves to something, by becoming supporters of a system, hoping thereby to change a clique of admirers into a real 'public'. One turns Republican, another Saint-Simonian, one is aristocratic, one *juste milieu*, one mediaeval, and another Germanophil, or whatever he decides. But if opinions don't give a man talent, they can always be relied upon to ruin it: as witness the poor fellow you've just seen. An artist's views ought to be confined to belief in his own productions . . . and, when nature has granted him the sacred fire, his sole means of arriving at success ought to be hard work.[17]

Léon de Lora, here speaking, was the single artist in the *Comédie humaine* who, from humble beginnings and through his own unaided skill, achieved both wealth and well-merited fame. His judgment, therefore, is worth something.

The last of Balzac's artists to whom I wish to refer is the sculptor, Wenceslas Steinbock. Appearing in the first part of *Les Parents pauvres*[18] as the protégé of Cousine Bette, then later as the husband of Hortense Hulot d'Ervy and the lover of Valérie Marneffe, he is the personification of human weakness, at the mercy of each succeeding female influence. Yet in Steinbock Balzac gives us his most penetrating study of creative genius.

This Polish exile anticipates the sculptors of the 1830's and 1840's (the story is set in the period of the Restoration) when small-scale decorative bronzes, ceramics, and wood-carvings won an immense popularity. In part, such activity was the result of circumstances unfavourable to larger work; in part, it reflected the re-awakened interest among collectors, stimulated by biography, fiction, and music, in Benvenuto Cellini. The artists of the period were frequently engaged in turning out elaborate clocks, inkstands, candelabra, and trophies of all kinds. Barye himself began in this way; and sculptors like Préault and David d'Angers frequently lent their full-scale models to be reproduced in little in the famous workshop of Froment Meurice.

Steinbock, discovered attempting suicide in an attic in the Doyenné, is befriended by Lisbeth Fischer, financed by her, and forced out of his apathy to produce a magnificent piece of silver-smithing in the manner of Cellini. This, admired by everyone who sees it, gains him the favour of Lisbeth's relations, the Hulot family, and, through the baron, that of the Government. His success is immediate. He marries Hortense Hulot, and is commissioned to produce the official monument to Marshal Montcornet. But it soon becomes apparent that Steinbock will never fulfil his brilliant promise. He has an aristocratic disdain for the drudgery of art, and his weakness of character allows him to become a pawn in the game played with such skill by Lisbeth Fischer and Valérie Marneffe. After three misspent years, in which he just manages to complete a clock and the Montcornet monument, he falls victim to Lisbeth's wiles and the fascination of Valérie. Finally, he leaves his wife and is content to share his mistress with Hulot, Crevel, and Montès de Montéjanos. His return to Hortense, which takes place only after Valérie's death, is (like all his other actions) a concession to expedience. We leave him as a sculptor who writes and talks about his art but no longer practises it.

In his earlier *La Fille aux yeux d'or*, Balzac had made no exception of artists in a lengthy condemnation of the vices of contemporary Parisians: 'What power is it that destroys these people? Passion. And every passion in Paris resolves itself into two simple terms: money and pleasure.' [19] Steinbock, who affects to despise money, has lavish tastes and is quite ready to indulge them at the expense of his wife or his mistress. Social engagements, though they have to be paid for, offer a release from the lonely labour of creation. Balzac points out how easily and pleasantly success can come in this way:

> He discoursed admirably on the subject of art, keeping up his reputation as a great artist among fashionable people by means of the spoken word, by criticisms and explanations. In Paris there are men of genius who spend a lifetime listening to the sound of their own voices, and are satisfied with a species of drawing-room fame. Steinbock, as he followed in the footsteps of such charming eunuchs, acquired a growing distaste for hard work.[20]

There follows a detailed examination of the part that sheer manual labour must play in the production of a piece of sculpture, a play, or a concert-performance; and we have to admire Balzac's choice of profession in this particular instance, since sculpture perhaps, of all the arts, makes the severest physical demands upon the creator. There are, however, more general conclusions to be drawn from Steinbock's failure:

> When Lisbeth had chained him up in his garret, Wenceslas Steinbock was on that arid path, travelled by so many great men before

him [Balzac has just given a list of them], which leads to the very heights of glory. Happiness—in the guise of Hortense—then drove him to idleness, the natural condition of artists; for, with them, idleness is always fully occupied. Theirs is the enjoyment of pashas in the seraglio: the caressing of ideas, a pleasant little tipple at the springs of the intellect. Great artists like Steinbock, much given to *rêverie*, are justly called *rêveurs*. Such opium-eaters come to grief; whereas, bracing themselves to meet the world on its own harsh terms, they might have been great men. On the other hand, these half-artists are charming fellows: they are popular; indeed, become intoxicated with praise. They seem actually superior to real artists, who are accused of self-love and boorishness and of rebelling against convention. This is because the absolute detachment and devotion to their work of the latter make them look like egoists to the stupid; especially as they are expected to keep up the same appearances as the dandy, performing those social evolutions known as 'duties' in the world of fashion: for people would love to see the lions of Atlas combed and scented like the lapdogs of a marchioness! The real artists, therefore, having hardly a peer and little hope of meeting one, fall into the exclusivism of solitude. They become incomprehensible to the great 'majority', which, as we know, is composed of clowns and ignoramuses, of the envious and the superficial.[21]

Whom, one wonders, had Balzac in mind when he wrote this? Himself, perhaps: awkward in fashionable company, a ruthless, solitary worker. Perhaps there was also some criticism here of Delacroix's social life, involving energies which, like Maxime Du Camp, Balzac may have thought would have been better employed in correcting faults of drawing. But in the Hugo circle, or at Nodier's, Balzac must have met a number of young artists whose limited talent encouraged them to seek a parallel career as drawing-room entertainers; and in the 'bohème galante' of the Doyenné there were still others. Paris of the 1840's possessed in Fromentin, Delécluze, and Théophile Gautier himself, distinguished enough examples of Steinbock's last, substitute, occupation, for 'finally he became a critic, like all impotent creatures who fail to live up to their early promise'.[22]

The *Comédie humaine*, alone, covers a period which begins in the first flush of the Romantic movement and ends on the threshold of Realism; and during the course of it certain changes take place in the attitude of the artist, as Balzac depicted him. Delacroix, the type of lonely aristocrat raised above, or cut off from, fellow-strivers after fame, becomes a little outmoded. As Lousteau tells Lucien: 'You're arriving in Paris where the battle is thickest and most desperate.' This 'battle' between the old guard of Classicism and the young Romantics could not be won by a leaderless, undisciplined army. The older symbols of independence—Hamlet on the horns of his dilemma, pirate and Arab chieftain wasting blood in berserker rages—had outlived their usefulness, and it was necessary to substitute others more suited to the emergency. The artist and the poet must discard their Byronic isolation and join together with other artists and other poets to form a compact and powerful group.

In this new orientation something, of course, was lost. With the concession to circumstances, the artist forfeited his seigniorial rights. There was a democratization of the brevet 'Romantic': the group, however proud its members, *corporately* could hardly be more than genteel. On the other hand, there was all the exhilaration of embracing a common purpose. The highest standards were insisted upon. To remain in the group, the artist must give of his best, whatever the sacrifice involved. To fail in this, to compromise, might bring him material benefits but would banish him from the society of those whose good opinion alone counted. The success of Grassou, therefore, Officer of the Legion of Honour, major in the National Guard, member of the Institut, means nothing. Of this, Grassou himself is well aware: 'Good father and husband though he was, the painter could not rid himself of a fatal conviction: artists made fun of him, his name was a term of contempt in the studios, and no mention of his work was ever to be found in the columns of the weekly journals.' [23]

Yet, if we can admire, we can also have our doubts about, the group of the Rue des Quatre-Vents, which included Lambert the mystic, d'Arthez, later the great literary master of the age, Bianchon, its famous physician, Ridal, its most distinguished playwright, Meyraux, an eminent scientist, and Chrestien, who would achieve immortality too, martyred in the Cloître-Saint-Merri. The group's high standards were excellent in their way—but might they not prove dangerously inflexible? The creative artist in its midst found himself presented with a *programme*.

We are, indeed, not altogether comfortable about Joseph Bridau's frequenting the Rue des Quatre-Vents, however disinterested the advice of his literary and scientific friends. The ban on worldly pleasures, even on potboiling, seems regrettable. Though Balzac sketches out a certain *succès d'estime* for Bridau, there are moments when we can imagine him withering away in this hothouse atmosphere like poor Louis Boulanger.

The hint of such changes in the *vie d'artiste* suggests that it is time to pass on to particular historical events, the formation of the Hugo group and the group of the Doyenné. In them we shall find the reality which the *Comédie humaine* reflects.

III

Mutual Admiration

i

In Balzac, not a single artist of importance lived, or worked, on the left bank of the Seine. His Latin Quarter swarms with petty bourgeois, publishers, the bookish generally, and students of all kinds from the University, the Law School, and the School of Medicine: but the École des Beaux-Arts, for any influence it brings to bear on the district, might not exist.

On the contrary, it is to Montmartre and the neighbourhood of the old Opera House (which, before the erection of Garnier's building, stood in the Rue Le Peletier) that Balzac's artists are to be traced, a quarter where they found themselves surrounded by the newly rich and by actress-courtesans of the type of Esther, Florine, and Héloïse Brisetout. Bridau's studio was in the Rue de Berlin, together with those of Schinner and Léon de Lora; then, later, in the Rue de Clichy. Grassou lived near by, in the Rue de Navarin; Steinbock, after his escape from the Doyenné, in the Rue Saint-Dominique-Saint-Germain (Montmartre). There is no need to extend the catalogue: his circumstances may vary, but one feature is constant, the *artiste balzacien* keeps to the Right Bank.

Yet, before and during the time when Balzac was writing, a steady drift across the river had been taking place. Perhaps his omission of any reference to this movement is an instance of the 'double' substituted by the author for the actual contemporary world of Paris; or another example of a habit of throwing his stories slightly into the past. At all events, the Louvre ceased to be the hub of the art world when, by *arrêté consulaire* of August 20th, 1801, Napoleon expelled the artists from the palace, and the men who had so conveniently lodged there were forced to find alternative accommodation.

The Left Bank was by no means a country unexplored by

artists, for the Rues Saint-André-des-Arts, du Pont de Lodi and de l'Université, the Hôtel Bullion and the former Capuchin convent had all, at the beginning of the century, a traditional link with the profession. David himself took up residence in the Rue de Seine in 1802, transferring his school and studio on first arrival to the Rue Saint-Jacques, where the Emperor and his suite halted their carriages in order to inspect the finished painting of the 'Coronation'. Later moves followed, but still in the same locality: David and his family from the Rue de Seine to the Rue d'Enfer; the school to premises above the Bibliothèque Mazarine, off one of the courts of the Institut.

The drift continued, for Academicians and rebels alike. Ingres, setting up his school in 1825, chose for its location the Rue des Marais-Saint-Germain (now the Rue Visconti) on the doorstep of the École des Beaux-Arts. When Suisse and Boudin, or Boutin, founded life-classes without instruction at 25 centimes *per diem* to suit a new mood and the purse that went with it, they chose convenient positions in the same neighbourhood. The Seine was explored in both directions. Upstream, the Île Saint-Louis, hitherto avoided on account of the toll-bridge and the notorious reserve of its inhabitants, began to attract an occasional journalist-lithographer; and its washerwomen, climbing the stone stairs, were observed by Daumier (and recorded) in his large converted attic over the Quai d'Anjou.

In the other direction from the Île Saint-Louis, on the Quai Voltaire, was the studio taken by Delacroix in 1829, in exchange for the one in the Passage Saulnier to which he had moved in order to paint his 'Sardanapalus'. Delacroix, it is true, returned to the Right Bank; but when he settled finally, in 1858, it was in the Rue Furstenberg, in the corner house now so well known. By that time, the network of little streets to the east of the old Abbey church of Saint-Germain-des-Prés had served a whole generation of struggling artists: the Desbrosses brothers in the Rue Gît-le-Cœur; Courbet in the Rue Hautefeuille; 'Chien-Caillou' and his like in the Rue des Noyers, where the disillusioned attic-dweller inverted Béranger's axiom, to complain, 'Dans un grenier qu'on est *mal* à vingt ans!'; and when Balzac decided to lodge Nicolas Poussin in the Rue de la Harpe, he may well have had its more modern clientèle in mind.

By chance or choice, perhaps a mixture of both, the most

illustrious Romantic artists and writers to form a group were a march ahead during the earlier stages of this invasion. Taking the 'collines savantes' in their stride, they had established themselves, by 1827, on the very summit of the Montagne Sainte-Geneviève. It may be unwise to read too much into the flight of the artist to the haunts of the scholar, the dramatist, and the poet; but certain facts speak for themselves, and for a period following 1827 the Sorbonne, the Odéon, and the Luxembourg provided the transit marks by which the painter set his course. In particular, the Jardin du Luxembourg became Romantic territory for artists and writers alike.

ii

It was in 1824, the year of Géricault's death and of the stormy reception of Delacroix's 'Massacre', that Victor Hugo, a gifted amateur artist as well as the poet of the *Nouvelles Odes*, set up house in the Rue de Vaugirard, at the very gates of this celebrated public garden. Its literary days were yet to come, however. Then it belonged to a quarter of Paris forlorn, even squalid. The Hugos, troubled by the racket in the carpenter's shop below their apartment, found it necessary to cross the river at least once a week to keep in touch with civilized society. Through the *Muse Française*, they were already known to Charles Nodier, and during 1824 the friendship ripened. It was with Nodier that Hugo went to Rheims for the Coronation ceremony of Charles X, and shortly afterwards (together with Adèle) made the journey to Mont Blanc. On their return to Paris, the Hugos became regular guests in Nodier's rooms at the Arsenal.

These Sunday mornings and evenings constituted only one of many brilliant salons of the day, but they must have had a particular appeal for Hugo. Though the company might be impressive, there was little ceremony. Refreshment took the form of lemonade, with gooseberry-wine for special occasions, and when candlesticks and chairs proved insufficient, room was found for candles and guests on the floor. Here was a simple, unaffected style of entertaining that merited the attention of an ambitious young man of limited means. For the moment, he could hardly hope to compete with Nodier. The latter's racy, apocryphal yarns of the Revolution, and skill in encouraging others to extemporize brilliantly, were inimitable. And the remoteness of the Rue de Vaugirard and the restricted space of his own apartment were disadvantages that would still have to be overcome.

Much could be learned, however, from these encounters with the writers and artists who flocked to Nodier's at-homes. The latter, forming a particularly strong contingent, included Isabey, Delaroche, David d'Angers, the Johannots, the Devérias, Louis Boulanger, and Delacroix. Hugo had always been clever with his pencil, and since his marriage he had been surrounded by others with a taste for art: Adèle Hugo herself, for instance, and his sister-in-law Julie Dudival, who won a second-class medal at the Salon of 1824. It may even have been in Julie's studio that he first met Delacroix, since the latter is known to have given her a small sketch for his 'Massacre'.

At Nodier's, Hugo, like Mme Ancelot, may well have been impressed by the independent attitude of these latecomers to polite society. Titles and famous names weighed less with them than with their literary colleagues. If, as he hoped, he were one day to establish a salon of his own, the goodwill of some of these clever young men ought not to be too difficult to obtain.

Towards the end of 1824, a chance meeting outside the Odéon brought the possibility a great deal nearer.[1] Hugo and his wife had arrived at the theatre early for a performance of *Robin des Bois*—the title under which Weber's *Der Freischütz* was played in Paris—and soon found themselves in conversation with a tall, pleasant-faced stranger, waiting for the same purpose. It was Achille Devéria. In the course of their talk, the young man asked Mme Hugo if she kept an album. Her reply, 'I shall get one to-morrow', shows that she knew to whom she was speaking: Devéria, indeed, at twenty-four, had become one of the most popular artists in Paris. The promised drawing was made on the following evening and so warmly appreciated that the artist planned more visits and produced more drawings. A close friendship resulted. The Hugos saw a great deal of Devéria from now on, and he in turn welcomed them to his parents' home in the Rue Notre-Dame-des-Champs and to his studio in the Rue de l'Ouest.

Only a few months before Hugo's introduction to this society (which made weekly excursions to the Arsenal rather less necessary), Delacroix had paid his first visit to Devéria's studio. It was there that the two Romantic leaders met, the early impression on both sides being favourable enough. But Hugo encountered personalities less difficult to please: Émile Deschamps, Alfred and Paul de Musset, Chenavard, Amaury-Duval, and Edgar Quinet; while Vigny was already a close friend. The name of Émile Deschamps is a sufficient reminder that earlier Romantic circles existed. Many of the guests had met elsewhere and, like Hugo himself, would continue to frequent other salons. But the Devérias possessed just those qualities which for a time ensured them a position at the very centre of the movement. Achille was handsome, charming, and dazzlingly successful; while Eugène, younger by five years, promised to outstrip his brother in the race for glory.

Three years passed. Hugo, working on *Cromwell*, the play requested by Taylor for the Comédie-Française, could interrupt his labours from time to time to take an almost proprietary interest in the Salon of 1827. Eugène Devéria's 'Birth of Henry IV', the picture of the year as some thought, had been executed under his very eye. The success of Louis Boulanger's 'Mazeppa' was still more gratifying, for here was a gentle spirit who openly declared his dependence on Hugo. This Salon, which we chiefly associate with the 'Sardanapalus' of Delacroix and the solemn gage thrown down by the Classicist opposition, Ingres's 'Apotheosis of Homer', was also remarkable for the wide range of works shown by David d'Angers, rather older than the others but soon to become one of Hugo's most faithful disciples.

The artists had delivered their challenge; the Preface to *Cromwell* would follow shortly. The moment was one of tremendous enthusiasm: 'The younger generation seemed to emerge from its long period of exhaustion', wrote Paul Huet, looking back; 'drawn by an irresistible desire for liberty, it rushed to the very sources of life in order to sample the beautiful and the good'.[2]

In the spring, the Hugos moved to a larger apartment in the near-by Rue Notre-Dame-des-Champs, where Eugène Devéria and Boulanger would soon share a new and splendid studio, and Sainte-Beuve occupy a house only a few doors away; David d'Angers, in the Rue d'Assas, remaining near at hand to portray and publicize his brilliant juniors. The time had thus arrived to draw these practitioners of a sister art into closer relationship, and the publication of *Cromwell*, in December, gave Hugo the authority to do so. At last he could establish a salon of his own.

The sculptor David d'Angers, who was one of the initial audience at the reading of the Preface to *Cromwell*, wrote afterwards: 'What penetrating ideas! This Preface, by itself, contains all the rules that literature requires';[3] but it was as a charter of liberty applying with equal force to all the arts that it came to be displayed so prominently in the studio of Duseigneur, a few years later. It would be foolish to insist that its arguments and parade of evidence were read and digested by every young painter, sculptor, and architect. For the majority, no doubt, a general impression of Hugo's aims sufficed.

But those who did study the Preface carefully—and, as we shall see, art students in those days were great readers—found an exhilarating attack upon the Classicist position, which, almost point for point, they could match from their own visual programme. When literary figures were being discussed by Hugo, the studio-reader, without altering the sense, could quite easily substitute his own choice of equivalents in the fields of painting, sculpture, and graphic design. Raphael would take the place of Racine (damned with faint praise by Hugo); Michelangelo, or Rembrandt, that of Shakespeare; Callot, that of Molière.

The young artist could further echo Hugo's plea for more vitality, variety, and local colour in the academic school of history-painting as well as in the drama. The cynicism with which Hugo regarded Classicist attempts to preserve the unities of time and place was the exact reflection of the Romantic artist's scorn for the archaeological solecisms and staginess of David. Again, he could agree with Hugo that, just as drama was distinguishable from melodrama, a Romantic canvas was distinguishable from the stereotyped Salon piece, *by the poetry of its execution*. Substitute 'painting' for 'verse' and a few technical terms of the pen for those of the brush, and it is not difficult to imagine Delacroix and Eugène Devéria expressing themselves in Hugo's own words:

> We demand a verse that is free, honest, and straightforward, that dares in all things avoid prudery and affectation; a verse that will pass quite naturally from comedy to tragedy, from the sublime to the grotesque; that is both realistic and poetic, at once beautifully wrought and genuinely inspired; that has depth yet spontaneity, breadth yet truth.[4]

The battle to be fought was identical, for the reception given by the critics to this dramatic poetry proved as savage as that which had greeted the 'Massacre of Scio'. And to the mingling of beauty with 'ugliness', of tragedy with comedy (the prime contention of the Preface) the artist came well prepared. Could he not look back to irreproachable models—to Leonardo himself?

The real force of the essay lay in its reiteration of the principle of liberty in the arts, a principle already stated in the preface to the *Odes* of 1826. In its call to arms, it was as intelligible to the young artist as to the young writer: 'Down with theories and systems! Let us tear away the old lath-and-plaster hiding the face of art! There are neither rules nor models; or, rather, no rules but the general laws of Nature!' [5]

iii

I have suggested that Hugo hoped to gain something for his cause, or for himself, by the introduction of artists into the salon whose dominating spirit he was to be. The question we can now ask is, what did artists themselves expect to gain from admittance to such gatherings? Of this I shall have something to say in a moment. It is obvious, however, that the overruling attraction from the very beginning was the personality of Hugo himself.

There are a number of portraits by David d'Angers, F.-J. Heim, Auguste de Chatillon, and others, which belong more or less to this time, and they confirm descriptions by Gautier in the *Histoire du Romantisme* of his 'grave and gentle countenance' and the 'truly monumental brow', resembling a 'pediment of white marble': Hugo, of course, had a very remarkable head. But it is the general impression of the whole man, dress, habits, peculiarities, that strikes the casual observer, and in this instance he would have been disappointed by the harshness of the voice, by the trunk too robust for the short legs, and a fashion in dress oddly bourgeois for the poet of rebellion. It was through some spiritual force, an innate *authority*, that Hugo conquered; and by an unwearied display of courage and enthusiasm. On these points most contemporaries are agreed.

The first-floor apartment of No. 90 Rue Notre-Dame-des-Champs included a dining-room, study, and drawing-room. It had access to a tiny garden, but the Luxembourg lay within easy reach, and it was only a step across the boundaries of Montparnasse to the open countryside. Having a picture in our minds of the leader of the salon, we can get a fair idea of the kind of entertainment to which artists and their friends were invited. It did not, like the Arsenal's, cater for both sexes: few women appeared and no one danced; so that Musset, on his occasional visits, had to forgo the pleasures of the waltz. All the same (as Balzac pointed out), in an avant-garde salon the newcomer had steps to practise quite as difficult as those performed in any ballroom. And it will not be unfair to give a short extract from Mme Ancelot's description of the Hugo evenings, satirically absurd though it is:

> When Hugo was the orator, and with bowed head and gloomy, anxious expression recited some stanzas from one of those splendid effortless odes of his, how could anyone use an epithet like *admirable*, *superb*, or *prodigious* in praising him, as had been done a moment earlier to flatter some mediocrity?
>
> Such a thing was impossible! Instead, there would be silence for a short while, then someone would get up, walk over to the poet, grasp his hand, and gaze heavenwards, the rest waiting with bated breath.
>
> At this point, to the astonishment of the uninitiated, a single word would be uttered, and re-echoed from every corner of the salon: '*Cathédrale!*'
>
> This spokesman, having returned to his seat, would be followed by another, who leapt up, crying: '*Ogive!*'
>
> A third (gazing round the assembly) dared a final: '*Pyramide d'Égypte!*'
>
> The company would applaud, relapse for a moment into a solemn hush, then explode again almost immediately, repeating in chorus the sacramental words.[6]

How did the artist, traditionally an awkward fellow, compose himself for these ordeals? The answer must be that, if he admired Hugo, such occasions never became ordeals. Perhaps, like Boulanger, he was half-poet himself; or, like David d'Angers, a worshipper of heroes who enjoyed the thrill of submission. Again, he may well have been schooled in these performances from boyhood: for the recitation of verses by the author, or by an amateur diseuse, had long been a feature of Parisian life and would continue so under the July Monarchy, when young women who regularly recited *Le Lac* and Arvers's *Sonnet* from *Mes Heures perdues* were estimated to number nine thousand! How splendid by comparison, then, four acts from *Cromwell*, or *Marion de Lorme* in its entirety!

But the compliance of the artist sprang from something deeper, from a long history of humility—and so from gratitude. For a century and more, art had served the libretto, the novel, and the pamphlet; for almost as long, the writer had minded the artist's business, and had not been careful to hide his condescension. Now, when he began to show a new sympathy and respect, the yoke ceased to chafe and a pleasant partnership ensued. Hugo's ascendancy suggests more, however; for the artist's admiration for him became a cult, signalized by the steady succession of busts and portraits, straight illustrations and freer reminiscences in painting and sculpture, produced both before and after the Revolution of 1830.

Hugo had something of greater value to offer the artist than prefaces and manifestos; there was in his works, as in Byron's and Scott's, a vast extension of subject-matter. To painters disgusted—the word is not too strong—with stereotyped academic themes, the novelty and variety of his invention provided an endless source of delight. We must remember that the 'morceau' and 'impression' were not yet thought of. Art was still closely dependent on literature, and the Romantics departed from this tradition only by banning one kind of literature and recommending another. In search of fresh subject-matter, therefore, the artist turned with enthusiasm to the *Ballades* and *Orientales*, as later to *Notre-Dame de Paris*.

Hugo, on his side, stood to gain more than Nodier from such a partnership, for the men he befriended were artists of greater talent and experience. In 1826, the editor of a paper friendly to Romantic tendencies made the comparison: 'M. Hugo represents in poetry what M. Delacroix represents in painting.' [7] Though this comparison became offensive to both parties, the writer of the article was, if tactless, substantially correct. The *Orientales* of 1828 do seem deliberately to translate the painter's passion for the East into poetic terms, to attempt in novelties of metre and rhythm a close equivalent of bravura on canvas. As Delacroix made notes from the costumes collected by Jal and Auguste, and careful documentary drawings on his Moroccan journey, Hugo was assiduous in consulting sources for *Le Derviche*. His experiments in pictural expression and the vivid 'paintings' that resulted were not all borrowed from artists, however: his genius found its natural outlet in images and colour. Such a stanza as:

> ' Oh! si j'étais capitane,
> Ou sultane,
> Je prendrais des bains ambrés,
> Dans un bain de marbre jaune,
> Près d'un trône,
> Entre deux griffons dorés' *

both borrows and lends Romantic currency. Pictures inspire the poem, the poem inspires pictures. Marie Nodier sang the *Captive* to Reber's music; but the number of paintings based on *Sara la Baigneuse*, on the other hand, shows the greater influence of Hugo upon artists. Since, however, the works of these artists are mostly forgotten, while Hugo's verse continues to be read, we find ourselves more often taking note of the reverse process. The names of painters and that of the sculptor David d'Angers occur frequently in titles and dedications. And when Hugo wrote a poem actually inspired by a canvas, *Mazeppa*, for example, how could Boulanger fail to be overwhelmed by the honour done him?

A new era had dawned, it seemed, in which the arts of writing and painting were to advance convivially together. This idea (of which Delacroix alone was suspicious) especially attracted David d'Angers and Louis Boulanger. David d'Angers's fame now rests entirely on the medallions which conveniently decorate—in reproduction—the pages of other men's biographies, while his fifty statues and numerous busts have passed into oblivion. Was he entirely altruistic, or a man secretly ambitious and aware that a good investment could be made out of his relations with the Hugo circle? I think the kinder interpretation is the true one, particularly in view of his generosity towards the unhappy Aloysius Bertrand. Boulanger, David d'Angers's junior by nearly twenty years, shared with Sainte-Beuve, before the 'affaire Adèle', a first place in Hugo's affections, and they were jointly

* 'Oh, were I a *capitane* or a king's daughter, I would take amber baths in a bath of yellow marble near a throne between two golden griffins!'

honoured in the *Feuilles d'automne* as 'mon peintre et mon poète'.

The career of Boulanger, however, suffered a steady decline after the success of his painting of 'Mazeppa' in 1827. His real talent seems to have been in the field of illustration, to judge from some admirable drawings for the *Fantômes* and the *Dernier Jour d'un condamné*; or in work on a small scale, for the little 'Mazeppa' at Montpellier is far more successful than the great canvas at Rouen. This picture was followed by a 'Death of Bailly' which, as Gautier informs us, met with harsh criticism; and a 'Triumph of Petrarch', in 1836, though better liked, failed to retrieve the situation.[8] In spite of the praises of Hugo, by whom he was placed in the front rank of a generation of painters likely to 'raise the French school to the level of Italian, Spanish, Flemish, and English magnificence', and other fulsome expressions of esteem scattered throughout the poet's works,[9] Boulanger was ready to throw in his hand by 1860, when he was appointed Director of the Musée and École des Beaux-Arts at Dijon.

His deterioration and its possible cause did not escape notice. In 1842, Planche wrote to Paul Huet: 'The *friendship* of Victor Hugo (if, in this context, the word conveys anything) has proved fatal to Boulanger; it won him three or four high-sounding odes. . . . But it rendered him deaf to all good advice, and finally prevented him from taking a line he could really follow to the end.'[10] Sainte-Beuve's opinion, expressed after Boulanger's death, made the same point: 'He was a Jules Romain [Giulio Romano] who had Victor Hugo for his Raphael.'[11] In an article written during the same year, 1867, Gautier admitted the painter's failings, but rated his positive achievement more highly. 'People have been rather unjust to Boulanger,' he said; 'if he himself admired too much, then he has not received even the admiration which was his due.'[12]

When Gautier came to write graceful obituaries on other artists of the 'cénacle' proper, the substance of them proved always the same sad record of decline and neglect. Achille Devéria ended up in the Print Department of the Bibliothèque Nationale, his brother as Keeper of the Musée at Pau. 'Tony Johannot', Gautier was at pains to remind the public of 1845, 'is beyond contradiction the king of illustration. *A few years ago*, no novel or poem could appear without an engraved vignette carrying his signature.'[13]

When we come to Célestin Nanteuil, another generation has arrived, and with it a new phase in the history of the salon in the Rue Notre-Dame-des-Champs.

IV

Up till the Autumn of 1829, artists had played only a social and cultural rôle in the 'cénacle'. After September 30th, when a reading of the completed manuscript of *Hernani* was applauded by a company which included Sainte-Beuve, Émile Deschamps, and Mérimée, they were called upon to give practical evidence of their belief in the founder. As this could hardly be expected of those who, like Delacroix, the Devérias, Boulanger, and David d'Angers, were busy men at the peak of their careers, Hugo opened his house to youngsters with a little more time on their hands, to the budding writer and the artist-elect.

On their return from the Rhine journey in November, Sainte-Beuve, the architect Robelin, and Louis Boulanger viewed with distaste the new recruits being marshalled by Hugo. No doubt it was stupid of them to expect that the old exclusiveness could be maintained for ever. To preserve the same circle, year in, year out, might suit baron Gérard, but not Hugo, whose career had hardly begun. Those, therefore, who wished to keep his friendship had to make a fresh declaration of faith and energetically support his plans for the future.

Before the ultimate 'battle' of *Hernani* there were many minor engagements to be fought. Aware of the vital importance of each step in the campaign against the censorship, professional jealousy, and green-room superstition, Hugo became less grateful for advice and criticism, prerogatives of friendship among equals, and began to prefer the company of those with neither the knowledge nor the experience to be critical. From now on dates his studied patronage of youth, for the results of which, in the pathetic lives of men like Berthaud and Lassailly, he cannot entirely escape blame.

But the immediate leaders of his youthful bodyguard, Gérard de Nerval, Borel, and Théophile Gautier, were not innocents from the provinces, nor without means. The first, recommended by a brilliant translation of *Faust* at a time when Goethe was just celebrating his eightieth birthday, could consider himself already an intimate of Hugo's and proudly undertook the distribution of the red slips. It was with these tokens of admission, inscribed 'hierro', that the playwright intended to pack the house and ensure a hearing for *Hernani* on its opening night, fixed for February 25th, 1830. Gautier has described the enthusiasm they aroused: 'Never in our lives, I believe, had we experienced a keener pleasure than when Gérard detached from the packet six squares of red paper and gave them to us with a solemn air, telling us to be sure to invite reliable men only.' [14] Gautier himself was responsible for the muster of artists, a service he was in the best position to render, since, while completing his studies at the Collège Charlemagne, he spent part of his time in Rioult's studio near by.

Still uncertain of his true vocation, Gautier tentatively practised art and was the friend of others similarly hesitating. His own account of these events is therefore of particular value. For one thing, it saves us the trouble of inquiring how young sculptors, painters, and architects could have been so ready to wish success to *Hernani*, when they were not, the majority of them, personally acquainted with the author. As Gautier explains:

> Much reading was done in the studios. The *rapins* were fond of literature, and their specialized training, which had put them in close touch with nature, made them readily appreciative of the imagery and colour in the new poetry. They took no exception at all to the vivid, picturesque detail so much disliked by the Classicists. Accustomed to a bold language of their own, bristling with technical terms, they found nothing shocking in the *mot propre*. We are speaking here of young *rapins*, for there were also the well-behaved students, faithful to Chompré's *Dictionary* and the Achilles tendon, highly regarded by the teacher and set up by him as an example. But these last had no following, and were pitied for their sober palette without a trace of Veronese green, Indian yellow, or Smyrna lake, or any of the seditious colours forbidden by the Institut.

Gautier goes on:

> What marvellous days! Walter Scott was then in the full flower of his success; we were being initiated into the mysteries of Goethe's *Faust*, a work that, to use Mmede Staël's expression, contained everything, and a little more than everything. We were discovering Shakespeare in the rather clumsy translation of Letourneur, and the poems of Lord Byron, *The Corsair*, *Lara*, *The Giaour*, *Manfred*,

Beppo, *Don Juan*, were reaching us from the East, not yet become commonplace. How youthful, fresh, intoxicating, bizarre in colour, and highly flavoured all this was! It turned our heads; we seemed to be entering unknown worlds. At every page we came upon subjects for compositions which we hastened to draw, or dash down furtively—for such motifs would not have been to the master's taste and, had they been discovered, would have earned us a sharp rap over the head with the mahlstick.

It was in this state of mind that the young artist toiled at his life-study, reciting to his neighbour at the next easel the *Pas d'armes du roi Jean* or the *Chasse du burgrave*. Though not yet affiliated to the Romantic troop, we had already been won over in our hearts. The preface to *Cromwell* was as radiant in our eyes as the Tables of the Law on Mount Sinai, and its arguments seemed to us beyond contradiction. The insults printed in the petty Classicist papers against the young master whom we regarded henceforth, and rightly, as France's greatest poet, made us livid with anger. We were burning to go out and fight the hydra of *perruquinisme* [old-fogyism], like the German painters you can see mounted on Pegasus, Cornelius at their head, after the fashion of the four sons of Aymon, in Kaulbach's fresco in the New Pinakothek at Munich. A less Classical mount would have suited us better, though: Ariosto's hippogriff, for instance.[15]

Such enthusiasm was in danger of wrecking *Hernani* before the curtain rose. The events of February 25th have been too often described to warrant more than the briefest summary here: the arrival of the Romantic train-bands outside the Comédie-Française at three o'clock in the afternoon; a four-hour wait in the locked auditorium; the disgust of the fashionable audience, arriving at seven o'clock and finding the theatre turned into a public restaurant—and worse; finally, the revolutionary nature of the play, given with evident disapproval by the actors themselves, and attended by scuffles and interruptions beyond the footlights. Neither Gautier nor Hugo was always prepared to remember the lighter side of this famous encounter with Classicist tradition. As regards the art students, fortified by a supper of garlic-scented saveloys, it provided a splendid opportunity for the release of animal spirits. While for fanatics like Borel and Charles Lassailly there was the joy of shocking a distinguished gathering which would not normally have acknowledged their existence.

Quaï and Perrier had demonstrated eccentricities of hair, beard, and dress, but in virtual isolation. Following them, in the grand era of the dandy, Eugène Devéria showed that the painter could vie with the literary man in sartorial invention. Unlike Delacroix, who cultivated an English sobriety long after others had tired of it, Devéria pushed his veneration for the sixteenth century to the point where elegance bordered on fancy-dress. As he could hardly adopt the gold brocade of a Venetian magnifico, he had set about modifying the costume of the day, and introduced a tail-coat with velvet facings and a waistcoat almost indistinguishable from a doublet. In addition, he had waxed a pair of Mephistophelian moustaches and wore his long, pointed beard at an angle well calculated to annoy the bourgeois.

By 1829, and particularly for the occasion of *Hernani*, self-expression in hair and dress was as general as it was various among the younger generation of artists and poets: '. . . wild whimsical characters, bearded, long-haired, dressed in every fashion except the reigning one, in pea-jackets, in Spanish cloaks, in waistcoats *à la* Robespierre, in Henry III bonnets, carrying on their heads and backs articles of costume from every century and clime, and this in the middle of Paris and in broad daylight' was Hugo's recollection of his faithful band of *claqueurs*, as they descended upon the theatre that afternoon.[16] And of these, Théophile Gautier seems to have been the most memorable, with his hair flowing over his shoulders and, blazing across his chest, the famous waistcoat of scarlet satin.

One of the youngest of the youthful company which supported *Hernani* during its run of forty-five performances was Célestin Nanteuil, then seventeen years of age. Scarcely eclipsed by Gautier, he wore on these occasions a long blue coat buttoned up to the chin in the style of a soutane. With his fair hair parted at the side and cut like that of a mediaeval student, it required little alteration to fit him for the title-rôle of Gautier's story, *Élias Wildmanstadius ou l'homme moyen-âge*.

Nanteuil did not become personally acquainted with Hugo till 1832. That, however, was a moment when he could make himself particularly useful, for Hugo required illustrators, and Nanteuil had a natural flair for Gothic pastiches. His first characteristic productions date from the year after his meeting with the poet; and though these etchings retain some of the clichés of the 'style troubadour' of the early 1820's, certain of them—the title-pages for *Notre-Dame de Paris* and the *Artiste* magazine leap to mind

—are brilliant and highly personal *tours de force*. But the demand for Gothic proved short-lived. The Goncourts, visiting the illustrator at Bougival, in 1855, found him dejected and hard-up; and thirteen years later he, too, was glad to apply for an official post, accepting, in fact, the one which had just become vacant on the death of Boulanger.

No atmosphere could have been better suited to Nanteuil's talent than that of the Hugo circle. Hugo himself had a passion for Gothic art and architecture, a passion that was the source of his inspiration in creating *Notre-Dame de Paris*; and, as a letter from Sainte-Beuve, written during the Rhine journey, shows, one that he communicated to other members of the 'cénacle'.[17]

The story of Sainte-Beuve's relationship with Hugo has no place here. But it must not be forgotten that he, too, played a leading part in bringing about this new association between writers and artists. Though friendly with Delacroix and Devéria, he found Boulanger and Victor Pavie more to his taste, and his closest alliance was with Paul Huet, whom he championed energetically for many years. When, in 1829, he published his *Poésies de Joseph Delorme*, he offered a first glimpse of that world of the artist which Vigny, Musset, Baudelaire, and Murger were all to elaborate later. And in 1830, as the first Romantic fellowship was about to break up, he wrote an article on Hoffmann, which shows a special sympathy for the artists of his own circle:

> Zacharius Werner, Berthold, Kreisler: all you restless geniuses with fear in your eyes, on whom the chill winds of the present age strike keenly; comfortless under the world's oppression, passionately attached to what is past, preserving a childlike belief in the future, mystics without faith, geniuses without proof, souls without bodies—how well he knew you, how well he loved you! [18]

If a close relationship with artists created in other members of the 'cénacle' sympathy and understanding, what was Hugo's own attitude and how far did he influence the development of a specifically 'artistic' self-consciousness? To the first part of the question it has often been answered, that his attitude was one of unqualified egoism, that he turned friendship to profit and lured those who admired him into ignoble dependence. Boulanger, according to this concept, threw up everything for a few kind words, and Nanteuil neglected art to act as adulterer's go-between.

Planche and Sainte-Beuve support that view, and Gautier's anxiety to be fair to both parties does little to combat it. But the facts and personalities involved certainly make for a more charitable conclusion.

While Hugo enjoyed playing the leading rôle, it is difficult to see what other he could have played. There may be something unattractive, but we can hardly call it sinister, about his relations with Boulanger. Even in a literary age of painting, artists are ill-advised to carry their regard for a writer to the pitch of adulation. But the weak will always admire the strong, and Hugo cannot be blamed outright for the failure of Boulanger, the Devérias, and Nanteuil to fulfil their early promise. A genius likely to stir the world would not have accepted Hugo so naïvely. Delacroix agreed to design the costumes for *Amy Robsart*, but (in spite of figuring in Albert Besnard's picture of the 'Battle of *Hernani*', painted over a century later!) did not, in fact, attend the Comédie-Française for that famous first-night. 'Homage' groups are usually composed of secondary talents, and Hugo's was no exception.

In fact, the poet has been blamed as often for neglect as for possessiveness. But it is clear that a small audience of artists could hardly have been expected to suffice for his restless ambition, and that sooner or later he would have to go out to win the allegiance of the great mass of middle-class readers whose natural spokesman he was. A comparison between his early prefaces and the reports of his views on art in later life reveals how little Hugo ever had in common with the young exhibitors of 1827. He took from them, as genius will, the particular elements of which he could make use, and was not entirely ungrateful in return. He fought in public on their behalf, as when he protested against the conditions leading to Antonin Moine's suicide; and, if he erred in raising false hopes among the young and inexperienced, he was far from being the only offender.

Hugo's influence exerted itself powerfully upon the conception of the artist; but not, like Balzac's, through the medium of the novel. There is no Sommervieux, no Frenhofer, no Joseph Bridau to be found in his work. Nothing in this way was offered to the public at large. The influence worked among writers and artists themselves. The 'grand cénacle' provided a new and exciting combination of the two professions, a combination for a purpose which was not mere social pleasure but an organized campaign in the Salon and the Theatre, in which both could play an equal part as brothers-in-arms. The leading spirits remained together for three brief years only, and the heights of Sainte-Geneviève were soon abandoned. But the example continued to provide inspiration. Though Hugo crossed the river in May, 1830, followed by his immediate admirers, the Latin Quarter had become the true soil of Romanticism. And on the stage thus temporarily deserted the scene is already set, not only for the Watteau-esque tragi-comedy of Musset's student-tales, but for the rough-and-tumble of Murger's *vie de Bohème.*

IV

Shocking the Burghers

i

When the Classicist stronghold had fallen and *Hernani* triumphed at the Comédie-Française, it was inevitable that the Romantic leaders should wish to resume their independence. The 'cénacle' dispersed. New interests engaged the attention of Vigny, Sainte-Beuve, and Musset. Hugo went into semi-retirement in order to satisfy the demands of his publishers. Thus the campaigners of February 25th found themselves unattached and without direction.

It was a grave moment for these young men of nineteen and twenty. Their zeal in securing the success of *Hernani* had brought them no personal advancement, and they had now to deal in earnest with the problems of art—and the problems of existence. The Revolution of July spelt disillusionment for this group, as for others, and its sense of isolation found expression in a line of Gautier's: 'Friends and foes, the masses and the kings, all mock and deceive us.' [1] Hugo retained his place in their affections, however; and it was a signed copy of *Cromwell* that occupied the place of honour in the studio of a young sculptor, Jean Duseigneur, or Jehan du Seigneur ('note well that *h*', as Gautier tells us, 'it is characteristic'), who occupied premises in a greengrocer's shop in the Rue de Vaugirard.[2]

Towards the end of 1830, the ablest of Hugo's lieutenants gathered here, among them Gérard de Nerval, Gautier, Borel, and Nanteuil, as well as Auguste Maquet, Alphonse Brot, Jules Vabre, Napoléon Tom, Philothée O'Neddy, and Joseph Bouchardy. When Gérard wrote to Sainte-Beuve, before the end of the year, 'I have become a member of the "petit cénacle", to which I find myself more and more attached', he was careful to add: 'Believe me, it has not been founded with intent to parody the other, the glorious "cénacle", to which you brought renown.' [3]

But Sainte-Beuve came to his own conclusions, on reviewing the episode in 1833. 'They thought it possible', he wrote, 'to continue, and reorganize on a broader basis, the "cénacle" sketched out by their elders in 1829'; an attempt, in the critic's opinion, bound to fail. And Sainte-Beuve deplored the exaggerated importance which the 'petit cénacle' gave to artists and their ideas.[4]

Indeed, the host and central figure of this group was the sculptor Duseigneur, and the concept of 'l'art pour l'art' came into existence along with his 'Roland furieux', exhibited at the Salon of 1831. But Duseigneur was only one artist among many. Gautier and Tom had trained as painters; Bouchardy was the son and brother of artists and himself a dabbler in engraving; Borel and Vabre had studied architecture. On the walls of the studio were sketches by Eugène and Achille Devéria and a copy of a Venetian painting by Boulanger. The group discussed, with enthusiasm, Delacroix, Ingres, and Decamps, 'our young great masters'. Excursions into the country beyond Montparnasse suggested the dual purpose of a notebook: one could either draw or write verses in it; and something of the art student passed into the group—more, into Romanticism itself. The older men of the 'grand cénacle' had felt the danger at the first performance of *Hernani*, and had been stirred to indignation by the display of animal spirits and the parade of the scarlet waistcoat which marked that occasion. Now, when the art student was gaining the upper hand in a society which pretended to imitate and prolong the 'grand cénacle', it annoyed not only the earlier Hugo circle but the general fraternity of letters.

It was not so much the ideals as the odd appearance and behaviour of Duseigneur's group that caught the eye. A newspaper invented the term 'jeunes-France' to describe the sculptor and his friends, and went on to ridicule the new *entente cordiale* between the arts:

> The poet said to the painter: 'You can paint, but you don't know how to use words; I will make you a present of my jargon'. . . . To which the painter replied: 'You can write, but you don't know how to use a brush; I will make you a present of my beard'. . . . And, from that day, painters have been able to write, and men of letters have worn beards.[5]

In discussing the second Romantic group of artists and writers, I shall not dwell at length on beards—nor on shock-heads, odd hats, and fantastic waistcoats. These had all been exhibited at the Battle of *Hernani*, and are in any case described with a wealth of detail in Gautier's *Histoire du Romantisme*. Contenting myself with that author's own explanation, 'we were out to discover something novel, strange, even a trifle shocking, in this line',[6] I can turn instead to a related, but more important, matter, which had not received much attention in the 'grand cénacle'.

ii

For it is now that the attitude, summed up in the phrase (sometimes attributed to Privat d'Anglemont) 'shocking the burghers', becomes really belligerent. A sudden intimate association with artists provided the impetus and established the attitude as a habit of mind. And when the writer had himself been brought up in the studio, it was harder to drop, than retain, the anti-bourgeois article of faith. What had up to now been a whimsical grievance confined to the scarcely articulate world of the *ateliers*, became, through the medium of the poem, the novel, and the newspaper-article, the most widely publicized attack upon society yet made on behalf of the artist. While the manifesto which expresses this point of view so forcefully, the Preface to *Mademoiselle de Maupin*, did not appear till 1835, its origin is undoubtedly to be looked for in the group presided over by Jean Duseigneur.

In the stormy months which marked the beginning of the July Monarchy, poetry and the *conte* almost disappeared from the daily Press, and the studio in the Rue de Vaugirard provided a refuge rather than an ambuscade. Those who met there insisted on the freedom of the artist and the autonomy of art as the first principles of their faith. Politics, which had begun to attract the former members of the 'grand cénacle', did not exist for these young men. None of them appears to have been 'out' during the *Trois Glorieuses* but Gérard, arrested for straying into a demonstration whose purpose was quite unknown to him! They took little interest in the 'People', in the Democrats, or Reactionaries. Only because it was impossible to avoid a pseudo-political label of some kind did the artists and writers of the Rue de Vaugirard accept the title 'jeunes-France', with its unfounded suggestion of Liberalism.

Yet it is true that the Revolution of 1830 left a mark on this community, for it changed baiting the bourgeois from a light-hearted studio prank into a serious demonstration. The Romantic writer and artist detested every representative of Louis-Philippe's triumphant bourgeoisie, from the 'progressive' industrialist who sought to fit art into his own pattern of social utility down to the mass of small businessmen, for whose benefit a new type of artistic and literary criticism was invading the newspapers. Even more detestable were the obstinate Classicists who still wrote and painted in that tradition, and seemed to have no other intention in doing so but to flatter the taste of the shopkeeper.

In the field of the visual arts, the patronage of the new king, though well-meaning, had stopped short of Romantic painting. Violent by its very nature, this new school was highly objectionable to Louis-Philippe himself and to the social group whose interests he supported. It is true that the Duke of Orleans, during his short lifetime, attempted to correct the prejudice. Delacroix, certainly, benefited by the change of government that brought his friends Thiers and Mérimée to power. But though the Duke purchased his 'Bishop of Liège' and the State his 'Liberty', the Salon of 1831, where these two pictures hung, filled champions of the new school with utter despondency, as witness the *Novissima verba* appended to Gustave Planche's review of the works exhibited that year:

> As we pen these final lines, the trial is over, the Royal ceremony concluded; medals and honourable mentions have been distributed, purchases and commissions all decided. Lord, what a motley crowd! Impossible to know where we are in the confusion! M. Dubufe alongside M. Champmartin! An honourable mention for Mme de Mirbel and for the finest portraits in the Salon! The pen drops from our hands. M. Paul Huet is not even mentioned.
>
> Ignorance, stupidity, and contempt! Ought we, on our side, to feel indignation or scorn? Alas for the arts, alas for France! Criticism is powerless! May faith and solitude offer some consolation to our great and genuine artists![7]

Offended by the taste shown in the Royal collection at Versailles, the artist was only too ready to join forces with Republicans and Socialists in their hostility towards the Philistine

King. The hymn of rejuvenated art (to borrow Cassagne's phrase) developed into a hymn of hate. The bourgeoisie, Louis-Philippe's most faithful supporters, became the object of a humiliating analysis and endless mockery. It was from 1830 that the talents of Henry Monnier were directed to this end, but almost every young poet and journalist with 'advanced' opinions played his part in the attack; Balzac himself exposing with particular relish the questionable methods by which fortunes were being made in the shops, on the Stock Exchange, and in the private offices of a few powerful and unscrupulous financiers.

To this money-grubbing bourgeoisie was opposed the type of the artist, generous and disinterested. As increasing wealth enabled the bourgeois to rise in the social scale, so the painter and sculptor kept pace with their claims to spiritual superiority: 'The artist', declared Préault, 'has longer, higher, and sharper vision than other men. "You see this star?" he says to the vulgar. "You don't? Well, *I* see it!" '[8] And the artist was quite prepared to demonstrate his spiritual superiority by open contempt, not just for middle-class taste, but for middle-class manners and morals. It is only a short step from Préault's 'Guillotine the baldpates!', at the 'Battle' of *Hernani*, to Borel's 'In Paris there's a den of robbers and a den of murderers: the first is the Stock-Exchange and the second the Law Courts';[9] and it was Borel who became the 'petit cénacle's' 'individualité pivotale'.

iii

The violence and extravagance of the more politically-minded of the group (among them Lassailly, who offered to assassinate Louis-Philippe with a needle dipped in prussic acid) eventually split the 'petit cénacle' in two. Gautier himself was drawn away into a new, intimate relationship with Hugo, now a neighbour in the Place Royale, which led him to a more sober interpretation of Romanticism.

The episode of the 'petit cénacle' is reflected in a number of Gautier's poems, however, and in two works of considerable interest in a study of the close association between artists and writers in the 1830's, *Albertus* and *Les Jeunes-France*. Albertus, the painter-hero of the poem of 1832, is the type of character that other young authors have invented to amuse their friends and annoy their elders, the type of Mardoche and Pelham, *beau cavalier*, conceited, amoral. The poem, though a mosaic of borrowings, contains much that is new. The element of word-painting, carried to lengths Hugo had never envisaged, would alone make it remarkable. But we find here, too, a complete portrait of the painter-poet of the 'petit cénacle'. As I have pointed out, the workshop of the artist had been a refuge for this group during the troubles of 1830, and afterwards a sort of intellectual fastness from which to view with disdain the bourgeois world outside. In *Albertus*, I believe, begins the now familiar trick of embellishing the artist's environment, of tantalizing the layman with hints of mysteries and forbidden pleasures to be enjoyed only in the studio.

Thus Gautier lingers over a description of the *atelier* of Albertus in the Hôtel du Singe-Vert:

> Savez-vous ce que c'est que l'atelier d'un peintre,
> Lecteur bourgeois?—Un jour discret tombant du cintre
> Y donne à chaque chose un aspect singulier.
> C'est comme les tableaux de Rembrandt, où la toile
> Laisse à travers le noir luire une blanche étoile.
> — Au milieu de la salle, auprès du chevalet,
> Sous le rayon brillant où vient valser l'atome,
> Se dresse un mannequin qu'on croirait un fantôme;
> Tout est clair-obscur et reflet.
>
> L'ombre dans chaque coin s'entasse plus profonde
> Que sous les vieux arceaux d'une nef. — C'est un monde,
> Un univers à part qui ne ressemble en rien
> A notre monde à nous; — un monde fantastique,
> Où tout parle aux regards, où tout est poétique . . .*

* 'Do you know what a painter's studio is, bourgeois reader? A discreet illumination, falling from the arched window, gives each object there a strange character of its own. It is like those pictures by Rembrandt in which the canvas shows a white star shining through the blackness. In the centre of the room, beside the easel, under the lambent beam whither the dancing mote revolves, stands a lay-figure, which you would take for a ghost: all is chiaroscuro and reflection.

'The shadow piles up in every corner more profoundly than under the ancient arches of a nave. It is a world, a universe, apart, in no way resembling this world of ours; a fantastic world, in which everything has visual eloquence, in which everything is poetical. . . .' [10]

From the single piece of Hungarian leather which modestly decorated the studio-wall in the Rue de Vaugirard a vast inventory of Japanese vases, Chinese fans, and mediaeval bric-à-brac is multiplied for the studio of Albertus. In the fictitious painter's works, finished or unfinished, we find the style of Delacroix mixing freely with that of the Italian fifteenth and seventeenth centuries—'Salvator would have signed' the landscape on the easel, at the moment of interruption; but when Albertus summons his valet: 'Quick, man, my cape and my sombrero!' and stalks off to his Faust-like consummation, we feel we have encountered an image of the artist even less real than Nodier's Charles Munster.

Though invented artists must always, alas, fall short of conviction, the special absurdity of Albertus calls for some explanation. It is to be found partly in the satirical attitude inseparable from the Gautier of the *Jeunes-France* stories and the Preface to *Mademoiselle de Maupin*, but, more subtly, the absurdity derives from the works of E. T. A. Hoffman which Loève-Veimars began to translate in 1830.

It would be impossible to consider adequately here an influence with such universal repercussions. A mild vogue for the 'fantastique' had preceded the Hoffmannesque in France with the demonstrations of Mesmer, echoes of which can be found in Cazotte's *Diable amoureux*, so eagerly read by young Alfred and Paul de Musset. Long before the translations of Loève-Veimars began to appear, Chateaubriand had memorably linked the idea of beauty with *les choses mystérieuses*. But Hoffmann's art gave a new twist to these 'mysteries', charming immediately both generations of Romantics. In 1829, in the same issue of the *Mercure*, were published the initial extracts of a story by Hoffmann and the translation of an essay by Walter Scott in which Hoffmann was directly attacked. The fact that Scott's denunciation fell upon deaf ears enables us to date the rise to popularity of the *conte fantastique* from that year. Now, 1829 was just the moment when artists and writers began to enjoy a new phase of intimacy in the Rue Notre-Dame-des-Champs; and the first example of Hoffmann's talent made available to the public by the *Mercure* was the study of a painter, *Salvator Rosa*.

If Nodier, Balzac, and Hugo all eagerly followed Hoffmann, the first with his *Du Fantastique en littérature*, the second with *Le Chef-d'œuvre inconnu*, in which Frenhofer comes astonishingly close to Hoffmann's Berklinger, and the third with his description of the alchemistic experiments of Claude Frollo, it is hardly surprising that their juniors exploited the same material to which, as it happened, scientific research lent a particular contemporaneity. Artists, indeed, and the artists whom the 'petit cénacle' particularly admired, had prepared the way. Delacroix drew the lithographs for *Faust* in 1828. In the Salon, during subsequent years, appeared Boulanger's 'Witches' Sabbath' and 'Fire from Heaven'. Tony Johannot initiated a vogue for *diableries* with his engravings for the *Danse macabre* of the bibliophil Jacob. Artists, we know, were well acquainted with the *Capriccios* of Goya, but Delacroix, who had been studying them as far back as 1820, nevertheless invoked the German author to describe an element of the uncanny about a certain official of the French Embassy at Madrid, in 1832, observing: 'Hoffmann could make something of this character.' [11]

While there is a crudely melodramatic side to the *Phantasiestüke*, and this too had its appeal for the 'petit cénacle', the remarkable quality of Hoffmann's imagination is shown in the skill with which he delineates the complex mind of the artist. In the Lavigne selection (to choose at random one of countless French editions over the years), as many as seven out of the seventeen stories are built round the character and habits of painters and goldsmiths.[12] In *Salvator Rosa*—as I have said, the first of his works to be published in a French translation—a host of vital and topical problems are discussed: among them, those of artist *versus* bourgeois; individual *versus* academy; genius in love; and posthumous recognition, with all its ironies.

Hoffmann, himself a clever draughtsman and caricaturist as well as musician, infused his tales of the artist with an artist's rich imagination and passion. So haunting was his own personality that in several stories, written by admirers, he himself is made to put in a dramatic appearance. From the combined impression of the man Hoffman was imagined to be and the actual tenor of his writing emerged an image of the artist as a wild, unconventional genius, torn perpetually between ambition and despair.

If we keep Hoffmann in mind, Albertus becomes understandable: for the notion (unsupported by any evidence!) that works of art can be more easily created in an atmosphere of chaos arrives now, and stays. It helps to explain, and may well have been used to justify, the eccentricities of Borel and Gérard; and though Gautier himself had a sound respect for order, the element of disorder is still the chief characteristic of Albertus. We must remember that the author of this poem mixed only with artists (like himself) very young and inexperienced. He had never visited the studio of Delacroix, nor seen for himself how meticulous was the routine of the landscape-painter Rousseau.

In *Les Jeunes-France*, Gautier turned from fantasy to mockery, though more than a hint of mockery had been apparent in *Albertus*. In the satire that followed there was also evidence of an underlying seriousness, and—from what he wrote long afterwards—we know that Gautier never quite lost patience with his victims. It was here his purpose to make fun of them, but the thirst for glory, whose manifestations can be so ridiculous, also aroused in him another sentiment: 'A feeling of pity overcomes me, when I think of this terrible, devouring ambition to make our names universally famous.' [13] And he can hardly have been unaware of those less fortunate than himself and his friends, who, in pursuit of the same goal, were—too many of them—ending their lives by violence, or in the sanatorium of Dr Blanche and in the public wards of the hospitals.

Untouched by tragedy as yet, the egotism of the 'petit cénacle' had already been the subject of some sallies in the Press, and was even better material for a disciple turned informer. Albertus is made to step out of his imaginary Flemish studio and abandon himself to the mundane pleasures of contemporary Paris, to the short black pipe and the 'sweet little doll, capable of making you fall head-over-heels in love; for an hour, at least'.[14] In his description of the conversion of Daniel Jovard from Classicist to Romantic, Gautier seizes the chance of poking fun at the manners and speech of the 'petit cénacle', and its wonderful self-importance: 'Already at the full height of your genius,' the bewildered Jovard is assured, 'you are winging your way over the vile bourgeois as an eagle soars above a hen-run! From now on, you can call yourself an artist; from now on, you have a *profanum vulgus*.' [15] In fact, these young artists are far from original.

Onuphrius sees the streets of Paris—and even his mistress—through the eyes of Hoffmann; Élias Wildmanstadius has surrendered himself so completely to the craze for Gothic art that he becomes a figure of farce. The situation in the *Bol de punch* arises from a desire to imitate Balzac, Janin, and Eugène Sue.

In this last story, we find that the *rapin*'s tastes have undergone a curious transformation since the rebellion against David. Now, in the 1830's, Greeks and Romans are both anathema. The Italian primitives are worshipped only by a few eccentrics, and the cult of the mediaeval is definitely *vieux jeu*. Instead, it is fashionable to decorate one's studio with trophies from Africa and the East; and the Renaissance, in its many varied aspects, dominates all. But there is something in addition. This is a revival of interest in the masters of the late seventeenth and eighteenth centuries, an admiration for Rigaud, for Watteau, for the pastel-portraits, 'fardés et souriants', of the Regency, and for Boucher. We may take this as a sign that the rule of Borel is over. At any rate, the spirit of *fête galante* which hovers over the Doyenné, the next headquarters of artists and writers, owes nothing to the 'Lycanthrope'.

iv

These headquarters were shared by Camille Rogier, Gérard de Nerval, and Arsène Houssaye in the ancient and decaying quarter which then separated the Place du Carrousel from the Louvre. On a site somewhere between later monuments to Gambetta and La Fayette ran the Rue, and the Impasse, du Doyenné. To the south-east, the galleries of the Louvre and the river enclosed a stretch of waste ground dominated by the ruins of Saint-Thomas-du-Louvre, the appearance of which is nostalgically conveyed to us in words by Gérard and in paint by a charming little picture, the work of Mlle Jaunez, in the Carnavalet Museum.

Towards the end of 1834, Théophile's father, Pierre Gautier, was transferred to a post in the Customs at Passy. Théophile's new career as a journalist, as well as his desire to remain in close touch with Hugo and his friends, demanded that he should now set up a home for himself in the centre of Paris. Accordingly, he rented two rooms in the Rue du Doyenné, rooms—as it turned out—which were to be little more than a dormitory: 'I was hardly ever there except at night, for my days were spent with the friends who shared Rogier's room.'

It was in this salon of Rogier's, vast, ornate, and falling picturesquely into decay, that the famous fancy-dress ball was given; when, following Gérard's advice, 'refreshments were replaced by frescoes daubed all over the ancient grey panelling: to the horror of the landlord, who regarded these paintings as so many blots on his walls. Corot, Adolphe Leleux, Célestin Nanteuil, Camille Rogier, Lorentz, Théodore Chassériau, very young men at the time, put their brushes to good use and improvised charming fantasies.' [16] Information given by Gautier elsewhere, and by Gérard de Nerval, enables us to add to this list of artists and to arrive at some idea of the work itself.

We learn, for instance, that it was Marilhat (an unexpected visitor) who contributed the Egyptian landscape; while Gérard speaks of a 'Red Monk' by Auguste de Chatillon. When the Doyenné was finally demolished in 1850, the author of the *Petits Châteaux de Bohème* was able to buy up some of these sketches, and his acquisitions included, besides the picture by Chatillon, Chassériau's tiger-taming 'Bacchantes', and two pier-glasses decorated by Rogier, 'in which the Cydalise, in Regency costume—a gown of dead-leaf taffeta: sad omen—inhaled the scent of a rose, her Chinese eyes smiling up at the portrait of Théophile dressed as a Spaniard'.[17]

Lorentz's 'Siege of Lerida' and two small landscapes by Rousseau had disappeared by this time, but Gérard was able to rescue another panel by Lorentz, 'a powdered *maréchale*, in Louis XV uniform'. One would give much to know how Corot came to be connected with the Doyenné, and what form his contribution took in the embellishment of a room 'now legendary', so Houssaye wrote later, 'as the rendez-vous of the first literary Bohemia'.[18] Unfortunately, the period 1830–1850 is so thinly documented as far as Corot is concerned that we have little hope of finding the answer to our questions.

It was, then, in the spirit of the *fêtes galantes* of Watteau, Lancret, and Fragonard, that the ball for which these pictures were designed took place. 'Happy time!' sighs Gérard. 'We gave balls, suppers, fancy-dress parties, and staged comedies of the old-fashioned sort. . . . We were young, always in high spirits, even, on occasion, *wealthy*. . . .' [19]

We must not forget the material resources of the Doyenné, since this *salon-atelier* of Rogier's with its 'good-natured laughter', its delight in scandalizing the neighbours, and its 'Cydalises', comes so close to Murger's Bohemia, that one might suppose the Gautier group and the attic-dwellers of the Rue des Canettes had a great deal in common. They had not. While Murger and his associates were outcasts, this earlier society enjoyed a normal relationship with the world. Such members of the public as they cared to invite to their gatherings were glad enough to accept—and bring their ladies with them. In spite of some freakish costumes, a high standard of cleanliness, even of elegance, was observed, as became the peers of Roger de Beauvoir and Gavarni. Cash, in fact, was never seriously short. Gérard enjoyed financial independence, and Rogier earned a good living as an illustrator. Gautier's family, though never rich, did not press him to adopt a career and was always ready to assist when necessary. Distinguished poets and novelists and wealthy patrons of the arts paid frequent visits to this oasis in the heart of the city. There were no alarming debts nor serious problems of day-to-day existence.

And yet the use made by Gérard and Gautier of the term 'bohemia' to describe the experience of their early manhood is not ridiculous. By the 1850's, the flexibility of this fashionable word was such that its application, especially when qualified by the epithet 'galante', does not really ring false. It conveys the notion of a group of young artists and writers, with their mistresses, consciously withdrawn from society. Here, however, were no battles as yet with those formidable enemies of youthful genius, want, ill-health, disillusionment. The whole episode was like a flirtation with life, an entertainment in fancy-dress, which seemed, in Gérard's words, 'the ghostly re-enactment of a century-old play'.

Even the ardour of the battle between Classic and Romantic had somewhat abated. Growing towards maturity, the poets and painters of the Doyenné began to find a new enjoyment in life. The period of the barricades and the cholera was over. Little by little the attitude typified by *Werther* and *René* and the 'sup from the skull' was abandoned. Gérard's paper, the *Monde dramatique*, to which a number of his literary and artistic friends contributed, adopted a less militant view of things. Hugo still claimed their admiration as a writer, but his political ambitions roused no answering enthusiasm in them.

The war-cries of *Hernani* 'died upon the ear', and, older and wiser now, the *claqueurs* settled down at last to the cultivation of their own talents. Each showed his independence in his dress as well as in his books: Gautier remained as flamboyant as ever, Gérard as inconspicuous, Houssaye a splendid figure 'in the strict fashion of to-day—or the day after'; and works were produced as different from each other as Houssaye's *Pécheresse*, Ourliac's *Suzanne*, and Gautier's own *Mademoiselle de Maupin*.

V

Anxious as Gautier and his friends may have been to avoid the scandals stirred up by Borel and the left-wing, 'Bousingot' faction, they could not do so. The attack launched by the *Constitutionnel*, in May, 1834, against the immorality of certain articles published by Gautier in *La France littéraire* might equally well have come from other sources and on other pretexts, for moralists and 'utilitaires' let slip no opportunity of doing battle with those who treated art in so cavalier a fashion.

By insisting on the divine character of the poet and on his social responsibilities as 'pastor of the community' they had contrived to win over Hugo and Lamartine to their way of thinking. In the 'petit cénacle' and the Doyenné, however, such overtures fell upon deaf ears. Hugo's changes of opinion were now none of these young men's concern, and they chose to remember him only as the author of the Preface to *Cromwell*, who had urged them to avoid the commonplace, search out the 'characteristic', and never rest in the battle against rules and systems.

The weightier the arguments brought forward by the Saint-Simonian, the more stubbornly were they resisted. The aims of the 'petit cénacle' are set out in detail in the *Histoire du Romantisme*, and though, with the group's extreme youth, much of its early violence had passed away, not much goading was necessary to revive it. Gautier, for instance, lists these aims as follows:

> To develop freely every intellectual fancy, whether or not it shocks taste, conventions, and rules; to hate and repulse to the utmost what

Horace called the *profanum vulgus*, and what moustachoed, long-haired *rapins* mean by 'shopkeepers', 'Philistines', or 'bourgeois'; to celebrate the pleasures of love with a passion capable of scorching the paper on which we record them, insisting upon love as the sole end and sole means of happiness; and to sanctify and deify Art, regarded as second Creator: such are the underlying ideas of the programme which each one of us, according to his strength, tries to practise—the ideal and secret ordinances of Romantic youth.[20]

The year 1834—the Preface to *Mademoiselle de Maupin* is dated May—conveniently divides the era of the 'petit cénacle' from that of the Doyenné. In 1834, Gautier began to realize that defective sight would make it impossible for him to take up painting as a career; but his relations with artists were never closer. Artists and would-be artists, in fact, outnumbered writers among his friends; and the influence of the studio is to be found, not only in the prose and verse picture-making already alluded to, but in the very foundation of his vocabulary. In his early work, as well as adjectives meticulously specifying colour, words like 'chic', 'galbe', 'poncif', 'rococo', and 'bonhomme'—regular studio-slang—are of frequent occurrence. Referring at the end of his life to these days, he declared: 'I was the painter of the group. . . . I laid out all the colours of the sunrise on the palette of my style.' [21] Much might be said of the rôle that the painter's technique played in Gautier's writing, the conscious application of colour, as it is floated or scumbled on; the building-up of impasto effects; the controlled flourish of the brush performing an arabesque. But the real point made by *Albertus* and *Les Jeunes-France*, and then confirmed by the Preface to *Mademoiselle de Maupin*, was less esoteric. It amounted to a witty rejection of all that society—in its character of moralist, 'utilitaire', or critic—had come to demand of the artist and his work. And what Gautier rejected wittily he also rejected authoritatively, as the chief spokesman of the painters and sculptors of his generation.

First (thus the *Preface* begins), the artist is a man who laughs at conventional morality; conventional morality is 'a very agreeable grandmother, but still a grandmother', to whom it is only natural, 'especially in one's twenties', to prefer any 'fetching little bit of fluff'.[22] Virtue lacks variety and physical attraction, and the artist cannot be expected to make such sacrifices for its sake. And since religion seeks to mortify the flesh, Gautier has no use for that either.

The accepted duties and responsibilities he leaves to others:

> I would very happily renounce my rights as a Frenchman and as a citizen to see an authentic painting by Raphael; or a naked woman: the Princess Borghese, for instance, as she posed for Canova; or Julia Grisi, stepping into her bath.[23]

Discipline of any kind is hateful, but especially the kind of discipline which society delegates to its theorists and critics. Of these, the 'vertueux', the 'utilitaires', and the 'progressifs' are dismissed with equal scorn. It is an age of journalism. 'The newspaper kills the book', says Gautier, echoing Hugo's 'The book has killed architecture'; but he could hardly have added: 'The newspaper kills the picture', for, as Delacroix had already pointed out, publicity, however unpleasant in itself, was the artist's best friend, and daily critics of art had become necessary evils: 'In the very act of wounding you,' the painter was forced to admit, 'they prove that you are alive.'[24]

There is nothing high-minded about Gautier's artist, however. He is deliberately flippant, especially when opposing the idea that art has some service to render to the community. Insisting on the purposelessness of a work of art, he uses an analogy well calculated to offend the burgher: 'To the pot under my bed, which is useful, I prefer the Chinese vase, which is no use at all'; and, as a personal declaration of faith: 'It seems to me that civilized man's best occupation lies in twiddling his thumbs, or smoking his pipe or cigar *analytically*.'[25] The artist, in fact, is a dilettante, and his art ought to be encouraged and valued as a luxury. Provided he remains true to himself, and is prepared to supply the élite with the exquisite article that the élite alone can appreciate, he has fulfilled his social duty. There is no question of pleasing the bourgeois. If art were really important (as it had been during the Renaissance), the bourgeois would properly have no voice in the matter at all.

Whether or not the middle-class reader, peremptorily put in his place, threw the book down in disgust at this point, or went on to read the story of Mademoiselle de Maupin, the Preface must have confirmed his unease on encountering young writers and artists in the Rue de Vaugirard or the Rue du Carrousel; for the *claqueurs* passed on to the next generation all the outward trappings which had enlivened the performances of *Hernani*:

> One had a black beard trimmed in the style of Francis I [so Gautier describes the eclectic [band], another's had been brought to a point, hair brushed up *à la* Saint-Mégrin, while a third wore a *royale*, like Cardinal Richelieu. The rest, too young to possess this important accessory, made up for it by the length of their hair. One had dressed himself in the black velvet doublet and close-fitting pantaloons of a mediaeval archer; another in the coat of a member of the National Convention, together with a soft, pointed hat of the most delicate design; and yet another combined a dandified frock-coat of exaggerated cut with a ruff of the period of Henry IV. The remaining details of their costume were all equally contradictory, so that they gave the impression of having been picking about at random among the old clothes of centuries, from which they had fished out something that, somehow or other, made up a complete wardrobe.[26]

Gautier and his friends had struck a zigzag course between Hugo's self-discipline and the idleness of the dandy, crowning industrious days with white nights and interrupting serious discussion to indulge in the crude horseplay of the art school. The painter of 1835 had become a *painter-poet* who presented his card with a bow, but his smile was impertinent and the pasteboard scrawled over with indecencies.

V

A Philosophy of Despair

i

The July Revolution brought the bourgeoisie to power, and the bourgeoisie, according to its mood, expected to be soothed or diverted by the artists in its midst. Some were ready enough to comply. Others, as we have just seen, opposed with every extravagance and paradox at their command the monstrous suggestion that they should subordinate the aims of art to their 'mission' (whatever that might mean) as citizens.

We must remember, however, that the group of the Doyenné represented one coterie only within the Romantic movement as a whole. The doctrine of Art for Art's Sake, as presented by Gautier, was not likely to win approval from leaders of the original 'cénacle', from Hugo, Sainte-Beuve, Vigny, or Musset, much as it might please some of the younger writers and artists.

Gautier, in the enthusiasm of the moment, had overstated his case. In particular, the parallels between painting and writing were open to objection. His background and companions being what they were, he had tended to stress too much the importance of the *homme spécial* in the writer's approach to his work. He assumed too readily that an almost exclusive searching after effect—understandable (with certain qualifications) in a painter —might be used to advantage in literary production. It did not require much common sense to envisage the sterility to which such 'transpositions of art', as Gautier called them, were bound to lead. Sainte-Beuve, by no means reconciled to the younger friends of Hugo, was among the first to point out the folly of their attitude in this respect, as Musset was to mock its more obvious affectations, and Vigny to condemn its indifference to the larger problems confronting the artist.

Though Gautier, on behalf of the Doyenné, preoccupied himself with style and advertised his scorn for social conventions, other writers had pursued, and continued to pursue, a more traditional Romantic theme. This was the selection of a representative figure from the modern world and the idealization of his character and mission—as Balzac chose the doctor in his *Médecin de campagne*; and Léon Gozlan, the barrister and the journalist. Earlier, it would have been a matter of course to hand to the poet the part of sage and interpreter. Now, however, the aspirations of the people were being expressed by spokesmen of their own (like Michel Masson, in his *Contes de l'atelier*—'atelier' in the sense of industrial workshop), and the poet himself, having scornfully washed his hands of the responsibilities of everyday life, could no longer fulfil this rôle. In an uncouth and brutal society, what was the alternative to the provoking impertinence of Gautier's creed? Vigny found it in dignified resignation.

His *Consultations du docteur Noir, ou les Diables bleus*, with its three narrative studies of Gilbert, Chatterton, and Chénier, appeared in the *Revue des Deux-Mondes* between October and April, 1831–1832, and were published in book form, under the title *Stello*, in the following June. I deal with his conception of the artist *after* Gautier's, however, because it was not till nearly three years later, in February 1835, that the dramatic version of *Chatterton* received its first performance at the Comédie-Française; and it was the success of the play that forced the public to take Vigny's ideas on artistic martyrdom seriously.

Since these ideas are closely related to his own character and experience, I may be forgiven for drawing attention, for a moment, to events which helped to crystallize them. Hugo had been immediately attracted to Vigny, and the attraction proved mutual until internal jealousies began to disturb the 'grand cénacle'. In a group where Hugo's robust talent commanded more and more attention, Vigny's own small, exquisite production was regarded—with Sainte-Beuve's connivance—as a sign of impotence. The first coldness between the two poets arose in 1829. After the Censor's rejection of *Marion de Lorme*, Hugo attempted to follow it immediately with *Hernani*, then in process of composition. But Vigny's *Othello* had already been accepted and he was determined that this arrangement should stand. The difference was patched up, but not forgotten. *Othello* was staged in October 1829, and four months later Vigny had the satisfaction of believing that the triumph of *Hernani* had been made possible by the *succès d'estime* of his own play.

But, in July of the following year, the Revolution brought a more serious break. Hugo, embittered by the new régime's banning of *Le Roi s'amuse*, developed sympathies that Vigny thought prejudicial to good order. Political events, in fact, forced the underlying antagonism between the two men to the surface. Hugo's sympathies were with the People, Vigny was an aristocrat; or, to use the term sarcastically employed by Sainte-Beuve to weaken Hugo's regard for his friend, a 'gentleman'.

Between the years 1833 and 1840, the Romantics divided themselves into two groups, Boulanger and Gautier remaining faithful to Hugo, Vigny attracting into his separate orbit Brizeux, Barbier, and the Deschamps brothers, who had been his closest friends before the institution of the 'grand cénacle'. Increasingly aware of his inability to satisfy popular taste and hypercritical of a world which, he felt, underestimated him, Vigny began to shape a philosophy to meet the circumstances.

In his *Journal* for 1829 and 1830, he had already expressed the pessimism which was to form so important a part of his outlook, together with his disdain of applause: 'A man of intellect ought to value his work according to its *lack* of popular appeal'; and his self-sufficiency: 'An artist must, and can, love no one but himself.' [1]

The year 1831 marked a further stage in Vigny's dislike of society: it was the beginning of the agonies and complications of his association with Mme Dorval. The Theatre, though he wrote for it *La Maréchale d'Ancre*, seemed to him to symbolize the growing vulgarity of the day, and he refused to sign a playwright's protest against the Censorship. In spite of his old friends' successes, among them Hugo's *Notre-Dame de Paris* and Dumas's *Napoléon*, or perhaps because of them, he turned to a more recent group of acquaintances, particularly to Brizeux.

The curious attraction for Vigny of the unfortunate had a bearing on his conception of the artist. I have already mentioned his attitude to the popular success that had always just eluded him. There were other grievances, and one that loomed especially large: 'To be born poor is the greatest evil of all. In a society based on wealth, one can never get over this.' In more than one autobiographical passage in his *Journal* he laments the loss of the family estates; and the vexations of an interminable law-suit which ultimately deprived his wife of her inheritance, though 'stoically endured', made him more conscious than ever of his own narrow means.

By the standards he set himself, he was a poor man; in comparison with more fortunate or prolific writers, he could believe himself a neglected one. The companions most to his liking, therefore, were others whom misfortune had prepared for the revelation of martyred genius. An early favourite in this character was the Breton poet, Auguste Brizeux. While still a student (he was nine years younger than Vigny), he had written glowing appreciations of *Héléna* and *Éloa*; and, by 1831, their grateful author was sending letters to him that read like preliminary drafts for *Stello*, then appearing as a serial in the *Revue des Deux-Mondes*.

Quite apart from the difference in years, there seems something rather odd about this exchange of confidences between Vigny, the aristocrat and dandy, and Brizeux, the publisher's hack, obliged to refuse invitations because he had no decent clothes. Brizeux, however, was never sordid, and he justified Vigny's belief in him as much by his courage in adversity as by the naïve simplicity of his verse. When he did complain of his lot, his correspondent offered various remedies. 'What you have told me', wrote Vigny, on one occasion, 'is the exact, sad truth of the matter. . . . I have been all through this myself, and have found a strange cure for such unavoidable despair: *scorn*. . . .' And he goes on:

> The pariahs of society are its poets, the men of soul and feeling, the superior and honourable men. The powers-that-be detest them, for in these poets they recognize their own judges, those who will condemn them before the bar of Posterity. But the third-rate fellow, who can be bought cheap, they love—they fear him too, because he knows how to sling their kind of mud. However, they fear those who soar above them less than those who walk in the gutter. Oh, how horrible it all is! *Desperatio!*[2]

Though at the last generously pensioned by the State—a move Vigny himself had prompted—Brizeux died in 1858 as a result of his long years of privation. A similar tale could be told of Antoni Deschamps; of Fontaney who, with his mistress (the daughter of Mme Dorval), perished from hunger and cold in 1837; of Mickiewicz, the poverty-stricken author of *Konrad Wallenrod*; of Gustave Planche, perpetually hard-up and disreputable; and of others still who were befriended and assisted by Vigny. But the letter I have just quoted leads us directly to the personification of the new point of view, to 'Stello' himself.

ii

The studies of Gilbert, Chatterton, and Chénier, which make up the novel of 1832, are linked together by discussions between a young poet, the Stello of the title, and a distinguished 'physician of souls', the docteur Noir. The Doctor has no difficulty in diagnosing his patient's illness as the 'blue devils', and to cure them he prescribes three stories to be told by himself. Poison counteracts poison, and the real misfortunes of other poets—'We are in complete agreement in understanding by "poets" *everyone dedicated to the Muse or the Arts*' [3]—will charm away Stello's imaginary sickness. Without enthusiasm, Stello agrees to undergo the treatment; and the Doctor embarks on the first stage, or the first of his three stories, the *Histoire d'une puce enragée.*

Taking advantage of the good humour of Louis XV and Mlle de Coulanges, who have summoned him to the Trianon on a farcical errand, the Doctor decides to speak to them of a young poet who lies starving in the house of the Archbishop of Paris, and begs assistance on his behalf. The King is furious, reads the Doctor a lecture on the fickleness of versifiers in general, and abruptly dismisses him. In the Archbishop's house, to which the Doctor hastens next, the poet is dying. He has refused food, asking the Archbishop's blessing instead. With his last breath he recites the famous passage beginning:

> 'Au banquet de la vie infortuné convive . . .',

which identifies him as Gilbert.

In the *Histoire de Kitty Bell*, the ubiquitous Doctor is once again an eye-witness, this time in the London home of John and Kitty Bell, where Chatterton lodges. The narrator makes Kitty's acquaintance over the counter of the confectioner's shop which she manages for her husband, and is shown a letter to her from the poet. This reveals the secret of the 'Rowley' manuscripts, their author's destitution, and his last remaining hope that the Lord Mayor, Beckford, will come to his aid. But when the two meet in Bell's shop, it is evident that Beckford has no great opinion of poets. After a passionate declaration of faith by Chatterton, the Lord Mayor tosses him a note containing, so he says, an offer of employment which he will do well not to disregard. Chatterton reads the note, and promptly throws his manuscripts into the fire. 'Good! I've reformed him: see, he renounces his poetry', says Beckford, misinterpreting the action. The catastrophe follows swiftly. Kitty begs the Doctor to go to her protégé, who has retired to his garret and may, she fears, be contemplating suicide. But it is too late. The poet, having destroyed what is left of his literary projects, takes poison. As a last request, he begs the Doctor to purchase his corpse and pay the debt to his landlord. John Bell receives the guineas owing to him with every token of satisfaction; but Kitty, who has returned the young man's pure affection, suffers a mortal blow, and when the Doctor returns to the house after the funeral, she too is dead.

This is how poets are treated under a monarchy and a constitutional government! What they may expect from the rule of the People is made plain in the third and last tale, *Une Histoire de la Terreur*. Here Chénier is the victim not of neglect but of active malice and brutality. In the last days of Robespierre, the docteur Noir enjoys the dangerous privilege of being medical adviser to both Jacobins and aristocrats. At the Maison Lazare he gives what assistance he can to Mme de Sainte-Aignan and other pathetic enemies of the State; in Robespierre's lodgings he is forced to listen patiently to the platitudes of the demagogue and to the bigotry of Saint-Just. A visit from Chénier's father involves him in the ill-fated attempt to rescue André, which has the opposite effect of bringing the poet more certainly to the scaffold. Here, private sources of information and recently-published material enabled Vigny to draw convincing pictures of the last terrible scenes in the refectory of the prison and the Place de la Révolution, as well as of the confused events that lead to Robespierre's fall.

Such are the carefully-selected backgrounds against which Vigny presents his triple portrait of the poet, in whom, as the Doctor says, we are to see also the painter and the sculptor. But it is clear that Vigny's 'homme de la Muse ou des Arts', be he ostensibly Gilbert, Chatterton, or Chénier, is as much a Romantic, a man of 1830, as any hero of Balzac's.

In his *Journal* for 1831, the author wrote: 'What has done me more harm than anything else in life is to have been fair-haired and slight in build'; and in 1834: 'If I were a painter, I would be a dark Raphael: angelic in form, sombre in colour.' By making his poets dark, melancholy, beautiful—and ever beautiful, since, like Raphael, they die young—Vigny subscribed to a vogue most perfectly summed up in the early self-portrait of Delacroix as Hamlet (or Childe Harold) and in the same artist's poetic rendering of his friend Baron Schwiter, now in the National Gallery. Consider the description of Chatterton: 'Dark, unpowdered hair falling over his ears; the profile of a young Spartan; a fine brow; large, steady, deep-set, piercing eyes; a firm chin under thin lips, which seem never to have been able to smile.' [4] Of Chénier, the Doctor says: 'I noticed particularly the pale, sad, passionate, careworn face of this young man, who wandered silently through the crowd with sunken head and arms folded.' [5] In both (Gilbert he saw only vaguely, as 'very noble and very beautiful') [6] he observed the same dark hair and large dark eyes.

The clothes worn by Chatterton are not without interest, since we have had occasion to notice how boldly the artist expressed himself through dress. 'Chatterton's attire', says Vigny, 'was unrelieved black from head to foot; his coat, tightly buttoned up to his cravat, gave him an air both military and clerical.' [7] Indeed, Chénier's *air d'officier* suggests not only the soldier in Vigny himself, but those military-style dandies of the Empire and Restoration who, as I have pointed out, supply an early model of the emancipated artist.

Having excited his readers' interest in the beauty and gallantry of his hero, the author calls for their sympathy or, unashamedly, their tears. The lengths to which he was prepared to go in this direction are illustrated by the last moments of Gilbert and Chatterton. Chénier, under the cold blade of the guillotine, makes, of course, the most melodramatic exit of all.

Nevertheless, Vigny considered that the moral still needed underlining, and conversations between Stello and the Doctor provide commentary and post-mortem. The Doctor recognizes in Stello the eternal artist, the spirit of Gilbert, Chatterton, and Chénier incarnate. And yet Stello is also an artist of the 1830's, as Vigny envisaged that ideal contemporary who would have absorbed his own teachings, brooding in a darkened room, the very name a symbol of detachment from the world.

To some extent, this was the artist already created by Hoffmann and, latterly, by Hoffmann's imitators. Thus, when the vogue for the *conte fantastique* began to wane, Vigny's desperate young poet and his mysterious docteur Noir, ought by rights to have suffered the common fate of stereotypes. As far as the young and impressionable were concerned, they did not. *Stello* appealed to the rising generation of 1840 as it had to that of 1830: a proof not only of Vigny's genius as storyteller, but of his skill as prophet.

The commentary had begun with a fierce argument between Stello and the Doctor; but towards the end of the book, their differences are resolved. 'Of the three kinds of Government, then,' says Stello, 'the first fears us, the second scorns us as useless, the third hates us and regards us as aristocrats because we are its superiors. Are we therefore to be the slaves of society for ever?' 'Its slaves, or its gods . . .' the Doctor replies enigmatically. 'The Mob nurses you in her arms, but observes you—as she does all her children—with a malicious eye; and every so often she hurls you to the ground and tramples you underfoot. She is an evil mother.' [8]

Suffering, maintains the Doctor, is the proof of genius. The 'lovable spirits', Gilbert, Chatterton, and Chénier, deserve special regard, but the list can be extended to include some sixteen others who have bestowed priceless gifts upon the world and experienced poverty and neglect in return. Nor does he forget Brizeux and his fellow-unfortunates, adding to the Roll of Honour 'all those also whose names are written in each nation's Valhalla and on the registers of its hospitals'.[9]

What is the sum-total of the Doctor's advice on the attitude the public ought to adopt to its poets and artists? It is contained in his simile of the swallows, who cry: 'Protect us, but let us go free.' And the poet, since all social systems are bad, and solitude alone is blessed, must derive what comfort he can from cultivating a patient and resigned despair.

iii

The production of the three-act drama, *Chatterton*, based on the story of *Kitty Bell*, took place at the Théâtre-Français on February 12th, 1835. It turned out to be Vigny's most successful venture, and thirty-nine performances were given before its withdrawal on July 8th.

If we take for granted the natural ambition of a Romantic to succeed in the theatre, there were two further reasons for Vigny's risking a stage version. The first is expressed by the docteur Noir, when he says: 'O Multitude! . . . the poet must subdue you through his interpreter, the actor';[10] and the second by the author in his own person: 'With *Chatterton*, I have tried to read a page of philosophy in the Theatre. I wanted people to say: "It is true"; not: "It is beautiful".'[11]

While the presentation of Chatterton's story is broadly the same in the play as in the book, there are some differences of detail and a new emphasis. The former have to do with Chatterton's social position. Vigny went as far as introducing a fictitious peer to conjure up a wealthy and aristocratic background for his poet: 'Upon my word,' Lord Talbot addresses Chatterton, 'if you spend your money as nobly as you did at Oxford, it will do you honour!'[12] But the more important change is the emphasis given to the act of suicide, merely by its translation into theatrical terms. The problem of whether or not a man has the right to take his own life is one that Vigny frequently discusses in his *Journal*. Suicide was the final solution he had planned for Stello's sickness of mind, and the docteur Noir would clearly have had no professional scruples about giving his patient every practical assistance to this end.

But the violent death which an author recounts on the printed page acquires an entirely different aspect in the theatre. For an hour or more the audience has lived with the stage character, has entered into his hopes and difficulties, as if he were a real person, and has become vividly aware of the grief his death will arouse in the sympathetic heroine, in this case superbly played by Mme Dorval. The taking of the opium in such circumstances, therefore, is immeasurably more shocking than the same act described at second-hand by a character whom no one was expected to believe in. It would certainly anger people—unless the playwright succeeded in making the crime appear just and inevitable. Of this Vigny was well aware, and in Chatterton's concluding speeches he deployed all his skill to ennoble the poet's wretchedness:

'I have sold my soul', cries the unhappy youth; then, raising the draught of poison, 'but with this I buy it back. Skinner will be paid. I shall be independent of all, I shall be no one's inferior now! Hail, first hour of peace that I have ever tasted, last hour of my life, dawn of the Day Eternal, hail! Farewell, humiliation, hatreds, sarcasms, degrading tasks, anguish, poverty, tortures of the heart, farewell!' And, setting fire to his manuscripts, he continues: 'Away with you, noble thoughts, written for all those connoisseurs of scorn and ingratitude, purify yourselves in the flames and mount with me to heaven!' [13]

The introduction of the Quaker (who had not appeared in the book), as the representative of true Christian humility and compassion, now made possible an impressive *coup de théâtre.* The old man has done his best to prevent the catastrophe; finally he falls on his knees and offers up a last prayer for Chatterton and Kitty: 'Into Thy bosom, O Lord, into Thy bosom, receive these two martyrs!' And so the curtain descends.

On the night of February 12th, the applause continued unbroken for ten minutes, and in a *Journal* entry, dated and particularized, 'February 12th, midnight', Vigny was for once able to express his gratitude to the public in the long passage that begins: '*Chatterton* has succeeded!' [14] The facile emotions of a theatre audience were certainly aroused, and, before leaving the Français that evening, the comte de Maille-Latour-Landry had made up his mind to found an Academy award for the special prevention of this kind of tragedy.

But the excitement of the first night gave way to misgivings, even hostility, when the critics settled down to consider their verdict. I shall not dwell on this, being more concerned with the effect the play had upon another section of the public—the young. It is sufficient to note that, with very few exceptions, the papers described *Chatterton* as unreal and subversive. 'Instead of giving a picture of human nature in all its variety', wrote the playwright's old enemy, Sainte-Beuve, 'Vigny merely describes a literary disease and a literary vice that attack ambitious, oversensitive, and more or less impotent, poets by the score.' [15]

From the start, a fundamental weakness in Vigny's picture of martyred genius was his manipulation of the facts. History shows that, far from being the famished poet of *Stello*, Gilbert enjoyed a life of careless gaiety and died as a result of a fall from his horse; that Chénier (at thirty-two, no romantic boy) was a captious political journalist who went on obstinately asking for trouble until he got it; while Malfilâtre, mentioned in the Doctor's roll of honour and later a name to conjure with, died, not of starvation, but of venereal disease. Even further removed from reality is Vigny's conception of Chatterton.

It was not he, of course, who invented the legend. Extravagant tributes to the young poet had long been the order of the day, among them the moving lines of Coleridge's *Monody*, first published in 1794, and the preface to Nicolas Bonneville's *Choix de petits romans imités de l'allemand*, of 1786, which speaks of Chatterton as the 'most powerful genius who has ever existed'! It did not require Vigny's English friend, Henry Reeve, to point out how unsatisfactory had been the real character of the 'marvellous boy': in the essay which introduced the drama on publication, its author admitted, 'It was the Poet alone who mattered to me; Chatterton was merely a man's name; and I have intentionally left out the true facts of his life, so as to concern myself with just that part of his fate which makes it an ever-lamentable example of noble poverty.' [16] By adding legend to legend, in fact, Vigny was determined to create a new 'truth'; and with a certain section of the public, between 1835 and 1845, he was only too successful.

iv

In his *Journal* for March 11th, he noted: 'Eighteenth performance of *Chatterton* at the Odéon: audience of young students. This is the most intelligent in Paris—ten times superior to that of the Français: grateful for everything, deeply touched, and so afraid of interrupting that it applauds by gestures. At the end, it expressed its appreciation vociferously.' [17]

With that audience Théophile Gautier was well acquainted, and the occasion itself remained one of his most vivid memories:

> We young people of the time were intoxicated with art, passion, and poetry; our heads were all in a whirl, our hearts all pounding

with extravagant ambitions. The fate of Icarus had no fears for us. 'Give us wings, wings, wings!', rose the cry on every side, 'even though we plunge into the sea!' To fall from heaven, one had at least to climb as far, a finer course than creeping along the ground all one's life. . . . The pit before which Chatterton ranted was full of long-haired, pale-faced adolescents who firmly believed there was no tolerable occupation on this globe but to write verses or to paint, to 'faire de l'art', as was said. These looked on the *bourgeois* with a scorn scarcely matched by that of the *renards* of Heidelberg or Iéna for the *Philistines*. . . . You can imagine the effect, in such surroundings, of M. Alfred de Vigny's *Chatterton*.[18]

The problem of suicide was of more than academic interest to this section of the audience. Henry Monnier, in his *Grisettes*, nearly ten years earlier, had made fun of it—a young woman addresses her lover: 'Go on, then, commit suicide, if it amuses you!' But the number of incidents of this kind increased so alarmingly after the July Revolution that Mrs Trollope, on her travels, felt impelled to make some inquiries. 'I will not venture to repeat the result in figures,' she reported in 1835, 'as I doubt if the information I received was of that strictly accurate kind which would justify my doing so; yet it was quite enough so, to excite both horror and astonishment at the extraordinary number which are calculated to perish annually at Paris by self-slaughter.'[19] In 1836 the French Government, among other attempts to get at the source of the trouble, offered a prize for research into the psychological effect of atmospheric disturbances. And Cantagrel, four years later, at a loss to explain the popularity of a play he detested, came to the conclusion that *Chatterton* had succeeded because it advocated suicide at a time when a government, generally disliked, was trying to check it![20]

For young writers, however, Vigny presented no shocks. Want, disease, and suicide were part of their daily life. In Chatterton they saw themselves; in the *dénouement* what had happened to their friends and to the friends of their friends. The emotions of those who dined 'chez Flicoteaux', and viewed the world from an equivalent of the Holborn garret in the Rue de la Harpe, were deeply stirred—and among them were some whose names would soon be added to the sacred trilogy.

A typical 'enfant perdu', both in his physical wretchedness and the fatalistic character of his poetry, was Hégésippe Moreau, author of a single volume, *Le Myosotis*. The experiences of Chatterton pale by comparison with Moreau's efforts to end his life and avoid the death by starvation which eventually overcame him in 1838. Associated with Moreau, so closely indeed that they shared the same disreputable frock-coat, were Veyrat and Berthaud, jointly responsible for the poem, *Avant mourir*. Berthaud's attempt to shoot himself with what turned out to be a chocolate pistol reduces to pitiable farce the 'pistolet de Werther' and the 'pistolets solitaires' to whose muffled reports Vigny listened so anxiously.[21] In his *Journal d'un poète* are collected a number of examples, of which perhaps the most important is linked with the names of two pathetic youths, Victor Escousse and Auguste Lebras, for their double suicide by charcoal-fumes made an impression that continued to be felt throughout the 1840's.[22]

So much for the struggles, despair, and suicide of poets during the July Monarchy. I have said that Vigny intended his chosen heroes to represent the painter and sculptor as well as the poet: and that he regarded them as of equal importance is made clear by statements in his *Journal*, such as: 'The priests of modern society are its poets, its painters, and its sculptors.' [23] He himself, it is true, had not the same lively sympathy with the modern movement in art felt by some other Romantic writers. He preferred Ingres's 'Apotheosis of Homer' to the 'Sardanapalus' of Delacroix, though he was friendly with the latter, and with the Devérias, David d'Angers, and Boulanger, and remained always on affectionate terms with Jean Gigoux.

While we shall find a number of echoes of *Stello* in the Salon *livrets* of the period, its most striking interpreter is the sculptor Préault, who was a great reader and theatre-goer. The titles of his works exhibited at the Salon of 1832 showed a ready appreciation of the novel Vigny had just published: 'Agony of the Poet Gilbert', and 'Starvation', bas-reliefs; 'Poverty', a terracotta group; and, in the following year, another group, 'The Pariahs', was refused by an indignant jury.[24]

The severity of the Salon's adjudicators added to the difficulties in which painters and sculptors now found themselves. Dominated by the Institut and composed not only of members of the Beaux-Arts section but of government nominees, it set itself deliberately to stifle the rebellion against Classicism. If it was not entirely successful, this must have been because public taste really had undergone some change; but the younger painters, and particularly those specializing in landscape, met with bitter opposition. Nor was their elders' fate reassuring. In 1835, Vigny's insistence upon the unhappy destiny of the artist in modern society seemed to receive fresh confirmation from two suicides which staggered the art world of the day. The first was that of baron Gros at Meudon, the second of Léopold Robert in Venice at the very moment when Paris was expressing admiration for his most recent work. The correspondence of Robert contains passages which might have been written by Vigny for any one of his forlorn poets. 'Alas,' he laments, 'I tried to achieve the impossible, and suffer the torments which attack those who fly too high.' [25]

Under such stresses and struck by such recent examples, which the tragic ends (though not self-inflicted) of Prud'hon, Sigalon, and Géricault had already anticipated, it is understandable that many youthful artists adopted Vigny's philosophy and began to look upon the world with rather more contempt than it deserved. It was against this attitude, and the real damage it was doing to the public's idea of the artist, that Thoré complained. There were young people calling themselves artists, he said, in 1836, before they had earned the right to call themselves men. They were too conceited to bother about learning their craft, yet, while still students, adopted the language and behaviour of experienced professionals. That the public refused to accept the value they set on their work didn't matter to them in the least, for they had the lowest opinion of the public. Some of these stupid fellows were so convinced of their own importance that, when their childish compositions failed to astonish the world and command universal admiration, there was nothing left for them but to kill themselves.[26]

And in 1844, Thoré was still counselling a celebrated Romantic landscape-painter against seclusion in Vigny's 'ivory tower':

> You, my dear Rousseau, have naïvely yet deliberately cut yourself off from all that lies outside your art. You have never given a thought to those passions that agitate the rest of us and to the normal concerns of everyday life. Instead, you lived like the hermits of the Thebaid, sunk in a somewhat godless preoccupation with self. It is true that your Thebaid was a veritable paradise of the imagination, splendid

with life and colour. Yet your secret uneasiness and anxieties, your instinctive depressions, and your failure at times to express the poetry that is in you: are they not the result of this excessive isolation, this suicide of a part of your faculties? [27]

No doubt, it would be possible to assemble a double list of poets and painters who shared the fates of starvation, insanity, or suicide in a state of mind flattered by Vigny's *Stello* and *Chatterton*. However complicated it may have been by purely economic problems, the neglect to which Vigny had drawn attention could not be disputed. And the despair and high mortality-rate among artists and writers in the third and fourth decades of the century exercised a profound influence upon the Romantic stragglers of 'Bohemia' who were now growing to manhood.

For the rest of his life, the creator of the Chatterton legend, with its sombre device, 'Despair and die', received the homage of struggling poets in Paris and the provinces. He answered their letters, he opened his house to them, he became their acknowledged champion. For those who belonged to this category of the 'neglected', or imagined that they belonged to it, gratitude and hero-worship created a picture of seraphic elegance: 'When we think of Vigny,' wrote Théophile Gautier, 'there comes to us involuntarily the image of a swan, its neck curved back a little, the breeze half-filling its wings, as it sails the glittering, translucent waters of an English park. . . .' [28]

There was one weapon, however, against which all the resignation and aristocratic reserve of Vigny's poet proved an inadequate defence. This was ridicule. When another genius, Musset, as gifted and sensitive as Vigny himself, handled the weapon, the effect was devastating. The curtains of Stello's gloomy apartment were rudely flung back, and the Poet and Doctor, with their attendant phantoms, dissolved into the clear light of day.

VI

Art and Love

i

The success of the caricaturist depends on familiarity with his subject. Alfred de Musset, eleven years Vigny's junior, had been present as a boy at the reading of *Hernani* in July 1829, and in the following December read to the same group a poem of his own. This poem, *Mardoche*, won him an ovation: in a company remarkable for the early flowering of genius, Musset, at nineteen, astonished his elders. And, like most precocious artists, he discovered almost at once the vein in which he was to excel.

As a child, he had an aversion for make-believe. Tales of chivalry, then much in vogue, did not please him: he left them to students twice his age, and gloried instead in the satire of *Don Quixote*. Then, having carried off all the most coveted prizes at the Collège Henri IV, he deliberately turned his back on the serious-minded and consorted with profligate dandies like Roger de Beauvoir, who soon taught him to live beyond his means.

At nineteen, he was already bored by moral conventions, and suspicious of literary ones. In *Mardoche* he pokes fun at Hamlet. Yet, despite the banter, there was much in his attitude that resembled Vigny's. Like Vigny, he scorned the easy approach, and foretold as fatalistically the tragic destiny of the poet. As Vigny suffered checks in the pursuit of fame, so, for Musset, disappointments followed the brilliant début. *Un Spectacle dans un fauteuil* was grudgingly received by those who had acclaimed *Mardoche*. Then came a love-affair even more exhausting and unhappy than Vigny's. But it is true that, along with such broad resemblances, the differences, too, were striking. Because he was unable to make a living out of poetry, Musset did not shroud himself in gloom and gloat over the failure of other poets, real or imaginary. He compromised. He became, though he detested, prose, a journalist. George Sand was succeeded by other mistresses, and he attempted to dispel an ever-increasing melancholy by drinking. The world was necessary to him, as it had never been to Vigny. He found no solution, therefore, in proud retirement.

Instead, he forced himself to write stories and articles which would help to pay for the social pleasures he could not do without. Rapt spectator at the dramas of his own *vie intérieure*, Musset was even less of a man of action than Vigny. Rather, he became the model of elegant idleness, of youth, love, and pleasure idealized in an urban landscape, and this for a whole generation of impoverished poet-journalists. In Musset such admirers found a novel mixture of gaiety and despair, a good-humoured contempt for convention, a *mise-en-scène* fairytale-like yet familiar enough for them to feel able to share in an episode of passion or misalliance. These are the characteristics of the stories *Frédéric et Bernerette* and *Mimi Pinson*, stories which were preceded, however, by other, more serious, tilting at orthodox Romanticism.

ii

In 1833, Musset wrote *Un Mot sur l'art moderne*, in which, while sympathizing with originality, he complains of the vast numbers of mediocre artists all trying to attract attention at the same time. Though in 1835 he had dictated to George Sand two sonnets attacking the critics of *Chatterton*, in his *Salon* for the following year Musset opposed Vigny's belief that the artist was faced with alternatives of neglect or ignoble popularity.

Scorning, and fawning upon, the public seemed to him equally reprehensible. Why suppose the good opinion of the few more sincere than the applause of the many? Besides, when a man felt himself without a real public, he began to indulge in self-pity—or outrageous conceit. The artist, said Musset, should make every honest effort to win the public's sympathy.

What did Vigny's lugubrious examples from history amount to? Gilbert in his lifetime produced only a spiteful satire: true, he died miserably, but the path of hatred and envy never yet led to happiness. Chénier went to the guillotine without giving the world those poems for which we now admire him most. Genius must at least reveal itself, before one can properly speak of its being 'ignored' or 'persecuted'.[1]

When Musset went on to discuss the art of 1836, he emphasized the results of the point of view he had been attacking. The Salon gave an impression of confusion. There was no common purpose, no evidence of standards or taste. He had expected, he says, to find a noble independence of spirit: he found instead imitation, a feverish, illogical plagiarizing of almost every school and master. Of these *pasticheurs* there was hope only for Boulanger and Delacroix, who would soon grow tired of such barren exercises. There is no mistaking Musset's attitude, that of an artist who has himself been forced to compromise; nor his belief, that isolation of itself, however proud and obdurate, can work no miracles. The artist, he maintains, would achieve nothing by listening to Vigny, whose conclusions were as false as his premises. The world was far more complex than that, the answer to its problems far less simple. But finding himself more and more opposed to Romanticism, he decided that ridicule might finally drive home the arguments put forward in *Un Mot sur l'art moderne* and the *Salon* of 1836.

In September and December of that year, and in the following March and May, the *Revue des Deux-Mondes* published four *Lettres de Dupuis et Cotonet*. This was an ingenious attack upon the Romantic abuse of epithets and passion for exaggeration in every form, an attack upon Hugo as well as Vigny. For us, one caricature of the Chattertonian painter, seen through the eyes of the two imaginary inhabitants of La Ferté-sous-Jouarre, will suffice:

He is profoundly unappreciated; the newspapers tear him to pieces; the public is quite brutal; his colleagues are envious of him; even his servant is hostile. In spite of this, he [Vincent] exhibited a landscape representing three Louis XIII ladies on a gondola in the Park of Versailles. The picture measures four inches high by three feet long—and the Government did not buy it. True, he was commissioned to paint a picture for a church in the provinces, and this picture, conscientiously carried out, won him some praise. But for what was it praised? For precisely the sort of details that don't matter: the feet, the hands, the wretched outlines! No one caught a glimpse of the artist's real profundity. You see, looking at a canvas and saying: 'Ah, that's well drawn!' means absolutely nothing. If it did mean anything, a schoolboy would be a judge of art. The beautiful, the sublime, lies not in the picture itself, but in the philosophic idea that inspired the artist. It is an incalculable series of *theosophistical* meditations which has persuaded, nay forced, him to draw a nose snub rather than hooked, and paint a curtain amaranthine instead of crimson. That is what really matters in the arts. But we live among savages. One journalist in a thousand understands. He alone grasped the significance of Vincent's 'Descent from the Cross', showing that it combined the *Requiem* of Mozart, the *Letters of Euler*, and the *Life of Saint Polycarp.*[2]

iii

At first sight, the attack seems too comprehensive. After the dismissal of earnest individualism on the one hand and earnest art-to-please on the other, what is there left to praise? Diaz and Horace Vernet are equally futile, and between them the smaller fry dart about in purposeless confusion. There are some contradictions: while poking fun at the independent attitude of inferior painters, Musset praises just this quality in Delacroix; lamenting the decline of schools, he seems ready to accept the new anarchy in axioms like: 'There is no such thing as Art, there are only men.'[3]

Even so, Musset did have a positive contribution to make, and a very important one. Though he never cast a spell over artists themselves, as Hugo and Gautier had done, he greatly influenced literary interpretations of the artist during the 1840's by drawing attention to the conflict between art and human passion. The problem, discussed with deep feeling in the *Nuits* and with characteristic delicacy in certain of his stories, was to become the central theme of Murger's *Scènes de la Bohème.** There, sentimentalized, vulgarized, and parodied, it degenerated into a plea for promiscuity, which echoes and re-echoes down to our own day in almost all literature concerned with the artist as a central character.

The origin of this preoccupation, however, was sound enough. By instinct and intelligence, Musset revolted against the conception of the artist as an isolated being, either in the sense intended by Gautier or in that so eloquently argued by Vigny. The

* Such was the original title of the tales published in 1851, and in the interests of accuracy I have adopted it here, though the later, longer version, *Scènes de la vie de Bohème*, is a great deal more familiar.

artist, according to Musset, must live, not in a coterie or an ivory tower, but in the world. Only thus can he catch and interpret the spirit of the time; and to do that is his real mission. This subtle and elusive spirit exists both in the world outside and in the artist himself, so that its discovery is, to a certain degree, self-discovery. The artist's aim, therefore, should be to face life, to accept experience, even to invite experiences beyond the common run, in order to enrich the 'moi' and make it truly representative. Thus for the writer, the essential poetry is the 'poésie du moi', the essential life the 'vie intime', and the determining experience human passion. If the final impression made by the author of the *Nuits* on a stoic like Delacroix was one of plaintive pessimism, this was because the spirit is more sensitive to suffering than to happiness, and reveals its nature more clearly in crises of grief and disillusionment.

From 1830 onwards, Musset's attitude to the relationship between art and life underwent some changes. By 1838, life seems finally to have asserted its independence, becoming actually hostile to the labour of creation. The work in which he states this point of view most emphatically is his *Fils du Titien*, published by the *Revue des Deux-Mondes* in May of that year. Though the setting and initial incidents owe a good deal to Hoffmann, the autobiographical theme of the story soon becomes apparent. In the person of Pippo, Musset sought to justify his own impatience with art and excuse his own dissipation. Thus a taste for gambling and a congenital idleness blunt the edge of Pippo's talent, and he loses all desire to emulate the achievements of his illustrious father. Béatrice, playing in fiction the part allotted in life to Aimée d'Alton, does her best to revive his ambition. But when, at length, he completes her portrait, he takes an oath never to paint again. One cannot, so the author asserted, love and paint at the same time; and it is better to die in the arms of the Fornarina than in harness in the studio. Béatrice's anxieties once put to rest, the pair live happily ever afterwards: 'To the devil with painting; life is too short!' [4]

iv

Again because of the light they shed on later presentations of the artist in fiction, I turn now to *Frédéric et Bernerette*, a story published three months before the *Fils du Titien*, in January, 1838, and to another written more than seven years later, *Mimi Pinson.*

We know how wearily Musset undertook his *contes* or *nouvelles*, most of them for the *Revue des Deux-Mondes*; and the descriptions he gave his brother of the miseries of the professional storyteller had some basis in fact, for Bonnaire, the *Revue's* director, was obliged to press Musset hard on occasion. Detesting the work, he was nevertheless glad of the money, and the receipts were encouraging.

In *Frédéric et Bernerette*, Frédéric Hombert, a law-student from Besançon, arrives in Paris to complete his studies and lodges for convenience in the Rue de la Harpe. When the story begins, he has nearly finished his three-year course, after which he is to return home. One day, his uneventful, bachelor life is interrupted by the appearance of a young girl at the window opposite. An episode in which Musset was personally involved is now translated into fiction; and Frédéric, in spite of his friend Gérard's warnings, rents a furnished room for Bernerette near the Luxembourg. Having hurriedly concluded his studies, he makes use of a further sum of money from his father to continue this idle existence for as long as possible: at which point Bernerette's former lover discovers her unfaithfulness and commits suicide.

Frédéric leaves Paris precipitately, to find a marriage already arranged for him at Besançon. His fiancée pleads for time, however, and the period of a year having been agreed upon, he returns to Paris. On this occasion, he takes lodgings near the Palais de Justice. His acquaintance with Gérard is renewed, and since Gérard has inherited a fortune, Frédéric himself drifts into a mode of living he cannot afford. Having that very moment raised 3,000 francs on a bill, he meets Bernerette once more and their liaison continues until the money is spent. There follow further renewals and ruptures, until Bernerette attempts to take poison. Tormented by his family's efforts to part him from his mistress and by the girl's own determination not to let him go, Frédéric takes advantage of what appears to be a proof of her lightness to leave suddenly for Switzerland. Much later, Bernerette writes a full explanation, revealing a series of misunderstandings. By the time this letter arrives—it is

Frédéric's wedding-night—he has already been informed of her death.

What first strikes us about this story is that, in spite of Musset's graceful style, its events and characters are presented quite unromantically. Like Octave, in *La Confession d'un enfant du siècle*, Frédéric is the victim of weakness of character rather than of passion. In his feeble way, he can neither wholly enjoy nor wholly renounce the liaison with Bernerette. Once yielded to, it becomes a habit; and a habit of which he is ashamed, since he is not by nature gay or irresponsible. Nothing could be less like Béranger's jolly *Voyage au pays de cocagne* than Frédéric's conscience-stricken debauches. There is no attempt to idealize the Chaumière, or the Boulevard Neuf, or the 'chambrette garnie' near the Luxembourg. In their moments of tranquillity, Musset's lovers lead a life so dull that he begs leave to pass over it in silence.

The *grisette* herself is the very personification of idleness, and, though she is easily amused and this gaiety is a gift of the gods, the author makes no excuses for the aimless course along which she is content to drift. And yet she has her moments of heroism, of remorse, and good intent, before death overtakes her. In spite of her vanity and idleness, she has cherished her lover and been faithful to him. Mlle Darcy, the respectable young lady from Besançon, provides a contrast in character that is by no means to the disadvantage of Bernerette, whose heart is sounder than her head.

It was this mixture of realism and sentiment that gave *Frédéric et Bernerette* its special appeal. The sordid, yet not too sordid, setting; the author's indulgence towards his characters' failings; the gaiety and sadness of light love complicated by the clash between intellect and illiteracy: all were elements of which Murger could make good use when he set himself the task of romanticizing the humbler experiences of down-at-heel journalists, artists, and artists' models.

Mimi Pinson, published in Hetzel's *Le Diable à Paris* in December, 1845, nearly eight years later, presents characters identical with Frédéric and Bernerette, in a similar setting. Here, however, the note of gaiety is sustained throughout. There is no tragic fate reserved for the heroine; and for the secondary character, Rougette, starvation is merely a temporary inconvenience. Musset had been very ill in the spring of this year, and did not return to Paris from his convalescence at Mirecourt till the middle of August. This light-hearted study of the *grisette* of 1845 might have been penned as a distraction from such fits of ill-health, boredom, and melancholy as increasingly assailed him in his later thirties. When the theatre or the *Cercle des Échecs* failed to chase away depression, he now resorted more frequently to alcohol, horrifying his friends by the gusto with which he swallowed down unconventional potions of his own mixing. For the faults of Mimi Pinson, in fact, he showed the tolerance he expected for his own:

'Ah! ce qui n'est qu'un mal, n'en faites pas un vice.' [5]

As the nature of Hetzel's publication required, an air of reporting characterizes *Mimi Pinson.* Musset's innocent hero, Eugène, studied at the School of Medicine 'only last year'. He refuses to accompany his friends to the Moulin de Beurre or to dance quadrilles with them at the Chaumière, because he deplores the system of mock-marriages between students and *grisettes.* His best friend holds a different view: for Marcel, *grisettes* are admirable young women, and the flower of the species is their neighbour, Mimi Pinson. It is his intention that Eugène shall come to appreciate Mimi as he himself appreciates Mimi's friend, Zélia.

By a ruse, he secures Eugène's presence at a supper-party to which both *grisettes* have been invited. Eugène's unfavourable impression of the girls is strengthened by their careless manners and by an anecdote told of the extravagance of a certain Rougette. Returning to his room early in the morning, Eugène meets a girl, ill and exhausted, on her way to post a letter. He undertakes to perform this service for her, but cannot resist opening and reading the letter first. It is a note, begging assistance from the girl's lover and signed 'Rougette'. The letter re-sealed and posted, Eugène sets out to buy food to take to her address. To raise a louis for this purpose, he has to call at a pawnbroker's, where he finds Marcel. When the pawnbroker overhears Eugène blame Mimi for enjoying herself while her friend is in extremities, he tells them that she has just pledged her dress with him for four francs.

Since he remembers Mimi's song of the previous evening:

Elle n'a qu'une robe au monde,

Marcel hurriedly redeems it, and the two friends go out in search of the owner. Marcel is certain that his own estimate of Mimi is the right one. He persuades his companion to return to Rougette's lodgings, where, sure enough, they find the four francs, as well as a slice of pie which Mimi carried away from the supper-party. Rougette, however, is too much the coquette to permit her benefactors to see her in bed; and though they both find this comical, Eugène makes up his mind to lecture her on the error of her ways. Not long afterwards, while they are discussing the matter, the two young men see, to their astonishment, Mimi and Rougette herself, waving at them from the fashionable precincts of Tortoni's.

V

In *Mimi Pinson*, the lightly-sketched background of *Frédéric et Bernerette* becomes more detailed and definite, for by the time Musset wrote this gay adventure the Latin Quarter was showing signs of becoming popular material for the storyteller. The isolation of the earlier lovers is now succeeded by the impression of an entire *arrondissement* disembarked from Cythera, students and *grisettes* filing arm-in-arm through the Rue d'Éperon, the Rue Saint-Jacques, and the Carrefour de Buci, quite in the manner of Watteau's famous renderings of the *Trois Cousines*. Though the boundaries of this world were reached, apparently, at the Boulevard des Italiens (formerly the Boulevard de Gand) and the Pont d'Iéna, to which Rougette once retired with the intention of drowning herself, the rapid development of transport, 'those bulging omnibuses crammed to bursting-point with *grisettes* on their way to Ranelagh or Belleville', as Marcel describes them, was soon to have its effect upon the female members of the community. Indeed, the *grisette* had already a taste for luxury. Rougette boasts a titled lover, and, when money is available, Mimi deserts the Moulin de Beurre to eat ices with her at Tortoni's. Their creator, nevertheless, was still too much of a Romantic to relinquish the idealized portrait of his own light-of-love, the little actress Louise, for the cold, calculating 'lorette' whom we shall be considering in a few moments.

Alfred de Musset, though a man of fashion, had some opportunities of studying this quarter of Paris. The house in which he was born, No. 33 Rue des Noyers (a street not then the slum known to 'Chien-Caillou'), stood in the heart of it; and it was in the Place de l'Odéon that the Musset children saw, pasted up in the arcade, the first proclamation of Louis XVIII. In 1818, the family was living in the Rue Cassette, almost at the gates of the Jardin du Luxembourg; and after the death of Victor de Musset in the cholera epidemic of 1832, his widow and sons moved to an apartment in the Rue de Grenelle.

This neighbourhood was essentially an aristocratic one in the 1830's, though the Chaussée-d'Antin, where lived the wealthy heroine of the *Deux Maîtresses*, already rivalled it as a fashionable quarter. Between the Rue de Grenelle and the Rue de l'Université clustered the great mansions of the eighteenth century, divided here and there by a magnificent garden like that of the Hôtel de Brienne. But from the point where the Rue des Saints-Pères met the Rue de Grenelle, the aristocratic Faubourg ended and the Latin Quarter began; and for a man of Musset's temperament, instinctively drawn to gaming, absinthe, and *filles*, there must have been a pleasant piquancy about this abrupt transition. On the one side were the gloomy memorials to great names, the Hôtel Soult, the Hôtel de Mouchy, the Hôtel d'Aiguillon, now with a hint of declining fortunes; on the other, the garish Chaumière with its dancers and Chinese lanterns, and the impecunious and unconventional life of a score of similarly notorious establishments.

Apart from his early familiarity with this quarter of Paris and the famous walks of the 'grand cénacle' which he had shared as a young disciple, his friendship (while still in his teens) with Roger de Beauvoir and Alfred Tattet would have given Musset a taste for unexpected encounters in the little streets that fan out from the Place de l'Odéon, and for the hilarity and argument enjoyed in the cafés which thronged the larger arteries of the quarter. Tattet, under whose wing Musset had been initiated into the dissipations of the *jeunesse dorée*, approved such contrasts: as when, during the course of Musset's real-life affair with the Louise who becomes Bernerette, he entertained the lovers at his house at Margency. Beauvoir's own keen interest in what was picturesque and sordid in this part of Paris may be gauged from his *Écolier de Cluny*.

But over and above the particular characteristics of Musset

himself, and the instinct which drew him naturally to haunts of gaiety, a number of less personal influences must have contributed to the topographical detail in the urban settings for *Frédéric et Bernerette* and *Mimi Pinson.* I have already mentioned the popularity of Hoffmann. In Hoffmann's stories, the streets of a city acquire a kind of mysterious personality, which Gautier was quick to adopt for the French capital in the nightmare of Onuphrius. And though it is true that at this time the urban wanderings of Gérard de Nerval and Privat d'Anglemont had not yet borne fruit, Daumier and Gavarni were already selecting and labelling the idiosyncrasies of various streets and quarters of Paris. Between the appearance of *Frédéric et Bernerette* and that of *Mimi Pinson*, Eugène Sue had begun to publish his widely-read serial, *Les Mystères de Paris* (1842–1843), which, at any rate to begin with, makes a most effective use of the topographical approach.

In the tales we have been considering, Musset was concerned only with students. But, as I have shown earlier, the left bank of the Seine had long become an artists', as well as a students', quarter; and at first it seems strange that the author had nothing to say of the painters, sculptors, and graphic artists of every type, not to mention poets and journalists, who ought certainly to have been acquainted with such a famous personage as Mimi Pinson. When Mimi enters the Place Saint-Sulpice, wrapped in the curtain which replaces her pledged dress, she is almost within hailing distance of the Hôtel Merciol. Yet Musset ignored the existence of any persons answering the description of Murger or Champfleury.

The reason is not far to seek. Musset was the poet of youth. For him, the golden age of youth was the period of a boy's terms at the University or Medical School, a period of intellectual and emotional awakening when sins of pride and sensuality are as harmless as practical-jokes. The self-conscious artists and journalists who had puzzled Dupuis and Cotonet did not qualify for the same sympathetic acceptance. Murger and his friends were too vulgar, ignorant, and prematurely aged. We are so nearly in Murger's territory, however; Musset's Mimi is so nearly Murger's; Marcel the medical student approximates so closely to Marcel the painter—that we find ourselves searching for some other writer or artist who can successfully link the two worlds together.

vi

In the lithographs of Gavarni, a combination of artistic and literary skill which remains unique, we are presented with that link. The artist-journalist of the period provides an extraordinarily close parallel to the poet-journalist, being driven in the same way to study the requirements of editors and the taste of the larger public. Yet while he bowed to necessity, he sometimes achieved results more important, and recognized as more important, than the work of independent exhibitors at the Salon.

Gavarni won the high regard of Delacroix, and Sainte-Beuve devoted three articles to him in the *Nouveaux Lundis.*[6] And he deserved their admiration; for, Daumier excepted, he outstripped all competitors, when he was able to put fashion-plates finally aside and concentrated all his powers on satirical draughtsmanship. Beside this later Gavarni, fade into insignificance the coarse-grained Monnier, the crudely comic Bertall, Charlet the sentimentalist, and Achille Devéria (his only rival in delicate effects, but feebly and incurably *chic*), while Traviès, Grandville, and Cham hardly count as rivals.

It would be foolish to seek any resemblance between Gavarni and the poet of the *Nuits*, but with other aspects of Musset's character there are obvious affinities: with the versifier 'aux manches de chemise', for instance, and above all with the author of *Frédéric et Bernerette* and *Mimi Pinson*. 'Faintly tinged with corruption' is Baudelaire's description of Gavarni;[7] and, in the general sense in which the critic uses the term, the artist's 'corruption' was very much of the same order as Musset's. He, too, combined the characters of intellectual and dandy. He, too, haunted balls, theatres, and shooting-galleries. Like the other, he was fond of celebrating the ephemeral joys of youth, and regarded himself as a connoisseur of those 'moments of deliciously refined emotion [as he explains in his diary] which rock the spirit gently between pleasure and pain, but which the slightest sound, the least word, a mere nothing, a fleeting thought, can destroy'.

Like Musset again, he rejected the idea that an artist must work in seclusion. On the contrary, so he confides to the diary:

It is a stale or empty mind that can find no interest in the great mass of humanity around us. Flatten your nose against the attic-window, young man, and look at the maze of rooftops and the chimney-smoke floating up from it! Put out your lamp, pull on your breeches; slip off for twelve hours into the hundred-and-one activities that churn the streets into mud; go here, there, and everywhere; wipe your feet on drawing-room carpets, slake your thirst in the tap-room; watch the thief being tried, and the law being made; risk your money on the turn of a wheel, or in buying and selling in the market-place. You'll come back full of pictures.[8]

Gavarni's account of his activities for 1833 shows that he followed his own advice. The artist was then twenty-nine, and his energy, social and artistic, astonishing. His world, however, was not Musset's. In spite of certain friends in common (Alfred and Laure d'Abrantès, for example), Gavarni's pivotal point was the Feydeau household, and his day began and ended in Montmartre. Though the 'heights' were not yet part of the artists' quarter, he had a strong personal affection for them, and for the vast panorama of the city which it was his special delight to study and dissect.

The twentieth-century monument to the artist stands lower on the slope of the hill, in the little Place Saint-Georges. But its position is well chosen, for here the stone figure, pencil and sketchbook in hand, gazes down the Rue Notre-Dame-de-Lorette. This street, once notorious for the immorality of its womenfolk, inspired—so some believe—an invention all Gavarni's own, the term and character, 'lorette'. Musset's Mimi had been drawn with great precision as the shining example of a class 'good, kind, loyal, and disinterested'. While her beauty, in his eyes, could not compare with that of well-groomed Society women, he thought she possessed something 'more captivating than beauty'. On the other hand, her ability to take everything (including her poverty) as a joke produced a frank gaiety very different from the covetous, knowing smirk, as Gavarni recorded it, of the 'ladies' of the Rue Notre-Dame-de-Lorette.

In the neighbourhood of the Opera-House, surrounded by wealthy financiers as well as successful artists, the *grisette* naturally acquired a sophistication unknown to her sister of the Latin Quarter. By the time the series 'Les Lorettes' appeared, in 1841, some changes seem to have taken place in the manners of these women, and in the attitude of their observer: Gavarni has become a deadly realist, his model a cynic.

The artist's success with the 'Students' series of 1839 had been enormous, as the Goncourts record; and the same success greeted the 'Lorettes'. In 1842, Gavarni returned to the theme, and again in 1843. During the years immediately preceding the *Scènes de la Bohème,* therefore, Murger had ample opportunity of turning over these spirited satires at the café-table and in the bookshops. It is not necessary to dwell on the infinite variations of idleness and greed which Gavarni portrayed in his Montmartre 'lorettes', but we ought to consider for a moment the connexion between these models of his, who, by definition, did not work, and the *grisettes* of the *Scènes de la Bohème,* recruited from the shops and the milliners' workrooms. It is clear that a 'lorette' of the richer quarter of the Opera would not often make the journey to the world of students, struggling artists, and poets, when she found the *enfantement de la carotte* problem enough already. Being acquainted with the artists and journalists living more prosperously in the neighbourhood of the Place Saint-Georges, she would have reason to avoid the experiences of her poorer kind across the river. Yet the Place Saint-Georges had its indigent backwaters too—the Rue de la Tour-d'Auvergne, for instance, with the Bohemian character given it by Alphonse Karr. The masked balls at the Opera provided opportunities for the Right-Bank 'lorette' and the Left-Bank *grisette* to meet; while, on the extreme fringe of the fashionable world, in the Rue des Prêtres-Saint-Germain-l'Auxerrois, stood the most celebrated haunt of impecunious Left-Bank artists and their mistresses, the Café Momus.

There was also the link provided by modelling for the figure, a *pis-aller* to which 'lorettes' and *grisettes* down on their luck were both driven from time to time. The Classicist school of David, with its emphasis on masculine themes and its cult of the male nude, had naturally supported a number of men in this occupation. Some of them, Amaury-Duval notes, were so employed all their lives, from the pose of cherub to that of white-bearded saint: a certain Dubosc was even able to save sufficient to found a prize at the École des Beaux-Arts.[9] And when, in Romantic times, private classes and schools were less well-attended, the model was still able to earn his three francs a day at the Atelier Suisse or the Atelier Boutin. But with the increasing importance of the *genre* picture, he found his profession growing daily more precarious; as Ingres maliciously remarked: 'It is thanks to the vogue for costume that the painters dubbed "Romantic" produce their pictures so easily, without knowing the first thing about the human figure.' [10] In his *Les Français peints par eux-mêmes*, Jules Janin shows how, in 1840, the model was constrained to eke out his livelihood by peddling. 'If you do not want to buy or exchange anything,' says Janin, 'he re-closes his pack, puts aside the mixture of sawdust and shavings that he is accustomed to palm off as smuggled tobacco; and, returning to his principal business, offers to model for the bust or the whole figure.' [11]

While modelling had always been a respectable profession for men (in the eighteenth century, official Academy models wore uniform and carried a sword), for women it was a different matter. Amaury-Duval and the Goncourts all stressed the clinical atmosphere of the life-class and the 'relative' chastity of the female model; yet from other sources we learn that her calling was regarded as the lowest in the calendar. Delacroix's note of October 22nd, 1822, hardly recommends it. And nearly twenty years later, Janin wrote:

> Shall we speak of the female model? . . . While exercising it on the sly, she always disowns her profession: she's a dressmaker, a milliner, an embroidress, she waits in a shop, but a model, never! When an artist knocks at her door, she answers, without opening: 'You are mistaken, Sir, I am not a model.' The next day, however, she is invariably in the artist's studio, chattering her head off, yawning, and sucking lozenges.[12]

And when Mme de Girardin tells us of an 'elegant and original ball which was given [in 1838] for all the models of Paris in the studio of a famous painter',[13] we can imagine a troop of women which included the types of Balzac's Coralie and Esther, as well as those of Mimi and Musette.

With the 'lorette' and the artist's model, then, and in the hands of Murger, Musset's lightly-shadowed idyll developed into a *scène de la Bohème*. That sluts and prostitutes could loom so large in the life of Murger's heroes is indicative of other changes, however. Musset had accepted 'Bernerette' only as an *amour passager*, and she played an insignificant part in his life. Similarly, Delacroix never allowed girls like Émilie Robert to interrupt his serious friendships with the great ladies of the Faubourg Saint-Germain. Even Gavarni, who made a virtue of promiscuity, regularly renounced his adventures for the sake of conversing with Mme Feydeau or the duchesse d'Abrantès. But we are about to enter a world in which the degenerate *grisette*, or 'lorette', represents the norm of female society.

It is but one instance of an ignominious flight of all those social joys and graces that, from the Renaissance onward, artists have worked so hard to come by. Alas for the novice now! The Palace of Art,

> So royal-rich and wide,

which he has looked forward to inhabiting, proves a house of cards. It collapses, leaving him to camp in the city's meanest wynd and darkest rookery—*like a gipsy*.

VII

Attic Nights

i

When following the story of the artist in France from the Revolution onwards, we note two features in particular: an ever-increasing demand for freedom, coupled with an ever-increasing insecurity. As the conception of the artist put forward by his interpreters encouraged in him greater self-esteem and zest for independence, the actual conditions of his life grew more humiliating. Some historians throw the blame for this on the kind of society in which he lived; for, as we have seen, the triumph of the bourgeoisie under Louis-Philippe did not produce a sympathetic world in which to practise the arts of poetry and painting.

The artist was as obstinate in his attitude, however, as his middle-class critics were in theirs, and if he determined, often without adequate training or means of support, to risk an unpopular style, the bourgeoisie can scarcely be held responsible for the inevitable discomforts attending his decision.

From 1830 onwards, we have listened to indignant outbursts by Hugo, Gautier, and Vigny on behalf of the victims. Now the victims, mainly young people of humble background, speak out on their own account. It is hardly surprising that, when they do so, a change of accent is discernible which prepares us for the last revolt against Romanticism. If not professing socialists themselves, such artists and writers had often absorbed the socialist ideas of the working-class from which they sprang, inheriting also the materialist viewpoint inseparable from a class-struggle against bad conditions.

Though more often than not they were indifferent to politics, in France an indifference of this kind was as good as an opinion, and a seditious one at that, when couched in the violent language of the studio. Experiencing a squalid poverty which Gautier, Vigny, and Musset had been spared, the working-class painters and writers were forced to adapt the fashionable characteristics of emancipation—Gautier's scorn for the bourgeois, Vigny's dignified self-pity, and Musset's redemption of the soul through love—to an entirely new set of circumstances. Thus at first they strove to idealize their wretchedness, inventing for themselves a character which would rise superior to the threats of landlords and vulgar mistresses. Murger, 'spouting idealism like a tap',[1] was the demonstrator-in-chief of this approach.

But the contrast between the ideal and the real soon became painful, and after a phase of dabbling in fantasy or comedy, writers and painters began to make use of their unrivalled opportunities to observe poor folk and the incidents of their humble environment. These, as subjects *faute de mieux*, gradually penetrated not only the novelettes of Murger and Champfleury, but the sculpture of Préault and the paintings of Tassaert, Bonvin, and Courbet. Literary ideas were no longer inseparable from an aristocratic or exotic environment, but were worked out deliberately against a background of poverty. It was from the life of the streets, or the landscape of the Sunday excursion, that the painter built up his picture: 'There is no question', wrote the *Artiste*'s critic apropos of Bonvin and Chaplin, in the 1848 Salon, 'but that a new school is on its way, a school composed of young people whose lives are lived outside the studio.' [2]

Once more, the artist played a considerable part in the formation of a new school of literature. Representatives of the two professions met on the staircases of lodging-houses, at the Chaumière, in the Luxembourg Garden, in the café and cheap dining-room. Common poverty and enthusiasm formed an introduction, and the alliance was sustained by the mutual interest that had been characteristic of earlier groups of artists and writers. Once again, there were poets who dabbled with the brush, and painters who dreamed of becoming poets.

ii

While tracing the relationship between art and letters up to this point, I have shown how writers borrowed ideas, cant terms, and technical discoveries from the studio, and found a new subject-matter in studies of the artist. This process was continued and intensified by Murger and his friends. As we shall see, artists dominated their humbler 'cénacles'; and, later on, Courbet played much the same part as Delacroix in stimulating fresh experiments in literature. But the outstanding characteristic of the society we are about to consider is the writer's imitation of the artist's way of life; that is, the way of life common to the art student and certain young and struggling Romantic painters and sculptors, mainly in the Latin Quarter and the neighbourhood of the Mint.

I have pointed out how, since the early years of the century, the Left Bank had fast been acquiring the reputation of an artists' quarter. In this process the 'Childebert' must have played a not unimportant rôle. It was a disreputable block of studios that took its name from the street which then ran parallel to the south side of the Place Saint-Germain-des-Prés; and without the Childebert, without its traditions of gaiety and practical-joking, the fictional *vie de Bohème* presented by Murger might well have worn a different aspect. From the time when the State seized this vast Abbey property in 1793, it became the home of generations of students and young professional artists. Two years after its appropriation, it was bought by a Mme Legendre, who, resigned to her irresponsible tenants, steadfastly refused to carry out repairs and let the building degenerate into the shambles described by Privat d'Anglemont in 1851, the year in which it was finally pulled down. For over half a century, the premises had suffered from continuous dilapidation and defacement. The residents, however, were ready to put up with almost any inconvenience in return for congenial company and a nominal rent. We hear of Signol moving his mattress to the centre of the studio to avoid the bugs swarming over the wall near his bed; and of another artist, Émile Lapierre, who turned his flooded attic into a swimming-bath, to the consternation of the tenant below, Aimé Millet, sculptor of the allegorical figure that watches over Murger's tomb in the Cimetière du Nord.[3]

During the first battles of Romanticism, the Childebert inevitably became a den of conspiracy. Its painters followed every fresh vogue with enthusiasm, from novel styles on canvas to crazes for mediaeval names and Spanish costumes. Even after a separation into *Jeunes-France* and *Bousingots* (later, *Badouillards*), unity was preserved by a ferocious hatred of the bourgeois, perhaps christened 'épicier' in this very building. When, after 1838, a general school of fantasy absorbed both *Jeunes-France* and *Badouillards*, the Childebert continued to bait the *épicier* by every means in its power. Drolling and Labrouste conducted teaching-studies there, the pupils of which won for themselves an evil reputation in the Quarter. Awakened by unearthly noises, says Privat, the neighbours would groan in pitiful resignation: 'We'll get no sleep to-night: the Childebert is celebrating!' [4] At such times, the building would be lit from ground-floor to attic and fantastically-dressed men and women silhouetted against the uncurtained windows, shouting and gesticulating; while others worked off their grievances by setting fire to the shavings in the wood-carvers' workshop. Nor were the antics of the students confined to their own premises: a fierce dog, painted like a tiger, with a saucepan attached to its tail, terrified the inhabitants of the streets near by, and the citizens arriving for Mass at Saint-Germain-des-Prés found themselves, on one occasion, surrounded by silent 'Bedouins' smoking oriental pipes.[5]

Childish and localized as these escapades were, they must have been symptomatic of the free-and-easy arrogance of the budding artist everywhere in the city. And such lightheartedness accompanied him well beyond the student stage, mercifully enlivening the long struggle against poverty and disappointment. Small wonder that Murger and his friends, mere boys when they first encountered the enemies of convention, longed to be artists themselves, even at the risk of starvation. For to be an artist was to be free. Behaving as he pleased, working or idling as the mood dictated, ill-mannered, unpunctual, he could be forgiven all, provided he had talent.[6]

Though they were popular with students from the Schools of Law and Medicine, the Café Dagneaux, Viot's, the establishment of 'Rousseau l'aquatique' (where wine was unknown) were all favoured meeting-places for struggling engravers, painters, and sculptors eking out a living with plates in almanacs, signboards, and church-sculpture exported to the provinces. It was in such haunts that Murger and his friends were initiated into the slang of the studio, and, as young amateurs in painting, took to themselves the title of *rapins* and did their best to live up to the wild humour of the 'regulars'. In the same company there were visits further afield, during which the future critics among them began to acquire their admiration for Velazquez and Zurbarán.

For Murger's 'territory' may be said to have embraced both banks of the Seine, the Louvre as well as the Childebert. And when his young friends, Villain, Chintreuil, Tabar, and the Desbrosses brothers reached the point of submitting paintings and sculpture, the opening of the Salon must have provided an exciting, though, alas, almost always disappointing, journey across the river. Maxime Du Camp has given us a description of this all-important occasion in an artist's life.[7] The Salon opened at midday (normally on April 1st), and from eleven o'clock the courtyard of the Louvre filled up with young and old, none of whom—in accordance with the inhuman regulations then obtaining—had received any news as yet of acceptance or refusal: 'On all sides', says Du Camp, 'were flowing locks, pointed hats, and anxious faces.' Artists from the same studio clung together. There was much shaking of hands, shouting, and ribaldry. About a quarter to twelve, the crowd would begin to mass in front of the building. At the first stroke of noon, the doors flew open, revealing a fat Swiss, in scarlet uniform and three-cornered hat, carrying a halberd. This was the signal for loud cries of 'Vive le père Hénant!', followed by a mad rush for the catalogue and the Salon Carré.

But the jury at this period dealt ruthlessly with the artists of the Romantic School, and we can imagine how many returned to the Left Bank disappointed: among them, for certain, Chintreuil and the Desbrosses. Back they went with dragging footsteps by way of the Pont Saint-Michel, not yet restored by baron Haussmann, to the Rue de la Harpe, ascending to some lofty retreat where cares could be forgotten and confidence revived. Stimulated by alcohol on an empty stomach, the company presently felt strong enough to venture out into the street again.

For those with money in their pockets, and on great occasions during the Carnival season, the excursion could lead to three or four nights' revelry in masks and fancy-dress, the days spent sleeping and idling till the Variétés, the Palais-Royal, and Musard's opened once more: festivity, as it was called, 'à grand orchestre'. But ordinarily jaunts stopped short at a tour of the cafés where other friends, especially painters, were to be met. If in a sentimental frame of mind, the young artist made his way to the Prado or the Chaumière—though not on Sundays, when the *épicier* was too much in evidence; or to the less fashionable

PLATE III. Gavarni (1804–1866): ' "What a miserable exhibition!" "It's disgusting!" "You aren't showing anything here?" "Good Lord, no: are you?" "Certainly not!" ' Lithograph published in the *Figaro*, March 10th, 1839.

The artist caricatures a type of painter already made fun of by Musset in his *Lettres de Dupuis et Cotonet*, the 'profoundly unappreciated' Vincent. We are told by his close friends, the Goncourts, that Gavarni himself had the lowest possible opinion of the bourgeois public; but such a drawing as this (and there are others like it) shows him equally critical of the 'little clique'.

PLATE IV. Honoré Daumier (1808–1879): ' "Ungrateful country, you shan't have my work!" ' Lithograph published in the *Caricature* (under the general title 'Actualités'), March 15th, 1840.

Daumier makes the same general point as Gavarni, but, since he was the stronger artist, more forcefully. Nothing, it would seem, is further from the spirit of Vigny's preoccupation with the heroics of failure. Yet, in his room on the Quai d'Anjou, Daumier, we know, gave pride of place to a lithograph of Préault's 'Pariahs', itself a clear echo of the philosophy expounded in *Stello*.

theatres (the *grisettes* adored melodrama); or, in spring and summer, to the Luxembourg Garden, whose well-grown shrubberies provided favourite trysting-places. But elegant mistresses were something the young artist could only dream of. The Sylvius of Champfleury's *Confessions* loves a seamstress, a laundress, and the wife of a concierge: another's sweetheart smokes a pipe!

Before the arrival of Courbet, Murger's circle was confined to youths of small talent or hope of success. Chintreuil, certainly, belonged to a superior order; and I shall have something to say about him when I come to deal with Murger's own career, since the two were at first closely associated. But the miseries of these young people are not entirely explainable on the grounds of ignorance and incompetence. We can find artists of real skill and experience struggling in the same slough of despair. Octave Tassaert's is a case of this kind which we might consider very briefly.

Born in 1800, he committed suicide in a sordid lodging near the Barrière du Maine at the age of seventy-four. For five years up to 1849 he was living in the Rue Saint-Jacques and may even have been known by sight to Murger. At any rate, his charming picture of a young artist peeling potatoes, now in the Louvre, represents no doubt exactly the type of Murger and his friends, and was painted in 1845, at the very moment when Murger was embarking on his first story about the Bohemian brotherhood. An early reminder of Tassaert's lifelong association with poverty can be found in a little picture of the artist's room, painted twenty years before. Though surrounded by some of the finest works of the Bruyas collection at Montpellier, its truth and pathos catch the eye immediately. Thereafter, concentrating on small *genre*-pieces having poverty as their subject, he became known variously as 'the Prud'hon of the Poor', 'the Garret Correggio', 'the Gilbert of Painting'. Yet, though he exhibited at the Salon with fair regularity, he could never command good prices, and was obliged to sell nudes *sous le manteau* at four centimes each. Jules Claretie describes the shock experienced by the Director of the National Museums when, shortly after 1848, a man dressed in rags arrived in his office, and turned out to be Octave Tassaert.[8]

To be fair, however, this artist was his own worst enemy. If we allow that misery may drive a man to intemperance, it is more difficult to explain another weakness, Tassaert's doubts about his true vocation. It was an uncertainty much in evidence during the Romantic period, when many painters believed that they were writers, and writers that they were painters. 'I have finished with art,' this example of the former wrote to Bruyas, in 1864, 'I am a poet.' [9] Whereas long runs of success enabled a man like Pradier to indulge a similar error, for Tassaert, always on the verge of destitution, it spelt ruin.

He had at least the initial advantage of a sound education. François Bonvin, on the other hand, was one of those whom Corot must have had in mind, when he said: 'If in our day a painter still has to undergo training, it will be entirely self-training and the academies will play no part in it.' [10] But Corot, all the same, must have known that lack of a conventional apprenticeship made the struggle doubly hard: and so, in this case, it was to prove. 'You remember my early trials?' Bonvin reminded Lecour, at a time when things were beginning to be easier. 'I was already deeply embroiled in the struggle for glory and the hospital.' [11] Born in 1817, he began by working in a printer's shop, attending evening-classes in the drawing-school of the Rue de l'École de Médecine, at the Gobelins, and at the 'Académie' Suisse. At twenty-two he left the printer and started on his real career, the hard way, exhibiting at the dealers' mart near the Institut which Daumier has so often shown us. Here, along with Andrieux and Guys, Bonvin sold pen-and-wash drawings to Painel for twelve francs the batch of eight. Though befriended by Gautier and Gérard among the critics, by the actor Bocage and by Octave Feuillet, he did not achieve the distinction of acceptance by an official jury till he was thirty. Late in life, and even then only through circumventing the ruses of his cut-price dealer, Bonvin began to receive a fair reward for his labours. Starting with the 'Cook', a series of Chardinesque subjects flowed from his brush, among them the celebrated 'School for Young Orphans', which, winning him a second-class medal at the Salon of 1850, really marked the turning-point. But it had been a desperate struggle.

A third artist, typical of the period yet independent of the Murger circle, is Félix Trutat. This painter died in 1848 at the age of twenty-four. No one who knows the gallery at Dijon will be able to forget Trutat's 'Bacchante', offered to the city during the artist's lifetime and refused. The refusal is not difficult to understand: a nude girl in the attitude of Titian's reclining Venus occupies the foreground, while behind her is a window through which Titian would have shown a gracious landscape—but which Trutat fills with a sinister head, grotesquely enlarged. The 'Bacchante' failed to find a buyer, and two pictures exhibited at the Salons of 1845 and 1846 went almost unnoticed. Gautier, however, praised the second and last exhibit, a self-portrait. Into it, with the same whimsicality which marred the 'Bacchante', the artist had introduced another disembodied and apparently irrelevant head. Following Gautier, Champfleury hastened to draw the attention of the *Corsaire*'s readers to this novelty; and Murger, in the *Moniteur de la Mode*, added his kindly word of encouragement.[12]

Such meagre support could do little to assist the painter, by then gravely ill with tuberculosis, a disease once rather fashionable in artistic circles, but now, in the 1840's, a dreaded scourge. From Paris, Tassaert returned to his native Dijon, where he made pathetic attempts to complete some sketches, and died soon afterwards at Talant, just outside the city.

When, then, we are confronted with the dissipations, the eccentricities, the disappointments and, above all, the dire poverty of the Murger circle, we cannot regard these as solely the result of feebleness. Such characteristics come close to being the order of the day. They appear more pronounced in the stories written by Champfleury and Murger only because what interested these young men was not art but the artist's way of life, which taste and circumstances had led them to adopt themselves. Concentrating on this struggle for existence, they had the wit to recognize its commercial possibilities, and from its pathos and humour evolved a new, if highly artificial, literary form. With such skill did Murger accomplish the task that the man himself and the hard facts upon which he built his extravaganzas almost escape notice in the legend he created.

iii

Henry Murger was born in Paris in 1822. He spent part of his childhood in a house in the Rue des Trois-Frères, where lived the artist Isabey and the actress Malibran; but, as the son of its concierge, he could gain little from such happy accidents. A scanty education followed. And when his mother died during his adolescence, he decided to leave an unsympathetic home and explore the world of art and letters: thus entering on a life of privation which finally killed him before he was forty.

It was some two years after the production of *Chatterton* that he took up his duties as general factotum in a lawyer's office, where he met the brothers Bisson, would-be painters, and through them, Léopold and Joseph Desbrosses, scraping a living as painter and sculptor. The five of them were often guests of another pair of artist-brothers, called Lazare, who lived in a house, or more properly a barn, near the Barrière d'Enfer. Here, having crossed a dirty yard and climbed a wooden ladder, Murger and his friends were received in a loft 'furnished' with the casts and engravings from which their hosts earned a little bread—but no wine.[13]

For this barn was the headquarters of the sect known as the *Water-Drinkers*, which came into being about 1839 and lingered on till 1844. In its heyday, it numbered among its members Noël, Cabot, Tabar, Vastine, Villain, Guilbert, Chintreuil, Nadar, and Champfleury. Though there was probably a great deal of truth in Murger's view, expressed later, that the Water-Drinkers frowned on all activities tainted with commercialism, it appears that, from time to time at least, Noël gave drawing-lessons; and, of the two Desbrosses, Joseph ('Le Christ') designed ornaments for a monumental mason, while Léopold ('Le Gothique') painted signboards; still others, like Champfleury and Murger himself, who soon left the lawyer's office, keeping themselves alive by contributions to journals of no very exalted intellectual standard.

Chintreuil, as a landscape-painter denied a landscape, was perhaps the worst-off. Like Champfleury, he soon gave up a makeshift job as bookseller's-runner at Legrand's, only to find himself stranded in Paris without means or opportunity to pursue his real vocation. From his window, in the Rue du Cherche-Midi, a forest of chimneys stretched as far as the eye could range, and the thought of his native countryside at Pont-de-Vaux kept tormenting him: 'If only I had a hundred-and-fifty francs to support me for two months, day and night, right away from this city! A trip beyond the Barrières for a few hours doesn't give you time to study the effects of nature. For that, it's necessary to live with a landscape.'[14]

Champfleury, however, dwells happily on these excursions which, though tantalizing for Chintreuil, were such popular events in the life of the Water-Drinkers. He tells us how he and his friends would tramp across the plain of Montrouge as far as Châtillon, Bagneux, Fontenay-aux-Roses, Châtenay, and Bourg-la-Reine, and from the heights of Châtillon one could get a view of Paris that turned the harsh reality for the moment into a poetic dream.[15] In a story called *La Scène du gouverneur*, Murger too describes how his heroes regularly put by a few francs to enable them to spend the first Sunday of each month in the woods of Sceaux and Meudon. And Célestin Nanteuil drew many pretty groups of artists and *grisettes* picnicking in the country near Paris.

But, ardent nature-lovers as many of these young men may have been, circumstances forced them to earn their living in the city. As Chintreuil had to be content to 'countrify' Montmartre and other quarters of Paris, so Murger began by idealizing urban squalor to match the mood of Romantic poetry, and especially the poetry of Musset. Most of the verse he wrote at this time imitated *Rolla* and the *Nuits*. 'Musset, not Hugo, was his man', says d'Héricault. 'The *Nuits* he regarded as unsurpassed. On that point we were in agreement: where we differed was in his admiration for *Frédéric et Bernerette*, a long-winded, sentimental tale which he believed to be the masterpiece of Romantic art.' [16]

Houssaye gives us a picture of Murger about 1844, when he was trying to break away from the Water-Drinkers: 'A pale wreck of a fellow, who had been through Bohemia already without knowing it.' [17] Long afterwards, in 1896, d'Héricault added a malicious but more detailed portrait:

> Murger was exceedingly ugly, and ugly without a trace of distinction. He was very clumsy, very small, and very dirty. A voice that croaked; a long chestnut-coloured beard that looked as if it had been bleached; gummy eyelids, the eyes themselves dull yet prominent, gentle and rather frightened in expression . . . such was the poet of youth! [18]

Murger, whose range of experience was narrow and had to be drawn upon again and again, often returned to the theme of the Water-Drinkers in his books. He seems to have found himself temperamentally unsuited to a discipline borrowed from the famous 'cénacle' of the Rue des Quatre-Vents. In the *Manchon de Francine* he blames the Water-Drinkers for having presumed to imitate Balzac's group: that sort of discipline had to be judged by results—d'Arthez produced men who won fame in every walk of life, the Lazares nothing but failures. Balzac, of course, was not the chief influence here. As the principal character of Murger's *Poète de gouttières* complains, one could soon grow tired of the Water-Drinkers' at-homes, 'where a gang of down-and-outs, idle as professional beggars, debated the knottiest problems of art without a trace of humour, while wrapping themselves pretentiously in the mantle of their sacred poverty . . . evenings which it was customary to bring to a close with a reading from M. Alfred de Vigny's *Chatterton*.'[19]

Murger, no doubt, had inklings that success might come to him in a manner which would horrify these high priests of art. He had long since abandoned the idea of becoming a painter; and, while continuing to write poetry, made up his mind to earn a living from journalism. Even so, between 1844 and 1849 he was to live a life as wretched as the rest. Subsisting on a tiny salary from the Russian agent, Count Tolstoi, by whom he was engaged as secretary, he implemented this with the pittance paid for contributions to such papers as the *Gazette de la jeunesse*, the *Âge d'or*, and the *Naïade*—or 'moniteur des maisons de bain'. The greater part of his time was spent in search of the five-franc piece, an occupation less amusing than it is made to appear in the *Scènes de la Bohème*. In 1841, he paid his first visit to hospital, suffering (as he was to continue to do) from a scrofulous condition called 'purpura'. A bed in the public ward had its advantages, however. Meals, though poor, were regular; he was able to do some writing; and he could receive visits from his Paris friends. In a letter of May 30th, 1842, to another friend in the provinces, he gave this news of them:

> You may, or may not, know that, after the opening of the Salon, there was an exhibition for the *refusés* in the Boulevard Bonne-Nouvelle. The Desbrosses sent various things, and sold, 1. The little statuette of Marguerite; 2. The bust of Saint Anthony; 3. A little picture by Chintreuil; the total raised being 200 francs, which has helped them a bit. . . . In the meantime, Chintreuil, through the influence of his Deputy, has just obtained a commission from the Minister—for 800, or 1,500 francs: we are not certain yet.[20]

Alas, the Deputy did not live up to expectations, and Chintreuil had to continue the bitter struggle without official patronage, the victim of constant melancholia and exhausting fits of coughing. A little help came from Béranger: sixty francs for a small picture, and credit at Giroux's colour-shop. The painter's situation remained precarious and, ten years later, when Béranger came to his rescue again, he was actually starving. But about this time it was at last possible for Chintreuil to leave Paris for the country. Recognition did not come till 1862, when, settled finally at Mantes, he was already far advanced in consumption.

For Murger and his friends, 1842 proved one of the worst of a number of bad years, past and to come. He, Chintreuil, and Joseph and Léopold Desbrosses were constantly in and out of hospital, existing on a common purse, and sharing each other's clothing, in a condition summed up by Murger in October as an 'interminable ballad, whereof the refrain, "Poverty, poverty, poverty!", never varies'. In April of the following year, he declared: 'We are starving. We've reached the end of our tether. Without question, we shall have to blow our brains out, if we can't find a niche somewhere.' [21]

iv

Then, all at once, his prospects brightened. He must have been acquainted with Champfleury (Jules Husson or Fleury) from the first formation of the Water-Drinkers. Now, in 1843, the latter arrived back in Paris after two seasons' kicking his heels in Laon, and the two shared a lodging together in the Rue de Vaugirard. Murger explained the change of address thus: 'I am living with a young man, an old friend of the Desbrosses, who wants to be a writer, and would probably make a go of it if he were not so lazy.' [22] The importance of this experiment in housekeeping was that it helped Murger to discover his true direction, and so in the long run rescued him from the hopeless existence to which he had seemed doomed.

D'Héricault, their near neighbour in the Rue de Vaugirard, leaves a portrait of Champfleury even less flattering than the one of Murger: 'I can see him still, our Realist mischief-maker, his ugly, yellow, ill-tempered face, and his malicious little eyes ever seeking some excuse for a spiteful comment.' [23] But it was precisely this sharp edge to his friend's wit that benefited the sentimental Murger. Not prepared, as Champfleury advised, to give up writing poetry altogether, he was at least sufficiently discouraged by recent events to consider a more practical way out of his difficulties. 'I'm going to hunt round for newspaper-articles and try to get a footing in the smaller theatres', he writes, about this time. 'Under a pseudonym, mind you; for I have no intention of getting my real name mixed up in all the literary crimes I contemplate. I may be setting out on the wrong road, but what else is there for me to do? I've no job and I must live.' [24] Indeed, as Tolstoi's patronage seemed to be coming to an end, a monthly fifty francs from the *Commerce*, the first results of these renewed efforts, came opportunely. For the moment, however, he could not quite make up his mind whether to join Champfleury or return to the fatal 'cénacle' of the Barrière d'Enfer. As a consequence, he found himself at loggerheads with both.

By March 1844, the situation had again deteriorated. His engagement with the *Commerce* petered out. Tolstoi did not re-apply for his services. And with early summer came the untimely death of Joseph Desbrosses, called 'Le Christ' on account of his selfless character, an event of such real grief to his friends, and so terrible in its implications, that it continued to colour all that Murger was to write on the subject of the *vie de Bohème*. In the most factual report of this tragedy, the *Biographie d'un inconnu*, two gravediggers approach the dead man's friends for the customary tip, but the mourners cannot oblige. 'No matter,' cries one gravedigger, gaily: 'next time will do!' Murger continues: 'The lugubrious humour of this answer sent a shudder through all who heard it. In the circumstances, it seemed almost like a prophecy; and we turned pale with terror when the other fellow blandly added: "Why, yes, of course! These gentlemen are old customers: I know them well!" ' [25]

During the previous six weeks, Murger informs us, no less than three of the original Water-Drinkers had met the same fate, and from the same cause—starvation. The warning light shone clear: yet Murger still nursed a desperate hope that his old companions would achieve success. Of Bresdin, engraver, etcher, and hero of Champfleury's *Chien-Caillou*, he thought very highly indeed, referring to two or three of the plates (and with reason) as 'true masterpieces of their kind'.[26]

By setting up house with Champfleury again, this time in the Hôtel Merciol, Rue des Canettes, Murger increased his acquaintance with artists. For, besides a special interest in the Le Nains, masters of his native Laon, Champfleury was full of enthusiasm for every aspect of contemporary art in Paris. Under the mask of Sylvius, he records his own original intention to become an artist; how he was admitted to the society of the 'Treize' (another version of the Water-Drinkers), who carried their hatred of the 'picture painted for the bourgeois' as far as it could go.[27] For the *Artiste* he wrote serious studies, for the *Corsaire* a continuous stream of light articles and skits on artistic life. These last, composed between 1843 and 1847, just anticipate Murger's *Scènes*. Less amusingly, and probably no more accurately, they hit off life as it was lived in the attics of the Hôtel Merciol, to which Murger moved from the Rue de la Harpe where he had been staying with Alexandre Schanne, afterwards to figure, as 'Schaunard', in the famous Bohemian quartet.

Later, in his *Aventures de Mademoiselle Mariette*, Champfleury emphasizes the squalid side of the existence Murger did his best to exalt into some sort of idyll. The attics, no doubt, were dirty and overcrowded, and the type of woman installed in them cannot have been well suited to the rôle of Muse. With poetry fetching nothing at all, and prose at five centimes the line, she might well look elsewhere, leaving Murger or Champfleury to his own devices for weeks at a time. But the men, too, must have needed this respite; they certainly found it convenient to disappear at frequent intervals themselves, their refuge being the editorial-office or the café.

For the part it plays in the *Confessions de Sylvius* and the *Scènes de la Bohème*, the best-remembered of the cafés is the *Momus*. This was blighted by unsuccessful writers and artists, who habitually ordered one cup of coffee for three and left nothing for the waiter. Its proprietor lamented such behaviour, but, not daring to invite reprisals, was forced to watch helplessly while authors dropped in to write their articles; etchers and lithographers brought along copper-plates and stones to work on; and painters actually set up their easels on the premises, to take advantage of a better light than their own garrets provided.[28]

That other refuge, the editorial-office, was linked for Murger and Champfleury with such titles as the *Tam-Tam*, the *Silhouette*, and the *Corsaire* itself. The *Corsaire*, unforgettably associated with Murger's earliest work, was a paper that paid little but promised much. Modest paragraphs accepted by its editor could lead to short stories; the stories, published in book-form, or dramatized for the little theatres, might eventually attract the notice of a larger public, and the way would then be opened to well-paid serializations in such celebrated journals as the *Revue des Deux-Mondes*, the mark of solid success. So (with certain reservations) it was to prove in Murger's case; and the director of the *Corsaire*, Le Poitevin Saint-Alme, launched a number of other writers on the five-centime rate who were later to make a name for themselves.

The change in Murger's fortunes, then, may be dated from the moment when, exploiting a vein of farcical humour which he had up till now preferred to ignore, he began to supply the *Corsaire* with a collection of tales of artistic life. At the suggestion of Houssaye, he had already exchanged his baptismal *Henri Murger* for the more elegant form 'Henry Mürger' (the *umlaut* has disappeared again, but the Anglicized version of the Christian name remains), yet he was still too concerned for his reputation as a poet to sign the amusing studio-anecdote, *Un Envoyé de la providence*, which appeared in Saint-Alme's paper in February, 1845. 'Whether you approve or not,' he wrote to a friend in that month, 'I believe I've found my literary bent—in pure fantasy.'[29]

VIII

The Bohemian (I)

i

Fantasy and literary caprice play so large a part in Murger's earlier stories, those which particularly concern us, that, as I have already pointed out, the reality underlying them may very well —and very properly—elude a casual reader. This element of invention somewhat embarrassed Champfleury. Having been intimate with the author from 1843, he found it necessary to underline the absurdity of connecting the few diversions they had shared in the Rue de Vaugirard and the Rue des Canettes with the endless lark that life becomes in the *Scènes de la Bohème*. The stories, nevertheless, have a documentary value of their own.

To begin with, they are largely autobiographical. So dependent was Murger on one kind of material at hand, that Champfleury made a joke of it in his *Aventures de Mademoiselle Mariette*, where his friend is caricatured under the name of Streich: 'Streich had a peculiar mania: it was always his own life and love-affairs that he wrote about. . . . Every now and then he cut a slice of adventure out of his life, like a wedge of pie, and took this slice to M. de Saint-Charmay [that is, to Saint-Alme, editor of the *Corsaire*].' [1] Episodes in the fiction can easily be traced to Murger's own experiences with Marie Virmal, Lucille Louvet, and Marie Roux, from whom are derived Mimi and Musette, showing that Champfleury did not exaggerate.[2] Nor are the male characters in the *Scènes de la Bohème* difficult to identify. Schaunard represents Alexandre Schanne, Sunday-painter and amateur musician; Marcel is a combination of Champfleury and the painter François Tabar, a pupil of Delaroche; Colline is closely modelled on Jean Wallon with features derived from Trapadoux, whose portrait was once painted by Courbet. Rodolphe, the hero, is of course Murger himself.

His picture in *Comment fut institué le cénacle de la Bohème* is a good example of the distortions of that comic mirror in which Murger was determined to see everyone and everything, while preserving a perfectly recognizable likeness:

> A lively discussion was going on, as they entered, between two frequenters of that public establishment [the Café Momus]. One of these was a young man whose face was completely lost to sight in the depths of an enormous bushy beard of various shades of colour. By way of contrast, however, to this prodigious growth on cheek and chin, premature baldness, setting in above, had left his forehead as bare as a knee, save for a few straggling hairs (so few that you might count them) which strove in vain to hide its nakedness. A black coat, tonsured at the elbows, gave glimpses of other openings for ventilation at the armholes, whenever the wearer raised his arms; his trousers might possibly have been black once; but his boots had never been new, and the Wandering Jew might have tramped two or three times round the world in them already.[3]

The elements of a situation which must have been common enough in the life of a young artist are similarly handled in the 'scene' that follows (though in reality the earliest), *Un Envoyé de la providence*. Marcel has been invited to dine with a Deputy, but cannot accept since he has no black coat. With the connivance of Schaunard, he borrows the coat of a respectable provincial who comes to sit for his portrait, and so is able to keep the appointment after all. The sugar-refiner does not, perhaps, object as strongly as he should to the dirty dressing-gown he is persuaded to put on in place of his own coat: 'It is a strange-looking garment.' 'But very valuable', puts in the painter. 'A Turkish vizier presented it to M. Horace Vernet, by whom it was given to me.' Yet in spite of the artificiality of the plot, the story abounds in authentic detail. 'Y' avait quat' jeunes gens du quartier', Marcel's song of jubilation, when he first receives the Deputy's letter, is one particularly associated with the artists' quarter of the Rue de la Tour-d'Auvergne.[4] Chintreuil, as we have seen, had identical hopes of a Deputy, and from what Fizelière tells us of Chintreuil's mode of dress, a friend might really have said to him on an occasion like this, as Schaunard says to Marcel: 'You can't possibly go out to dine in a red jacket and bargee's cap!'[5]

Both painters, on Schaunard's admission, are *coloristes*, or Romantics, which partly explains their poverty and their need to listen politely to a middle-class Philistine airing his views on art. But this provides one more opportunity of ridiculing the bourgeois, as when Murger shows M. Blancheron requiring his portrait in *miniature*; 'for, to the worthy delegate, as to a good many other people, there are but two kinds of painting—"house" and "miniature" '. It also helps to make a more original point: how Marcel, quite unconcerned by principle in any non-professional connexion, is genuinely horrified at having to deny his artistic gods and simulate an admiration for (of all people) Horace Vernet!

Originating as sketches, the *Scènes de la Bohème* follow no strict plot. Rodolphe is a journalist, poet, and playwright; Marcel a painter; Schaunard a musician and painter; Colline a philosopher, who finds occasional employment as a private tutor. Mimi is attached to Rodolphe, Musette to Marcel, Phémie Teinturière to Schaunard, and the philosopher is similarly, though less circumstantially, provided for. These young men resign themselves to temporary poverty, while making every effort to catch the public eye and achieve the reasonable degree of success they consider their due. Theirs is a practical outlook and they have sufficient talent to overcome their difficulties in the end. The majority of the stories illustrate efforts to raise money, struggles for commissions, and the perpetual need to squeeze some enjoyment out of an unpromising existence in which they often go hungry. For these young men, optimism is a necessary armour. Their misfortunes, happily, never prove fatal, and are endured with such stoic gaiety that the sting is hardly felt. It is true that Mimi dies, and that tragedy comes to others known to Rodolphe and his friends, but the young men themselves escape unharmed, and leave this way of life finally with nothing more painful than a sentimental regret.

Having recounted thirteen of their adventures in pursuit of love or the five-franc piece, the author paused to sum up and defend a comradeship which had been in existence for six years:

> This long period, passed in daily intimacy, without altering the strongly defined individuality of each one of them, had bound them in an accordance of ideas and a unity which they would have vainly sought elsewhere. They had their own manners and customs and modes of expression, to which strangers would not have possessed the key. Those who did not properly know them called their free-and-easy

ways cynicism. It was, in fact, just frankness. Their spirits, restive against all constraint, hated the false and held the commonplace in contempt. Accused of exaggerated vanities, they retorted by proudly proclaiming the programme of their ambition, and, having the consciousness of their worth, they did not abuse it.

During the many years that they had walked together in the same paths, they had often of necessity been placed in rivalry; but they had never broken their ties, and had passed over personal questions of self-respect without heeding, every time attempts had been made to disunite them. Moreover, they estimated exactly their own individual value; and pride, which is the antidote of envy, protected them from all petty professional jealousies.[6]

Murger's life (thus transposed as the life of Rodolphe and his friends) boasted in reality but little of this *amour-propre*. It had never been enviable in any way. To succeed as a writer, however, it was necessary for him to make it seem so. As his 'dear reader', Murger had in mind the very bourgeois whom the heroes of the *vie de Bohème* affected to despise. All these enticing visions of freedom were cooked up for a respectable audience, leading a regular life, which could have no inkling of the real boredom of existence on the fringe of society. To make the visions easier to accept, Rodolphe ceases to be Musset's student of gentle birth, and takes on the character of a robust young man of the people with an uncle in the stove-business. Subscribers to the *Corsaire* needed only a spark of imagination to identify themselves with this erring member of their own family, and brave with him the *Cape of Storms*, join in his search for *Polar Violets*, and indulge vicariously in his *Lenten Loves*: properly appreciating the whimsical touches with which such episodes were embellished.

Murger recounted also the tragic death of Mimi, knowing that laughter is all the better for being mingled with a few tears. In doing so, he was offering another slice out of his own life, as Champfleury had said, and perhaps did right to remind his audience that Bohemia was not invariably cheerful. But he avoided lingering too long in the sick-room, and soon returned to the jollities of conjuring up a hundred francs or winning the goodwill of a creature, half *grisette*, half 'lorette', 'rather like a theme of Greuze's arranged by Gavarni'. Bad as things might seem from time to time, what compensations this life of freedom brought with it: getting up late, lounging and sponging one's way round the clock, and at the end of it, excusing everything, the observation: 'We're only young once!'

For, like Musset and Béranger, Murger made immaturity a complete excuse for the aberrations of the artist. As long as he can keep clear of thirty, what better occupation than to bait the *Garde nationale* or the 'old guard' of art and letters? Mimi and Musette will come and share his garret from time to time, despite the lure of more comfortable quarters, because in this chequered and fantastic existence are distilled all the noblest, most disinterested qualities of youth.

And in the absurd notion that there was something about the poverty-stricken artist which attracted the opposite sex, Murger flourished a trump card—to such effect that the ordinary public, caring little for art itself and knowing even less about the persons and habits of those who devoted their lives to such pursuits, was able to equate artistic freedom with sexual freedom. Especially since, by the time the *Scènes de la Bohème* became famous, Courbet's loud voice could be heard declaiming: 'If, to-day, I come across a woman blessed with one sort of quality, I take good care to enjoy it while the opportunity presents itself; then, to-morrow, I can take a fresh mistress, and enjoy some other quality in her!' [7]

Meanwhile, Murger scored no immediate success with these sketches. Perhaps we should never have heard of them, had not a dramatic author arrived, in 1849, to re-arrange them for the theatre.

ii

Though, from 1845 onwards, Murger had no difficulty in placing his stories in the *Corsaire*, he was a slow worker, the work itself was poorly paid, and his struggles were by no means at an end. Indeed, the fears expressed by those who had attended Joseph Desbrosses's funeral seemed day by day in danger of realization throughout 1846 and 1847. Chintreuil's fortunes were at their lowest ebb; first seven, then three of Courbet's pictures were rejected by the Salon jury; Nadar, Léopold Desbrosses, and Murger himself revisited hospital on a number of occasions; while his mistress, Lucille Louvet, died at the Saint-Louis, and her body, as a pauper's, was claimed by the authorities for dissection.

Champfleury, living alone on the Quai Malaquais, exclaimed: 'To spend one's days hungry and ill-shod, and making paradoxes about it, is really the dreariest kind of existence.'[8] Murger suffered equally the drawn-out crisis of a life dependent on miserably paid journalism, and confessed to Tolstoi (for whom he was once again fulfilling the duties of secretary) that creditors threatened even his fees from the *Corsaire.*

For Murger, indeed, the year 1848 was as disastrous as any he had known. At last an unfortunate accident brought his activities for Count Tolstoi finally to an end; he was once more in hospital, this time in the Midi, from which he wrote begging for a handkerchief and two sous' worth of tobacco.[9] On his release, he had not a rag to his back, and it fell to the lot of d'Héricault to lend him, somewhat ungraciously, the ill-fitting garments which would enable him to go out and look for work. 'Wisely,' says the latter, 'I refused to give Murger the address of my tailor, who, strangely enough, had no burning ambition to become *honorary* "outfitter to the King of Bohemia".'[10] Feeble in health and spirits, ashamed of the ludicrous figure he cut in d'Héricault's cast-off clothing, Murger took little interest in the political events of 1848.

'Its causes and consequences', says Jules Breton, of Louis-Philippe's abdication, 'made a lively impression . . . on the arts and literature. It was a violent stimulus to new experiments.' Murger's friends shared in the excitement: Baudelaire and Champfleury collaborated in the production of a short-lived newspaper, for which Courbet designed a title-drawing; and Nadar and Fauchery helped to give assistance to the Poles in their fight for freedom. In Murger's work there are only echoes of all this. Marcel, for instance, on renting a new room, arranges with the porter to call him every morning with a report on the weather and the form of government under which they are living; accordingly, the next day there is a knock at the door, and he receives the following bulletin: 'Monsieur, to-day is the ninth of April, eighteen hundred and forty . . . the streets are muddy and his Majesty Louis-Philippe is still King of France and Navarre.'[11] The only explicit reference to the new Republic (in the story called *Son Excellence Colline*) takes the form of a light-hearted dig at Jean Wallon, who secured a minor Government office.

It was early in 1849, when he was living in abject poverty in the sixth-floor attic at No. 78, Rue Mazarine, directly above Courbet's friend, the socialist philosopher Proudhon, that Murger received a visit from a clerk in the Ministry of War, Théodore Barrière. Barrière, as an experienced dramatist and play-doctor, proposed that Murger and he should collaborate in a stage version of the stories that had been appearing in the *Corsaire*. Murger accepted. With the help of a composer, Nargeot, a five-act play with songs and music was evolved, and the Théâtre des Variétés engaged for its production. The first night, fixed for November 22nd, 1849, was to prove the turning-point to which Murger had looked forward during eleven years of the blackest misery. Charles Monselet approved the conventionalized plot contributed by Barrière, and upheld Murger's own insistence that the harrowing death of Mimi should be retained to provide the final curtain. His judgment was confirmed by the play's resounding success.

The idea behind this dramatic version (entitled *La Vie de Bohème*)[12] is the same justification of the artist's way of life which had inspired the series originally published in the *Corsaire*. There are a number of differences in the unfolding of the plot, of course, and some alterations of character. In the play, for instance, Rodolphe is a gay young gentleman staying in the country-house of a wealthy uncle when he meets Marcel, Colline, and Schaunard, who have been picnicking in the grounds with their friends, Mimi and Musette. It follows, therefore, that his subsequent adventures in their company are little more than slumming. Nor is the Mimi of the play the Mimi of the stories in the *Corsaire*. She has become an 'angel of consumption', virtuous, hardworking—and seriously in love with Rodolphe. Far from sharing Musette's experiences in the gay *demi-monde*, she neither knows nor expects anything but a life of poverty. It is just that she cannot resist Rodolphe's poetic love-making, decked out with such compliments as, 'So you go to Pradier for your hands, Madame?' In various concessions to 'good theatre' and bourgeois susceptibility, the touch of Barrière may be detected. But Murger himself cannot escape all responsibility for the disappearance of much that had been really comic and spontaneous.

As Champfleury declared, Murger made his name with this success. Though in point of time, Champfleury had anticipated the *Scènes de la Bohème* in several less sparkling documents of artistic life, in the *Corsaire* and other journals, it was Murger who first roused general interest in this kind of material. He might well marvel at his luck, declaring himself the Emperor of Morocco, married to the Bank of France, for his finances immediately improved as sudden notoriety opened to him the columns of newspapers more generous than the *Corsaire*. From the spring of 1850, he began to spend frequent holidays at Marlotte, a tiny hamlet near Barbizon, on the edge of the Forest of Fontainebleau. In Paris, he was able to exchange his attic in the Rue Mazarine for more suitable quarters in the Rue Notre-Dame-de-Lorette. Schanne noted the splendour of this apartment, its grey velvet draperies, the mediaeval dagger fastened to the wall beside a Renaissance bonnet, the piano humorously furnished with a cast of Préault's 'Silence', and the fashionable lithograph of 'Maître Wolfram' by Lemud hanging near by.[13] For the first time in his life, their owner received invitations to houses where there were carpets underfoot and chairs to sit on. To d'Héricault he announced that Anna Thuillier, the actress who played Mimi, had consented to share his cab for a short distance. When d'Héricault smiled at his emotion, Murger added: 'Ah, you don't know what it is to find yourself sitting for the first time next to a woman *who smells nice*!'[14]

La Vie de Bohème succeeded in making the artist's way of life a subject of increased curiosity. This could be a nuisance. The Café Momus, for instance, began to attract sightseers; and serious artists and writers like Courbet, Baudelaire, and Gérard de Nerval, who had been patronizing Louvet's establishment for a number of years, found themselves suddenly the centre of vulgar interest. It must be admitted, however, that publicity brought to this group more advantages than disadvantages. *La Vie de Bohème* created a demand for fiction and *reportage* with a similar background, and, in 1851, Michel Lévy published a first collection of Murger's *Corsaire* stories under the title of *Scènes de la Bohème* (later to become *Scènes de la vie de Bohème*), followed by a second collection within the year, *Scènes de la vie de jeunesse*.

iii

Murger's circumstances had altered, therefore, by the time he came to arrange these tales for publication in book-form. He was now anxious to be accepted by the serious public of the *Revue des*

Deux-Mondes, and concerned—as never before—for the *respectability* of Bohemia.

'The Bohemia with which this book is concerned is by no means peculiar to the present time', he begins.[15] In the first part of the Preface he seeks to trace the history of unconventional and vagrant personalities in art and literature: Homer himself; Villon, 'poet and vagabond *par excellence*'; Clément Marot, Mathurin Régnier; literary figures under Louis XIII and Louis XIV; Molière and Shakespeare; Jean-Jacques Rousseau and d'Alembert; and, somewhat slightingly, Malfilâtre and Gilbert. Such references would serve, he hoped, to rid the term 'Bohemian' of any mistaken associations with sword-eaters and 'inventors of "infallible systems" '. He then returns to the present: 'To-day, as in the past, any man who enters the path of Art, with art as his sole means of support, is bound to pass by way of Bohemia.' The most illustrious contemporary writers and artists were Bohemians once, and often looked back wistfully at the courage and hope that had preserved them through their early struggles.

Next follows his definition, 'Bohemia is a stage in the artist's career; it is the preface to the Academy, the Hospital, or the Morgue'—then his classification of the various types of Bohemian. There were really three of these: the dreamers, the amateurs, and the stalwarts—or 'official' Bohemians. Each class is described in detail. As to the first, Murger has more scorn for its conceit than pity for its sufferings; nothing but contempt for the second; and a real admiration for the third (to which, by implication, he himself belonged). In fact, his contemptuous attitude to the 'dreamers' arose from his own early sympathy with their ideals; nor was he always immune to the flattery of 'amateur' Bohemians, as his enthusiastic reception of Whistler, in 1855, was to show.

On Bohemia, for Bohemia's sake, he launches a vigorous attack: '*Axiom.*—Unknown Bohemia is not a thoroughfare; it is a *cul-de-sac.*' It is a life that leads nowhere, extinguishing the intelligence as a lamp goes out for want of oxygen. The man who stays too long in Bohemia is doomed, or can escape only into the neighbouring Bohemia of crime. And the origin of this fatal attachment is to be found in the legends that have grown up round the names of Gilbert, Malfilâtre, Chatterton, and Hégésippe Moreau.

So much for the 'dreamers'. For the 'amateurs', as I have said, Murger felt nothing but contempt. 'We knew one of these amateurs who, after staying three years in Bohemia and quarrelling with his family, died, one fine morning, and was carried in a pauper's hearse to a pauper's grave; and he had an income of ten thousand francs!' Murger, conducting himself in the Preface as a man of common sense, dismisses the 'amateur' with this ludicrous example of the quixotic.

He concludes, however, on a note of enthusiasm, for he is now dealing with the 'official' Bohemians, the brave, independent young writers and artists who have already given proof of talent, but whose sales are still so moderate as to render life precarious. No obstacle can prevent their determination to get on; indeed, it is the obstacle itself that stimulates them to fresh efforts. They do not despise commissions offered by shopkeepers and industrialists: it is less honourable to be idle and starve. The 'official' Bohemian will not restrict himself to the society of the Café Momus and the garrets of the Quarter; he believes in visiting the world of fashion too, and in broadening his mind, when the opportunity occurs. At the same time, he is conscious of being a citizen of a special world of his own, a private world, and prides himself on a slang composed of the language of the studio and newspaper-office which is unintelligible to ordinary mortals. He leads a life, adds Murger, that only patience and courage make possible: 'No one can attempt the struggle unless he wears the stout armour of indifference, proof against fools and envious attacks; and no one can afford to lose his pride in himself for a moment; it is his staff, and without it he will stumble by the way. Delightful and terrible life, which boasts its conquerors and its martyrs, on which no one should enter unless he has made up his mind beforehand to submit to the ruthless law: *vae victis!*'

iv

Accustomed to a day-to-day struggle against sickness and starvation and prematurely exhausted by the experience, Murger wished to enjoy some of the comforts of life. Yet, though his aims were frankly materialistic and he had little interest in literary movements, he could not remain untouched by the endeavours of such a close friend as Champfleury to break new ground. Nor could he afford to turn a deaf ear to editors and the established critics when they began to express dissatisfaction with the *rapin-grisette* formula, a formula he had only somewhat shamefacedly adopted himself. The result was that, despite his deep attachment to certain ideas expressed in the *Scènes de la Bohème*, he felt obliged to raise the moral tone and social standing of his characters and, as time went on, to experiment, himself, in themes which might be classed as 'Realist'.

Meanwhile, his *Scènes de la vie de jeunesse*, also published in 1851, merely covered the ground made familiar by the first collection of stories. The characters comprise the same poets and artists, whose mistresses involve them in the same type of adventure in the Latin Quarter. The greatest debt is still to Musset.

But if nothing really new is added, our picture of the Bohemian would be less complete without the added touches given in *Un Poète de gouttières*. Here Murger was determined to explode the Chatterton legend once and for all. Melchoir is the personification of heroic genius (in so far as it is possible to be heroic and mediocre at the same time). '*Chatterton!*' exclaims Murger in disgust. 'This was the book with which Melchior had completed his spiritual intoxication, and how many young people like him have poisoned themselves with the prickly self-esteem contained in those violent pages!' He continues: 'The *Chatterton* play is certainly a fine work—but its success must often have weighed heavy with remorse on the conscience of the author. He ought, moreover, to have foreseen the dangerous influence which this play would exercise on the faint-hearted and over-ambitious. *Chatterton* is one of those productions which have all the attraction of the abyss; and this play, which represents in dramatic form nothing less than the apotheosis of pride and mediocrity, with suicide as its conclusion, has in all likelihood opened many a tomb. But there is no doubt that the performances of *Chatterton* created this lamentable school of snivelling, fatalistic poets which the critics have not attacked fiercely enough.' [16]

In the story of Melchior, Murger shows how Vigny's continual harping on the hardships of genius had led, in his weakest imitators, not to heroic resignation but to an enthusiastic *cult of failure*. No doubt, Melchior is a caricature, but if Vigny's philosophy had not been 'attacked fiercely enough', who was better equipped for the task than Murger, the life-long observer of such pathetic geniuses *en herbe*? It turns out, indeed, a vicious and sustained attack.

Although Melchior had been given many opportunities of escaping from his dismal situation, he was quite determined to remain where he was: poverty lent itself so admirably to the elegy and the dithyramb! There was, however, something lacking: the last thorn in the martyr's crown, a bed in hospital. Only by suffering on the 'pallet of Gilbert' could he achieve real distinction. Thus Melchior deliberately makes himself ill and manages to obtain admission to the Hôtel-Dieu. There he is questioned about his profession. 'I am a poet,' he replies, striking a pose; 'that is, one of those unfortunates whom the brutality of the day abandons pitilessly to every kind of hardship.' [17] His idea is now to write an ode, giving the hospital as his address, and to send it as soon as possible to the *Revue des Deux-Mondes*. This done, he settles down to imagine the general admiration and curiosity his poem will arouse. People will be clamouring to solve the identity of this 'second Gilbert', this 'brother of Moreau lying in agony on his wretched bed'. Fashionable ladies will come to visit him. Inquiries will be made on his behalf in the Chamber of Deputies, and a pension will be awarded him to prevent the Liberal papers printing headlines condemning the scandalous neglect of another great poet. In fact, the *Revue* does not publish Melchior's ode after all, and the modern Chatterton gives up literature for stockbroking!

Murger was a sad disappointment to Champfleury, when it came to style and presentation. *Les Vacances de Camille*, published in 1857, appeared over the subtitle, 'scenes from real life', but is just another story in the manner of *Frédéric et Bernerette*. No doubt the author was often at odds with himself, on the one hand hankering after the frivolous themes of his youth, on the other anxious to please Buloz and develop into a well-behaved novelist; his state of mind further complicated by a desire, fitful though it may have been, to advance along the path blazed by his more progressive friends. And throughout he remained oddly sensitive to the dissatisfaction of his oldest associates, the Water-Drinkers.

Thus, in the *Vacances de Camille*, his hero, Francis Bernier, is still frantically searching out Théodore, an earnest ex-Water-

Drinker, to explain his defection for the hundredth time and recover that painter's good opinion. Bernier himself has by now become a regular exhibitor at the Salon and, while not taken seriously by collectors of taste, is generally respected by the dealers and provincial Press. 'He had learnt', Murger informs us, 'to walk on carpets, to test every kind of chair, and to dance all the new dances. He made rapid strides in the science of puerile accomplishments; and he received the reward of being hailed as a *charmer*.'[18] If Murger could not resist exaggerating his own social success here, there is a touch of self-mockery, too, in the other 'improvements' he ascribes to Bernier: 'Renouncing all the memories of his youth, he had turned his sharp artist's humour into a gentle playfulness, and if, under cover of a lady's fan, he was invited to retail some exploit from his student-past, he did so in the disdainful terms of a sceptical social-climber, who speaks disparagingly of his impoverished native country in order to get himself naturalized in another, wealthier one.'[19]

In reality, Murger was far from enjoying the success or the financial security here suggested. Like Bernier, however, he had been decorated, receiving the award shortly after the publication of the *Vacances de Camille*, in 1858. He lived better, of course: for the first time in his life he was able to travel; and Delvau estimated his income during the later years at between three and four thousand francs. Yet though all this suggests prosperity, he was in constant difficulties with creditors, even forced on one occasion to leave his apartment and abandon his furniture in lieu of rent. No remarkable success followed the initial triumph of his collaboration with Barrière. The rustic novels, *Adéline Protat*, 1853, and *Le Sabot rouge*, 1859, failed to interest the public. Nevertheless, the one triumph had opened to him an assured living as a journalist, and Michael Lévy, despite occasional disputes, was always ready to republish his serials in book-form. Even as late as 1860, Murger had some encouragement from dramatic critics and the public, when his light comedy, *Le Serment d'Horace*, was successfully performed in the theatre.

His financial embarrassment seems to have been due to other causes, to his inability to manage his affairs (even with some assistance from the last of a long line of 'Mimis'), and from ill-health. On January 14th, 1861, Dr Piogey ordered him into hospital. The 'purpura', aggravated by habitual overdoses of strong coffee, had recurred in its most violent form, followed by a severe attack of arthritis.

During this last fortnight of his life, reduced at the age of thirty-eight to a condition of physical decay that horrifies us in the description,[20] Murger had at least some consolation in the widespread sympathy felt for him by the people of Paris. 'Since Béranger lay on his death-bed,' says Delvau, 'there had been seen no such compassion for a dying man.' [21] Ironically, it was an original member of the Water-Drinkers who tended him most faithfully, the kind and eccentric Nadar. Others awaited—with all the curiosity that Melchior had longed for and failed to arouse—some last words characteristic of a 'prince of Bohemia', and it was confidently expected that Murger's would prove sensational. Delvau, responsible for the report, did his best to furnish something worthy of the occasion: 'No more music! No more alarums! No more Bohemia!'—so the dying man is supposed to have muttered.[22]

Three days later, the funeral procession made its way to the cemetery. The pall-bearers were distinguished persons; and the Ministers of State and Public Instruction, as well as the Institut, sent representatives. It only required an onlooker to remark: 'This must have been some millionaire!' to complete the tragi-comedy of Murger's life.

But as the glories of Bohemia passed into history, the posthumous *Nuits d'hiver* appeared in the bookshops to revive once more the legend Murger had created. The respectable and mediocre novelist of the *Revue des Deux-Mondes* was forgotten. 'Murger's work is wholly dedicated to youth and poverty', wrote Paul de Saint-Victor. 'Success lifted him out of Bohemia, but there he remained in spirit, continuing to sing the joys and brightness of the fleeting hour.' [23] The *Nuits d'hiver* belonged in reality to Murger's youth; and Baudelaire could slyly remind the public, a little later, how very differently the poet spoke of Bohemia among those who had been through the long, gruelling experience with him.[24]

IX

The Bohemian (II)

i

The term 'Bohème', in something like the sense intended by Murger, is almost certainly contemporary with the Preface to *Cromwell*, inspired (as Derôme once suggested) by some Romantic *orgie de truands*.[1] Literary and artistic Paris of the 1830's was crowded with rebellious and impoverished young men, and for its appositeness the word 'gipsy' was no doubt soon seized upon and given currency. George Sand, arriving in the capital shortly after the July Revolution, would early have been familiar with it. In succeeding years, her personal grievances led her to see in this 'gipsy' life of the artist a noble protest against the pettiness of convention: as, in *La Dernière Aldini*, Lélio declares: 'An artist's fatherland is the whole world, the great *Bohemia*, as we say.' [2] In this novel, the word 'Bohème' occurs five times, and its importance is emphasized in the climax of the final paragraph: 'Lélio hesitated a moment, replenished his glass, and sighed deeply. Then, his beautiful dark eyes wet with tears, yet flashing youth and gaiety, he gave us, in a voice of thunder, a toast which we echoed as one man: "Vive la Bohème!" ' The setting of *La Dernière Aldini* is Venice, and its tale of grand passion has no obvious connexion with Paris of the 1830's; but the author is certainly up-to-date in her use of the word 'Bohemia'.

On the other hand, the picturesque life of street dancers and singers was already attracting attention, and not only the attention of Daumier. The female 'busker' had acquired literary fame in Hugo's Esméralda, and had sat for her portrait, as the 'Petite Mendiante russe', to Émile Deroy, painter-friend of Baudelaire and Banville.[3] Indeed, the feminine character of the 'vie de bohème' and 'vie bohémienne' cannot but strike the reader rather forcibly, when, in Balzac's *Illusions perdues* and *Splendeurs et misères des courtisanes*, these phrases are applied exclusively to the raffish existence of Coralie and Esther; just as the same aspect had always been dwelt on by Béranger in describing the follies of his *grisette*-rhyming Lisette. Rather than George Sand's historical Venice, it is Béranger's working-class Paris, his student-idylls and sentimental sermons on the girl of easy virtue, that lead in a direct line to the Bohemia of Murger. Yet neither he, nor (in the 'legends' attached to his lithographs) the observant Gavarni, uses the term 'Bohème' in quite the same sense.

Balzac recognized its possibilities first. In 1839, he had invented that imaginary 'cénacle' of the Rue des Quatre-Vents which, though on a different social level, certainly anticipates the fanatical society of the Water-Drinkers: but the title 'Bohème' is not applied to it. When, in *Une Fille d'Ève* and *Un Prince de la Bohème* (originally, *Les Fantaisies de Claudine*), he does give us a specific definition of Bohemia, it is not of a small, dedicated group that he speaks, but of the whole vast clearing-house of worldly ambition, as it exists in Paris, crammed indifferently with amateurs and charlatans, stockbrokers and politicians, as well as with genuinely struggling poets and artists.

Were the date given to *Un Prince de la Bohème* in the *Comédie humaine* its date of first publication, it would seem strangely significant that this story, Musset's *Mimi Pinson*, and Murger's own first 'scene', *Un Envoyé de la providence*, all appeared in the same year, 1845. But Balzac's title, '*Un Prince . . .*', covers only minor alterations to a tale first published in 1840; so that his definition long precedes any references, implicit or explicit, by the other two authors to the idea of 'Bohème'; a term, indeed, that, even as late as 1845, they had not yet begun to use. Balzac, by this reckoning, must also be three years ahead of Dennery and Grangé, whose play, *Les Bohémiens de Paris*, is usually, and probably rightly, regarded as responsible for the general introduction of 'Bohème', though without any artistic undertones, as a popular catchword.

We must suppose that Murger took his cue direct from the great novelist, since Balzac is the only modern writer mentioned and approved in the *Scènes de la Bohème*,[4] and the notion itself of presenting his stories as 'scenes' must have come to him from the same source. While wider in scope, as we have noted, Balzac's definition comes very close indeed to Murger's:

Bohemia [says Balzac] is made up of young people, all of whom are between twenty and thirty years of age, all men of genius in their own line, as yet almost unknown but with the ability to become known one day, when they will achieve real distinction. Already you can pick them out at Carnival-time, giving rein to their superfluous high spirits—kept in check for the rest of the year—in comic escapades of one kind or another.

He continues:

This word 'bohème' is self-explanatory. Bohemia possesses nothing, yet contrives to exist on that nothing. Its religion is hope; its code, faith in itself; its income, in so far as it appears to have one, charity. All these young people rise superior to their misfortunes: poverty they must endure, but their destiny they can shape for themselves.[5]

Though the so-called 'Bohème galante' of the Doyenné actually preceded Murger's Bohemia, it did not receive its title till some years after the events recorded. To the veterans of *Hernani*, the society of the Café Momus and the Hôtel Merciol must have represented a very degenerate version of their own little band—Houssaye, at any rate, gave it as his opinion, in 1845, that literary standards were becoming deplorable on account of the 'progressive invasion of Bohemia'.[6] Yet Théophile Gautier, looking back in 1848 at the group of the Doyenné, was quite happy to describe it as an 'encampment of picturesque and literary Bohemians'.[7] And in 1852 appeared Gérard de Nerval's recollections of the same group under the title of *La Bohême galante.*

Murger himself came only gradually to appreciate the force of the word 'Bohemian'. In the first nine of the *Scènes* (leaving out the later, introductory tale) 'bohème' occurs once. It is in the eleventh and twelfth, *Un Café de la Bohème* and *Une Réception dans la Bohème* that the term begins to appear frequently. These stories, it can be no mere coincidence, describe a ruse on the part of Rodolphe and his friends to whet the curiosity of Barbemuche, a simple-minded bourgeois. For his benefit, 'Bohemia' is paraded as an exclusive club, election to which is most desirable and difficult to achieve! Apart from this view, there are others often quite contradictory, which seem to slip out at times by chance. Thus, in the *Flots du Pactole*, Rodolphe speaks of Bohemia as a disaster to be avoided at all costs: yet, in *Donec gratus*, it is held up as worthy of the highest admiration. And in the *Manchon de*

Francine we learn that the marks of a 'true Bohemian of true Bohemia' are industry and unselfishness. Jacques, this exemplary sculptor, had a less positive qualification: he was still under thirty. As we have noticed, Murger was always insistent on the importance of this age limit, at which Balzac himself had hinted. In the *Épilogue des amours de Rodolphe et de Mlle Mimi*, Marcel warns Rodolphe: 'We are nearing our thirtieth year'—for, after that, no man of talent could afford to stay in Bohemia.

But however early the word itself came into fitful use, its real acceptance must date from the first performance of Murger and Barrière's play of 1849. According to the *Corsaire*'s dramatic critic, the audience at the Variétés had been a little puzzled to begin with, but by the end of the evening all doubts were dispersed, and everyone now understood exactly what was meant by the *vie de Bohème*.[8]

ii

Once notorious, it acquired another significance, though not a lasting one, as the breeding-ground of 'Realism'. Many had been shocked by Murger's caddish 'heroes' and street-corner 'heroines' and the sordid circumstances that brought them together; and he was often to take the blame for anything that happened to displease critics of contemporary trends in literature. For a brief period, indeed, Realism did borrow from Bohemia, sieving the bare facts of low life from its elaborate fantasies. Champfleury's *Chien-Caillou*, a story with the penniless engraver Bresdin as its hero, might easily, with a facetious twist or two, have been turned into another *scène de la Bohème*, but becomes in his hands a fine piece of unadorned *genre*. *Chien-Caillou* appeared in the *Corsaire* in 1845; and by the end of that year the same author had embarked on a series of character-studies which illustrate even better the transition from punning anecdotes to police-court plain-speaking. In these *Excentriques*, Champfleury abandons (for a change) the Bohemian brotherhood itself, and takes stock of the poor Bohemian's even poorer relations gathered round his doorstep, such as the mountebank Miette, the decayed *rapin* Cannonier, and the model Cadamour.

This did not mean that Champfleury felt any less interest in art and artists. Through his sympathy for Chintreuil, he came to think highly of the new landscape school. Then, tiring of the eternal cattle and forest-clearings of Troyon, Dupré, Flers, and the rest, he stumbled upon Bonvin. Here were subjects human, humble, and *urban* and an artist who looked the part: for, though anxious to escape the bounds of his old world, Champfleury still in his heart subscribed to Murger's 'It's the rags that make the poet'. Bonvin might have gone on monopolizing his admiration, had he not made the further discovery, in 1848, of a painter with a quite startling belief in himself and contempt for the whole school of Classics and Romantics.

The identification of Bohemia with Realism must have seemed complete when Courbet began to catch the public eye. Champfleury believed he had found the heaven-sent pictorial interpreter of his own creed in this artist, who had indeed burst upon the world of art 'comme un aérolithe'.[9] He was immensely impressed by the seven paintings and drawings exhibited at the crowded Salon of 1848, and in February, as co-editor of the short-lived *Salut Public*, called upon Courbet, then twenty-nine, for a vignette to head the second and last number. In the following year, the painter attracted considerable attention with an 'After Dinner at Ornans', and Champfleury, delighted, was able to congratulate himself on the prescience of his earlier criticisms.

No doubt the two men had some previous knowledge of each other, for Courbet had been living in the Latin Quarter since 1840, and was a close friend of Bonvin and an acquaintance of Schanne, both of whom he had met at the 'Atelier' Suisse; but up till 1849 there had been no intimacy between the boisterous young painter and the original Bohemians, almost all of them loosely associated with the Water-Drinkers. Now that group was breaking up. Some of its members, like Karol and Joseph Desbrosses, were dead; others, like Murger and Champfleury themselves, had forced their way into the larger world of journalism and the theatre. A new meeting-place succeeded the Café Momus. Though Champfleury was understandably ready to exploit the fashion for tales in the *rapin-grisette* formula which he had helped to initiate, he was moving at the same time in another direction and, as we have seen, trying to persuade Murger to go along with him. At the Brasserie Ändler, conveniently situated on the ground floor of Courbet's house in the Rue Hautefeuille, Bohemia proper comes to an end, and is followed by a 'cénacle' involved in Realism and under the spell of an artist who, though powered by a creative energy not usually associated with Bohemia, indulged to excess in its familiar preoccupations: wine, women, and interminable theorizing.

Schanne, in his memoirs, fixes the origins of this new 'cénacle' from about 1850, and there is mention of the word 'réalisme' in an article by Champfleury for the *Ordre* on September 2nd of that year. The article deals with Courbet's 'Burial at Ornans': 'M. Courbet's history pictures, which will be an event at the Salon,' says the writer, 'are bound to give rise to important argument. From to-day critics can get ready to embark upon the battle for, or against, realism in art.' [10]

iii

It would be a mistake, however, to assume that the spread of the Bohemian idea was halted by the establishment of an offshoot creed. We have seen, in fact, that Bohemia was very much in the Parisian mind on the occasion of Murger's death, as late as 1861; and its wider popularity had then scarcely begun. Baudelaire himself points out how much the youthful Realists of his generation admired Murger. And, in spite of opposition, Bohemia would go from strength to strength. Such a thing could never have happened solely on the authority of cardboard characters like Murger's Rodolphe and Marcel, and Champfleury's Tony and Sylvius. During the period following the production of the play, the public became more and more curious about the habits of artists and authors in real life. Its curiosity was rewarded. For in picturesque and tragic qualities, illuminated by literary ability of the first order in at least two instances, the Bohemians of flesh and blood outshone all that the trivial talent of Murger had been able to invent.

The fact that Gérard de Nerval and Baudelaire had almost nothing in common with the general run of patrons at the Café Momus does not make them less part of the legend. They came from a different social class, and that difference was sharpened by their superior intelligence; but to a public suddenly presented with the sordid circumstances of Gérard's suicide or with the scandal aroused by the *Fleurs du mal*, such differences would not be very striking. To the squalor from which Murger and his friends sought desperately to raise themselves, Gérard and Baudelaire voluntarily descended. The perverted pleasure that a refined man can extract from familiarizing himself with the gutter was not new when Restif de la Bretonne composed the recollections of M. Nicolas; but Gérard's wanderings through the poorer quarters of Paris in the mid-nineteenth century, his apparent destitution, and tragic end in the alley of the Vieille-Lanterne seemed to his contemporaries a striking example of the fate reserved for modern genius.

The public, while amused, had always prophesied with relish that no good could come to Rodolphe and his kind, and here was the retribution Murger's puppets had only miraculously escaped. As for the *Fleurs du mal* and its author, whom the court-case transformed into a figure of scandal, were not obscenity and blasphemy just what one might expect of an artist who deliberately flouted the conventions by which decent people lived? The public argued foolishly, perhaps; yet, in respect of certain weaknesses and eccentricities, both Gérard and Baudelaire did fall into the category of Bohemian. And the more remarkable their powers were acknowledged to be, the more contagious their example proved throughout the world of art. Thus, ludicrous as it may seem, the vagrant, anti-social characteristics of these really gifted men—and of some others—contributed to the same result as the penny-a-line concoctions of Murger. They strengthened the view that an artist must be an eccentric: they perpetuated the conception of the artist as a Bohemian.

iv

The *Petits Châteaux de Bohême* was published in 1853, the *Bohême galante* in 1856.* Neither add anything to the Bohemian concept, and we see here only a dextrous manipulation of the fashionable word of the moment by Gérard himself or, as is more likely, by Houssaye, since to the latter fell the task of editing these papers after the tragedy. While the author is very obviously on familiar terms with Hoffmann, it is Villon who guides Gérard's thoughts, just as he inspires Gérard's own Godinot Chevassut in the story, *La Main enchantée*. And though

* Strictly Gérard's titles still keep the form 'Bohême' which, for reasons more important then than now, soon gave way to 'Bohème'.

this Romantic nostalgia derives also from Mortefontaine and the eighteenth century, in the end it leads us back to the streets of Paris, as they were known to the poet of the Testaments or to Gérard himself.

For he had Champfleury's interest in the city's highways and byways and their humbler inhabitants. In the *Femme Mérinos*, he tells us about gipsies and mountebanks, in the *Nuits d'octobre* about cheap eating-houses. He prides himself on being a connoisseur of thieves' slang, and—perhaps it was not very difficult—finds fault with Sue in that respect. Such tastes, combining the old world of Villon and the new one of the nineteenth-century cut-throat, were destined to become an obsession. With the *Voyage en Orient* selling well, the traveller might have settled down and earned a comfortable living. He preferred to pursue a furtive independence, writing his copy on the backs of envelopes and flitting from one common lodging-house to another. As Murger looked a middle-aged man while still in his twenties, Gérard at forty-six might have been taken for sixty. And it is not unfitting that a detailed account of his death should have been included in the *Histoire de Murger*, for, that night of 1855, he seemed to sum up all the tragic elements in the *vie de Bohème*:

On the morning of the previous day, he had called upon the most devoted of his friends, Charles Asselineau, and begged of him the few sous' entrance to a library where he was in the habit of working. Asselineau, seeing his poor friend dressed, despite the bitter cold, in a wretchedly inadequate coat and without his little cape, at once offered his whole purse. But Gérard obstinately refused to take more than the trifling sum he had asked. He was nervous and preoccupied. 'I don't know what has happened to me,' he said, 'but I'm worried. For several days I haven't been able to write a line, and I very much fear that I've reached the end of my ability to create. To-day, I shall make one more effort . . .' He made it, in fact: and it seems that his spirit, already broken by this terror of sterility, failed him once again. Then, ill-clad, on the verge of starvation, his brain teeming with wild fancies, he set out into the bitter night, growing ever more hysterical on the lonely, purposeless route he took through those nameless streets of the ancient city which he knew better than anyone, and seeing more clearly at every step the menacing phantom of his existence from now on—unproductive and contemptible—till he stopped abruptly and made an end of it.[11]

Baudelaire gave a rather different impression. Whereas Gérard was always shy and unassuming, Baudelaire, or the apparent Baudelaire, delighted to call attention to himself and impose his views on anyone he happened to find in his company. Of Baudelaire, the art critic, I shall have more to say later; here, for a moment, I want to recall the man who made the conventional his *bête noire*, the man who enjoyed shocking, not only the burgher, but even his cronies at the Brasserie.

Though he might on occasion adopt some extreme measure—such as painting his shaven head green—to assert his individuality, Baudelaire was determined to avoid being confused with the kind of Bohemians who modelled themselves on the Romantics of 1830, wearing their hair and beards long, and the *rapin*'s pointed hat, red blouse, and velvet jacket. As early as the epoch of the Hôtel Pimodan, on his first meeting with Théophile Gautier, he is described as close-cropped, with a faint moustache —which he soon removed. Like Whistler, however, he contrived to make of his very cleanliness something shocking. As he himself wrote, 'Le dandy ne se pare que pour se séparer'; * but remarkable as his simple and elegant dress must have seemed in the company of tramps like Murger and Planche, it was his original and forbidding beauty, according to Gautier, that made the real impression.

Before the scandal associated with the *Fleurs du mal*, the poet's reputation, owing something to his *Salon* of 1846 and brilliant renderings of Edgar Allan Poe, was confined to a limited circle. As a poet, some of whose work had been published in the *Artiste* and more recently in the *Revue des Deux-Mondes*, and a great deal of it read from manuscript to his fellow-writers, he was regarded as cynical, erotic, and violent. And whereas these characteristics appealed to those who considered it admirable to experiment and describe new feelings, they were liable to less friendly interpretation in other quarters.

'From the first whiff people got of them,' writes Barbey d'Aurevilly, 'the *Fleurs du mal* aroused universal indignation':[12] that is, from the moment the first poems from this collection were published separately in the newspapers, trouble began to brew. On the appearance of the book itself in July, 1857, two articles,

* Which might be rendered: 'The dandy *cuts a dash*, just to *cut himself adrift*.'

one closely following the other, came out in the *Figaro*, attacking the author on moral grounds. Since this paper was generally held to enjoy Government protection, a prosecution was to be expected; and Baudelaire and his publisher, Poulet-Malassis, were in fact sent for trial on August 20th.

The main objection to the *Fleurs du mal* advanced by the *Figaro* critic, Gustave Bourdin, arose from the 'unpleasantness' of the subject-matter. But Bourdin was spurred on by his dislike, also, of what he took to be the *breeding-ground* of such compositions:

For fifteen years or so, M. Charles Baudelaire has been a prodigious poet for a tiny circle, whose vanity, in honouring him as God, or near-God, has not been altogether unprofitable: the members of this circle consider themselves *his* inferior, it is true; but, at the same time, superior to *everyone else who denies their Messiah.* You ought to hear these gentlemen venting their opinions on the sort of genius we ourselves admire and pay homage to: Hugo is a poor fish, Béranger a bounder, Alfred de Musset a crackpot and, as for Mme. Sand, she should be locked up! [13]

What is interesting here is the attempt to fit the poet into a 'school'; a school of sycophants and iconoclasts, dwelling in a little world of their own, the *world of Bohemia*, where all fine ideals die a natural death. According to the *Figaro*, Baudelaire's predilection for the morbid and indecent is the natural result of this.

Pinard, counsel for the prosecution, may well have held the same views himself, but his experience of the *Madame Bovary* case had shown him the advisability of avoiding a general attack. 'Charles Baudelaire', he declared, 'does not belong to a school. He is entirely independent.' [14] Counsel therefore kept to specific objections, to the immorality and blasphemy of certain passages for which Baudelaire alone must take responsibility. These tactics were, in fact, facilitated by the defence's apologetic argument, which ignored Baudelaire's own view that art was quite independent of morality. As a result, the poet was found guilty and fined 300 francs. To the man in the street, unaware of the disintegration of Murger's group, it must have seemed a judgment against Bohemia.

Poetry, unless scandalous, was something that rarely attracted the public's attention. Painting came into a different category, for the annual exhibition at the Salon was considered everybody's business. Thus Courbet's pictures, with their unusual subject-matter and treatment, were written about and discussed in a steady glare of publicity which touched Gérard and Baudelaire only on isolated occasions. Here was the modern artist at his most spectacular and intimidating. Whether one regarded the pictures or the man, one scented the Bohemian, amoral, anti-social.

Though he was not bound to the Murger group by the same close ties as Chintreuil, from 1840 Courbet had shared many of its experiences; and, since he came of peasant stock, might be said to belong more or less to the same social caste. He enjoyed a small allowance from his family, but this barely supported him during his early years in the Rue Pierre-Sarrazin and the Rue de la Harpe. True to the popular notion of Bohemia, he lived always in the student quarter, and this long after Murger and Champfleury had departed for more fashionable addresses.

Courbet, perhaps, had never quite the touch of dandyism suggested by Baille's drawing of 1840: d'Héricault quotes the remark of a friend who saw the artist for the first time regaling himself at the Café Dagneaux: 'Upon my word, if butchers' boys begin to make a habit of coming here, I shall have to give the place up!';[15] but the hair which at that time barely covered Courbet's chin and cheeks was subsequently encouraged to the magnificent growth that so impresses the spectator in the early self-portraits. One might dislike the mature artist, but one could never ignore him!

Like the other Bohemians, he began as a Romantic. His 'Lovers in the Country', refused by the Salon in 1845, is full of Wertherian melancholy. Other early pictures include an 'Odalisque' inspired by Hugo, a 'Lélia' illustrating George Sand's novel, and a 'Walpurgis Night' also derived from Goethe. It is difficult to believe that Courbet had actually read the *Captive*, *Faust*, or *Lélia*: such was his contempt for books in general. He could have found pictorial versions of these subjects in any Romantic studio, and had but to produce one more of his own.

This stage did not last long, however. In 1848, Champfleury discovered a fresh and distinctive element in his work; and in the following year the 'After Dinner at Ornans' pleased not only this new champion but a number of other critics who were growing weary of the Romantic school. There was no exhibition at the Salon in 1850. In 1851, those who had pleasant memories of the 'After Dinner' and the 'Grape-Harvest at Ornans' were astonished to find themselves presented with a picture more than seven yards long, entitled 'A Burial at Ornans', together with two other works, the 'Stone-Breakers' and the 'Peasants of Flagey', which they felt they could no longer enjoy as inoffensive *genre*-subjects. These pictures appeared to have been specially composed as a protest against the existing social system; but, of them all, it was the vast 'Burial' painting that aroused keenest resentment.

For here morality and religion themselves seemed to be under fire. Parisians took the meticulously 'realistic' portraits of the villagers for a piece of malice, accusing the artist (whose friends and relations they were!) of assembling the most repulsive human types he could find, with the object of ridiculing the ordinary, decent Christian mourner's attitude to death.[16] The critics now fell savagely on Courbet, who was a self-confessed atheist and a close friend of P.-J. Proudhon and Max Buchon, both regarded as dangerous men and punished for their socialist convictions. From the verbal and pictorial attack in the contemporary Press, one is able to realize just how unpopular Courbet had made himself.[17]

The artist gave his enemies every assistance. He made as little secret of his revolutionary opinions in politics as in art. 'This philosopher Proudhon who shares our way of looking at things' (so he wrote)[18] had profoundly influenced him from the time when they first met, about 1848. In his *Du Principe de l'art et de sa destination sociale*, of 1865, Proudhon congratulated Courbet on having freed painting from Gautier's 'art for art's sake', which he himself detested. But the two men did not always see eye to eye. Proudhon disliked the crude anti-clericalism of his friend's 'Return from the Conference', and was disgusted by his praises of free-love.[19] When, however, Proudhon went to the Sainte-Pélagie prison, and afterwards to the Conciergerie, and Buchon was exiled, following on the Coup d'État, Courbet, the mere painter, was allowed to remain at liberty. And, though under surveillance, he continued to preach his violent (but usually contradictory) doctrines at the Brasserie Ändler for a long while to come.

It was there, more or less regularly and always on Thursdays, that he presided at the large table, surrounded by artists,

Plate V. Gustave Courbet (1819–1877): 'The Painter's Studio' (detail), 1855. *Louvre.*

'Bohemia, 1855' was a misinterpretation of this picture (of which the lower portion only is shown here), but a pardonable one. To begin with, Courbet himself is so much the braggadocio, his 'Muse' so like a blowzy model. Though ideas, not people, are being entertained here in the Rue Hautefeuille, the bourgeois spectator, already suspicious, we may suppose, of certain figures to the left of the central group, would not be reassured as he went on to make out, to the right of it, P.-J. Proudhon, Champfleury, and Baudelaire. The first of these, a social reformer, had been sent to prison for attacking the principle of private property, the second was still best known as the frivolous author of the *Aventures de Mademoiselle Mariette* and the original Marcel of Murger's novel, and the third, taxed with obscenity, would soon be publicly censured and fined on that account.

From left to right. Group demonstrating Courbet's sympathy for the underprivileged and concern at their exploitation: a Jew; a parish priest; a 'veteran of '93'; a gamekeeper; a farrier; two huntsmen; a reaper; a pedlar; a *curieux*; a clown; an undertaker's man; a prostitute; an unemployed labourer; an Irishwoman suckling her child; symbols (in the form of a lay-figure and still-life) of the painter's rejection of religion, Romanticism, and contemporary art-criticism. A small boy, suggesting the admiration of posterity; Courbet himself, with the Muse of Realism. Courbet's protégé, Promayet; his wealthy patron, Bruyas; Proudhon; Cuénot; the *proscrit*, Buchon; Champfleury; two lovers, possibly suggesting free-love; a child reading—no doubt to balance the still-life opposite; two anonymous visitors; obliterated at Baudelaire's request but faintly visible now, Jeanne Duval; Baudelaire.

PLATE VI. J.-A.-D. Ingres (1780–1867): 'Self-Portrait', aged seventy-eight, 1858. *Uffizi.*

Painted for the celebrated collection of self-portraits in Florence, at a time when the list of Ingres's honours required, to be complete, only his nomination as senator which came four years later. But to those who over-emphasized the importance of 'sensitivity' in an artist's character and expected to find some evidence of it in his appearance, Ingres, vulgar and even brutal as a man, presented an irritating contradiction. On the other hand, we may come to the conclusion that the life and work of this great painter supply the perfect antidote against those false values of Romanticism which produced their own ultimate parody in 'Bohemia'.

musicians, and critics. The Brasserie, says Champfleury, was Courbet's real studio, where he demonstrated his aim to concern himself only with the 'commonplace and the modern', and attacked the aims of other artists—the idealism of Ingres, the patriotism of Vernet, the orientalism of Decamps, and the Romantic melancholy of Delacroix. The authorities, no doubt, recognized that there was nothing very sinister about this. Courbet oddly combined fervour and farce, and his quips were received with as much relish for their unconscious, as for their conscious, humour: announcements, for example, like, 'I myself passed over Tradition as a strong swimmer would cross a river: the Academicians have all got drowned in it!' [20]

Champfleury, though alive to the childlike conceit of the painter and the frequent absurdity of his remarks, was the most interested, first as one of a large audience, then as collaborator: for Courbet expressed a number of ideas he had long held himself. Soon he was spending time in the studio above the Brasserie, visiting Ornans with the artist, and exchanging letters. From 1850 to 1862, Courbet was the subject of a series of articles by Champfleury, whose enthusiasm, however, began to cool off from that point.

The year of closest collaboration was 1855. To that year belongs Courbet's most aggressive demonstration of his ideas, the independent exhibition of his paintings in the Avenue Montaigne, on the threshold of the *Exposition Universelle*. This selection included his latest and most important picture, to which he gave the title, 'Realistic Allegory: Interior of my Studio, particularizing a Seven-Year Phase in my Life as an Artist'. Champfleury not only assisted in writing the catalogue's introductory manifesto, but published an article defending Courbet in the *Artiste*, 'Le Réalisme, lettre à George Sand'. The artist was already proving somewhat difficult to manage, and his literary interpreter found himself embarrassed by the expression, 'allégorie réelle'. 'One must take care not to twist words to suit symbolic ideas, which the brush may be able to translate but which defy grammar', he said in his article; and, in private, complained to a friend: 'It is his desire to *write* that is Courbet's greatest danger.' [21]

In the 'Painter's Studio', as it is usually called, M. Prudhomme and his friends were at last presented with a conception of the artist by the artist himself on a scale bound to excite interest and discussion. The manifesto in the catalogue made it clear that the painter rejected the narrower meaning of 'Réalisme': 'The title of "Realist" has been thrust upon me, as the title "Romantic" was thrust upon the men of 1830.' His pictures, nevertheless, and this picture particularly, had to be looked on as the full and fearless expression of a modern artist's attitude to life.[22]

And so on the walls of the shed in the Avenue Montaigne, Bohemia became 'real'. The prettiness and the paradoxes were stripped away, and there remained what read like a bald statement of contempt—for religion, morals, and society. The public, used to approaching this little world of the Latin Quarter in the company of a romantic Rodolphe and a penitent Mimi, discovered in their place an arrogant materialist watched over by a naked woman, intended by the artist to represent his Muse, but accepted by the general public as a professional model of the coarsest type.

When, in the year following, Banville wrote:

> Avec nous l'on chante et l'on aime,
> Nous sommes frères des oiseaux.
> Croissez, grands lys, chantez, ruisseaux,
> Et vive la sainte Bohème,*

he felt, so he admitted later, considerable misgivings: 'In composing this song, I had to summon up all my courage to write the word "Bohème", which I loathe, though I wanted to rid it of its vile encumbrance of rags and tatters, and anoint it with the ambrosia which was its due.' [23]

And he made it clear that it was not the Bohemia of the Café Momus or the Brasserie that inspired him (he had already composed a skit on 'Bonjour, M. Courbet!') but the earlier Romantic conception found in George Sand's *Dernière Aldini*. A reaction against the artist's way of life popularized by Murger and now, it seemed, rendered unbearably banal by Courbet was indeed soon to establish itself.

* 'It is our nature to sing and make love, we are the birds' own brothers. Burgeon, you tall lilies, give song, O streams, and long live Bohemia the blest!'

X

Anti-Bohemian

i

The prime creators of Bohemia's *aura popularis*, Murger and Champfleury, took the earliest opportunity to put Bohemia behind them. In 1848, Murger was still caught fast in this environment—and hymning its charms; in 1849, as soon as collaboration with Barrière won him success, he left the old haunts and began to pick holes in what he had panegyrized. His strictures, all the same, were invariably half-hearted and nostalgic. Champfleury, with fresh fields already conquered, could afford to express a sense of disillusionment in less graceful terms: thus, for him, as early as 1849, Bohemia 'stank'.[1] Selecting Dupont, Baudelaire, and Bonvin as the only members of the community worth serious consideration, he went on, in 1851, to attack the work of Murger himself.[2]

The flight of the Bohemian from Bohemia was not, however, just a late bid for respectability. It had been meditated long before, in the Rue de Vaugirard and the Hôtel des Canettes; for both Murger and Champfleury knew, even at that stage, that they possessed a flair and a tenacity which, given a modicum of good luck, were almost certain to separate them one day from the general run of literary vagrants. Champfleury, as he became increasingly interested in the wider aspects of art and literature, left the *Aventures de Mademoiselle Mariette* far behind him. Murger lacked intellectual incentive and blazed no trails; he could but laboriously 'improve' the old characters and the old situations. And though his name on the title-page ensured some support for these drawing-room novels and for a few Realist experiments, it was as the author of the *Scènes de la Bohème* that he won and retained the Philistine's affection.

For readers by their thousands had been, and continued to be, delighted by the image of the artist which they found there: no epic hero, withdrawn from the world in lordly contempt, but a mixture of madman and buffoon who thoroughly enjoyed his rôle of general laughing-stock. And, as if to corroborate Murger, anecdotes, real or apocryphal, of Bohemian eccentricity began to flood the gossip columns of the newspapers; occasionally, as we have just seen, reaching climaxes of tragedy or public scandal, but more often continuing the comedy evoked by Murger. Among the better-known exhibitionists was Privat d'Anglemont, a creole as penniless and prodigal of deceptions as Rodolphe or Marcel. Accosted one night, while wandering in the neighbourhood of Montrouge, he had only to exclaim: 'But I'm Privat!', for the footpads to insist on his celebrating the joke with them at a champagne-supper by moonlight.[3]

Amusing, however, as some of Privat's exploits might be, it was becoming clear to self-respecting writers and painters that this notion of the artist as a clown (or lachrymose *buveur d'eau*) must be tolerated no longer. As early as 1861, in the very year, that is, of Murger's death, Léon Cladel submitted a manuscript entitled *Les Martyrs ridicules* to Baudelaire's friend and publisher Poulet-Malassis. This novel, which appeared in 1862, describes a Bohemia stripped of its humblest charms. The characters, wrapped each in his 'artistic or parasitic' pea-jacket, long-haired, uncouth, unclean, are in many ways only too familiar—yet appear utterly different. Along with the fun and the verbal fireworks, all the spirit has gone out of them. They are poor lack-lustre creatures, whom the reader, however impatient with his own bourgeois lot, would never wish to emulate.

Alphinien Maurthal, the hero, is not yet twenty-six, but his dull eye and dragging step suggest someone twice that age. Under Cladel's malicious direction, in fact, it is the Water-Drinker (in Murger, more often a 'voice off') who now elbows Rodolphe into the wings and monopolizes the centre of the stage. When Murger devoted a whole tale to such a figure, as in *Un Poète de gouttières*, farce joined forces with satire: Cladel dissects Maurthal in chirurgical earnest. And Mimi and Musette, new style, are of the same dismal tribe. To one, sheer stupidity gives the 'false air of a sphinx'; the other, an affected little milliner, adores George Sand, and never ceases to make herself ridiculous in consequence. Murger's characters may lack substance, but these are *shades* of shades. Such, of course, was the author's intention. After recording the uneasy diversions of Alphinien and Claire against the time-honoured background of garret and cheap *estaminet* (set here in the Boulevard de Sébastopol), Cladel really does convince us that these two will end by losing their identity altogether in a solemn mummery of Rodolphe and Mimi. For example, on their way home from a performance of *La Vie de Bohème*, the two young people quarrel and drop into the very words of the dialogue spoken in the theatre, even addressing each other by the players' names.

This dreary affair concluded, Alphinien is able to concentrate on his ambition. It leads him round the Paris cemeteries, kneeling and kissing the marble feet of the poets honoured there, and hysterically demanding of them the secret of genius: 'What must I do to become great like you?' The sensible answer never occurs to him. Indeed, it is probable that the advice offered by Baudelaire, who took much interest in the book, 'Stay at home, rack your brains, and scribble unceasingly',[4] would not have solved his problem.

Alphinien's misfortune is that which afflicts his friend, the painter Tulmont—self-doubt:

> He found Tulmont motionless before a large canvas, hardly advanced as far as the sketch. In one hand the painter held his palette, on which the colours had been thrown together in the greatest confusion; the other was empty, and the brushes it had let fall lay at his feet.
>
> Seeing Maurthal, and without altering his position, he said: 'Maurthal, don't you ever ask yourself the question: are we genuine artists, or have we allowed a mere thrill of excitement to take control and puff us up to a self-importance which nothing now, or in the future, is going to justify? For myself, I don't know, old chap, I just don't know. I'm very much afraid I've made a mistake; that I've been dreaming all this while!' [5]

Baudelaire's adoption of Cladel's book seems to have gone as far as insisting on certain emendations to the text itself. No doubt he was fascinated to see persons and events of his early life passing into legend: 'Here is Murger (poor ghost) transformed into an interpreter—a dictionary—of the Bohemian dialect, into a Lover's Companion for the Year of Grace 1861.' [6] If he found this somewhat flat tale worth fathering in an article which became its preface, it must have been because he (or a part of him) hated the cult of Bohemia as heartily as did Cladel.

No man, surely, conformed less to the Zingaresque than Baudelaire. That he could, all the same, couple with loftier preoccupations a delight in vagabondage, and 'what may be called Bohemianism',[7] was typical of the complexity of the poet, about whom nothing is simple or easy to understand.

ii

Baudelaire was a naturally fastidious man. He began by anointing himself like a young god; later, when they were all he could afford, he made do with a fanatical devotion to soap and water. The same fastidiousness characterizes the *Fleurs du mal*, just when the author of these poems seems most intent on shocking his own, as well as the reader's, sensibilities. The cruder his surroundings and the company he keeps, the more squalid the hotel-room, the more brutalized the mistress, the keener grows his apprehension of beauty. And into an artist's perverse enjoyment of what is wounding to his intelligence merges the agreeable *frisson* of the aristocrat in contact with what is inferior to his station. For Baudelaire, dandy and patrician, continued to regard the artist as an aristocrat long after the tide of opinion had turned against this Romantic conception. Gautier, Silvestre, the Goncourts themselves, all condescend to weigh imagination in the scales with manual dexterity. As far as Baudelaire is concerned the *côté ouvrier* hardly exists. He discovered the aristocrat in Guys, and praised him highly. Of Courbet he never really approved, for there the artisan could not be overlooked. He was the wholehearted admirer of two modern painters only, Delacroix and, after Delacroix's death, Manet, both as fastidious as himself.

Baudelaire was first introduced to Delacroix in 1840, so Tabarant informs us. The poet, then nineteen, stood enthralled before the 'Justice of Trajan'. Opposition and neglect were always to draw him nearer to the victim, and that the 'Justice' had given offence to so many friends, as well as enemies, of the artist had much, no doubt, to do with Baudelaire's embarking from that point on a lifelong advocacy of Delacroix.

Nothing suggests that the two were on intimate terms. Baudelaire's praise of him was politely acknowledged by the painter; but continual bludgeoning dulls a man's sense of discrimination when it comes to thanking his few defenders. The letters written to Baudelaire, acknowledging services of the kind, show that Delacroix was quite unaware of the stature of this particular champion. As a man of the world, he was often shocked by the poet's oddities; as an artist, he found Baudelaire's anxiety to draw attention to the 'morbidity' of his painting somewhat embarrassing. 'When all is said and done,' Delacroix was reported to have let slip, 'I find him rather tiresome.' [8]

Earlier, Baudelaire had made friends with artists like Fernand Boissard and Émile Deroy; and he met others at the Café Tabourey, the Café Régence, the Restaurant Cousinet, and at Philoxène Boyer's suppers. He was associated with still another group, which included Chenavard and the sculptor Préault, at the Divan Le Peletier. But he had the lowest possible opinion of artists in general, detesting the untidy notions they got trimmed into neat manifestos by their journalist friends. He preferred to form his own views, to which he held tenaciously while exposing the fallacies in others. He said once that, Chenavard, Préault, Daumier, Ricard, and Delacroix apart, he didn't know of a single artist capable of conducting a really intelligent conversation—that is, a conversation with a philosopher or a poet.[9] Ignoring the 'messieurs présomptueux' of the cafés, therefore, he educated himself in the galleries of the Louvre, admiring above all Bronzino, Van Eyck, and the Spaniards.

Then, in 1845, he met Delacroix, and found what he had been looking for: that confluence of the transitory and the eternal which had always been his own particular dream. Here was the 'universal man' of the Renaissance *re-born* once more, a man whose appreciation of music and literature was as profound as his understanding of art. The visitor's devotion became complete. The more he saw of Delacroix and Delacroix's work, the more he was able to persuade himself that the aims of the painter were the precise counterpart of his own. They had, in fact, much in common. A number of passages in Delacroix's *Journal* might have been written by Baudelaire. Both bore the stamp of the aristocrat, both were by nature reserved, both dedicated to the *goût du difficile*. Baudelaire's deep affection for Delacroix comes out very plainly in his description of the painter on his death-bed, and it was this affection that provided the most valuable element in his equipment as critic. 'I have the right to explain Delacroix's art,' Baudelaire seems to be saying, 'because I understand it; and

I understand it, because I have accepted the painter in all his strength and in all his weakness': *confessio amantis*, whatever complications were involved.

That which further distinguishes Baudelaire's artist, as he appears in the *Curiosités esthétiques*, is his profound isolation. In a review of 1846, the critic is still regretting this and optimistically suggesting remedies; suggesting, too, that: 'There is something a thousand times more dangerous than the bourgeois: the bourgeois artist; a type of practitioner created to stand between the public and real genius, who actually does hide one from the other. The bourgeois of limited intelligence goes wherever the loud voice of this bourgeois artist orders him. If only we could do away with the fellow, our friend the shopkeeper would be carrying E. Delacroix shoulder-high in triumph';[10] but he had already admitted that the master's talents were bound to arouse opposition, indeed ought to do so: it merely added to the glory of Delacroix's 'Marcus Aurelius', he had said, that no one understood it.[11]

In like optimistic vein, Baudelaire offered up a little hymn in praise of the much-scorned bourgeois himself; and, in the *Salon* of 1846, continued to flatter him, adding that he might go on to prove his natural appreciation of works of art by purchasing a few. These were experiments in popularization never repeated. For a moment, disgusted by the feebleness of the Romantic camp-followers, he had been tempted to appeal to the 'good sense' of an enemy reputed to possess at least that. Then followed inevitable reaction. And the idea of an alliance faded with his growing indignation at middle-class America's treatment of Poe (whose translator he now became) and the continued slights to Delacroix, a painter he had imagined—or affected to imagine—on the brink of popular acceptance.

The artist, then, must stand alone. Perhaps it was right and inevitable that he should. Having at first a little regretted Delacroix's isolated position, Baudelaire had to admit that it was not altogether the result of circumstances. It is in the nature of a genius to keep aloof, from the mediocre in his own profession as well as from the lay public: 'I know many who have the right to say: "*Odi profanum vulgus*", but who [if not Delacroix] can add victoriously: "*et arceo*"? Too much hand-shaking debases the character!'[12]

Such a genius does not belong to any school, nor does he create one. The art form thus invented communicates its mysteries only to the few, it is something 'invisible, intangible, a dream, a matter of nerves, of *soul*';[13] the skill of a man in a million, able to display a rare understanding of those subtle 'correspondances' which lay at the heart of Baudelaire's creed. The message itself will not be for men of the painter's profession, but for the poet. The poet's greater sympathy for Delacroix, Baudelaire tells us, has always been evident.[14]

To-day, this 'disloyalty' in the ranks which so astonished the painter's champion does not seem quite so puzzling. For the landscape-artist and Realist, the title Baudelaire gave Delacroix, 'painter-poet', might equally have served to describe Devéria or Boulanger: they suspected, and had a right to suspect, the literary implications of the term. But Baudelaire could not forgive them for having taken part in the attack on his favourite artist, or for having allowed it to achieve its object—since 1859, four years before the expression 'painter-poet' passed his lips (on the occasion of the Brussels lecture), Delacroix had finally ceased to show in public.

The masses, however, interpreted the painter in their own way. They concluded that he had taken some pleasure in outraging convention. And Baudelaire was not greatly concerned to defend Delacroix on this charge. Apart from a plea that the picture-poems are 'naïvely conceived' and may shock because they have been dashed off in a fever of inspiration, he accepts lightly enough an element he goes on to define as the 'customary insolence of genius'.[15] And in an illuminating passage which directly precedes his maxim, 'Beauty has always the quality of strangeness', he sees a merit even in the act of astonishing.

Delacroix, 'though he was a man of genius, or because he was a perfect man of genius . . . had a great deal of the dandy about him'.[16] At first a dandy in the more trivial sense, as the years passed he entered (so Baudelaire believed) the rarer category of 'spiritual dandy'. Now, for the artist, this dandyism, expressed in the 'cult of self', allows him to bear neglect and hostility with greater fortitude, as it absolves him from seeking or inspiring affection. Thus the dandy in Delacroix, diagnosed according to the theories of Barbey d'Aurevilly and Baudelaire, helps to explain his isolation and underline its aristocratic character.

But this proud loneliness of the soul, 'volcanic crater, artistically camouflaged by bouquets of flowers', has bred melancholy, if not melancholia. It was nothing new to recognize the melancholia in Delacroix's pictures; for Baudelaire, however, it becomes the vital point: it is this malady, he concludes, that raises Delacroix to equality with the masters of all time, an idea he expresses in the concentrated imagery of the *Phares*:

> Delacroix, lac de sang, hanté des mauvais anges,
> Ombragé par un bois de sapins toujours vert,
> Où, sous un ciel chagrin, des fanfares étranges
> Passent, comme un soupir étouffé de Weber.*

And in another stanza, after finding in Delacroix the same restless, unhappy spirit that he has noted in Leonardo, Michelangelo, Rubens, Rembrandt, Watteau, and Goya, he concludes:

> Car c'est vraiment, Seigneur, le meilleur témoignage
> Que nous puissions donner de notre dignité
> Que cet ardent sanglot qui roule d'âge en âge
> Et vient mourir au bord de votre éternité.†

While it is easy to accept the artist's mood of discontent as that in which he speaks most nobly for humanity, we turn from this poem rather less sure that Delacroix ought to be included among the giants. Did not Baudelaire at length fall into the habit of looking into Delacroix's paintings as into a mirror of his own genius, and finding in them a great deal more than they contained?

For the 'painter beloved of poets', continues Baudelaire, the satisfaction of work well done will bring its own reward. Yet he may long for some more human appreciation. Here, once again, the shadow of the critic blurs the silhouette of the artist: since Baudelaire writes for posterity, Delacroix must paint for it. Both, apparently, are to find solace in dreaming of that far-off, but

* 'Delacroix, lake of blood, haunted by evil spirits, in the shade of the pines' unchanging green, where, under a lowering heaven, strange fanfares pass like a stifled sigh of Weber's.'

† 'For, in effect, Lord, the best proof we can give of our dignity is this burning sob which echoes through the ages, dying away on the brink of Thine eternity.'

assuredly favourable, judgment. The princely painters and sculptors of the High Renaissance had received immediate recognition, the court-painters of the Baroque were showered with honours. Those who came after, domestic painters or glorifiers of Revolution and Empire, looked no further ahead for praise than the hour of completion. With Géricault and Delacroix, this tradition has come to a close, and all the artist can rely upon is the gratitude of future generations. They at least will be able to distinguish between originality and its counterfeit; they will not be taken in by the stock landscapes, the dull portraits, and dreary 'realism' of Delacroix's contemporaries, but will value as it ought to be valued the inventive power of the great painter who declared: 'Consult Nature, if you like, but only as you would consult a dictionary.'[17]

From 1845 till 1863, all roads in Baudelaire's criticism led to Delacroix. Delacroix's achievement was the standard by which every other man's work was judged. Delacroix was in the critic's mind when he delivered his most celebrated summings-up. Even when Delacroix's works did not appear in the exhibition under review, that would be advanced as one more reason for discussing them.

Could anyone have contested more fiercely than Baudelaire the Bohemian image that the public clung to, that curious combination of a tearful Melchior and a roistering Rodolphe, with which must now be joined the jolly clown personified by Privat d'Anglemont? Baudelaire's artist is once more an aristocrat, armed against inferiors, isolated, and seeking isolation.

iii

I have suggested that the energy Baudelaire gave to the defence of Delacroix was at least in part stimulated by an increasing neglect of the Romantic leader's work. Indeed, the group in which Baudelaire felt most at home numbered some of the first to desert the cause with which Delacroix was associated. Baudelaire himself, contradictory and disillusioned, typified the period of indecision between two creeds; but though he revered Delacroix and distrusted Courbet, he had no belief in Romanticism as such.

Indeed, the painters of this school had never consolidated their success of 1827. One painter only, Baudelaire's hero, achieved distinction, and that in the face of ceaseless attacks. Decamps came nearest him. Roqueplan merely satisfied a taste for anecdote and the picturesque. Diaz's genuine feeling for colour degenerated into virtuosity. Devéria, Sigalon, and Champmartin remained, even when working on a large scale, vignettists. Ary Scheffer and Jean Gigoux slipped into insipidity; and Chassériau, a much stronger artist, did not quite succeed in his difficult aim of combining the best elements in Classicism and Romanticism. As we have seen, the July Monarchy brought to power a middle class demanding an art it could understand, a dramatic or sentimental story told clearly and correctly in every detail. Colour appealed to the baser emotions, so it believed, and was therefore best avoided.

Providentially for those who embarked on this line of attack, and Lamennais in his *Esquisse d'une philosophie* of the 1840's was one of them, there existed in France an artist whose singular prestige could be used to enforce the argument. The sensual, the erotic, the gaudy even, in Ingres could be conveniently forgotten, and a deaf ear turned to Silvestre when, in a malicious phrase, he drew attention to the oriental character of Ingres's Classicism.[18] Ingres himself raised no objections to the part he was called upon to play, though it led him often enough into strange company; since those who best satisfied the witch-hunters' desire for a 'serious' art were not Classicists at all, but costume-piece men like Gérôme, Delaroche, Horace Vernet, and Schnetz.

Compared with such public idols, the landscape artists were forgotten men, exiles whose poverty put them into a special category of rural Bohemians. The sympathy of Taine for these holiday friends of his, encountered in the Forest of Fontainebleau, was exceptional.[19] With their blouses and berets and peasant clogs, the men who shouldered an easel through Barbizon and Marlotte became stock figures of fun in the humorous papers and the music-hall world. A severer view seemed justified when it dawned upon reactionary critics that men like Dupré, Chintreuil, and Daubigny might have had something to do with initiating the 'subversive' movement known as 'Realism'. And the Second Empire, underestimating Daumier, mistrusting Millet, and alarmed by Courbet, turned with relief to the pretty pictures of Winterhalter and Meissonier.

On the face of it, the Exhibition of 1855 appeared to provide Delacroix with a long-deserved, long-delayed, triumph. Ingres and he were the only painters represented on the Committee, and, when the Exhibition opened, visitors were able to see as many as thirty-five examples of his work. He took part in all the important ceremonies, was awarded a grand medal, and advanced to Commander of the Legion of Honour. Moreover, dealers and private buyers for the first time seemed really anxious to acquire his pictures, old or new: the 'Marino Faliero' (withdrawn from the Salon of 1827) made 12,000 francs. But not all the critics waxed enthusiastic. Academy spokesmen were hostile; Delécluze complained of Delacroix's incompetent drawing; Maxime Du Camp, on behalf of the Socialists, declared that the veteran Romantic was quite out of touch with the ideas of a later day.[20]

The Goncourts, whose views reflect the taste of the younger intellectuals, were almost as disapproving. Granting the verve of Delacroix's composition, they roundly condemned his paint. It had been common practice to object to this artist's colour, as we have seen, *on principle*; here, inheriting the Doyenné's cult of the eighteenth century (indeed, carrying it much further), the Goncourts based their criticism *on aesthetic grounds*. Delacroix, they believed, lacked above all the 'colourist's supreme gift, harmony'.[21]

What the Academy still found unpardonable neither critics nor public would be likely to accept wholeheartedly. That very concern for art which struck Thackeray as so admirable in the average Frenchman by no means proved always an advantage to the artist. M. Prudhomme felt certain he knew everything there was to know about pictures, and when presented with something fresh and original grew most indignant. In a canvas by Delacroix, in Millet's rustic subjects, in a figure-study by Courbet, or even a clump of trees by the ageing Rousseau, he felt that something escaped him—the logic of a new argument, the rules of a new technique—and he hardened his heart against these painters.

There is no doubt that, for a public accustomed to the Classicist's 'ideal', Romanticism inspired pictures that were difficult to comprehend, and Realism others so commonplace as to appear equally puzzling. The shock of visual innovation then, as always, was keenly felt. How could the Sunday gallery-goer realize that it was a matter of just one more 'ideal' establishing itself: this time, the artist's own simple delight, free of the dictates of any school, in the subject of his choice?

IV

As Romantic painting fell into discredit through its own weaknesses, through the opposition of critics faithful to an older formula, and through the sustained hostility of the great mass of picture-fanciers, Bohemia, a sort of Romanticism in little, shared its fate. Already commercialized by popular novelists and boulevard playwrights, it naturally disgusted those who were making strenuous efforts to branch out in a new direction. The brothers Edmond and Jules de Goncourt constituted themselves its most implacable enemies.

To begin with, their suspicions of Murger had been snobbish or political: they thought they saw 'Bohemianism' dominating and socializing the whole literary world. And for a time they had to work side by side with representatives of the school which they looked down on and disliked. In the offices of the *Éclair* they met Pouthier; contributors to the *Paris*, representing another phase of their journalistic career, included Alphonse Karr and Murger himself. But, mixing with painters, haunting the dealers' shops and the salerooms in search of drawings (the modest basis of their great collection), the Goncourts, keen amateurs themselves, were splendidly equipped to write on almost every aspect of artistic life. Nifa, in *En 18 . .*, is a model; the *Voyage du no. 43 de la rue Saint-Georges au no. 1 de la rue Lafitte* is almost entirely concerned with painters and pictures. While the brothers' gifts are displayed at their most brilliant, perhaps, in the three series of biographies dealing with eighteenth-century artists, it is to *Manette Salomon*, published in 1867, that I want to confine myself here.

This novel returns to the problems discussed in an earlier story, *Charles Demailly*. Against a studio background, now, it shows how the vulgar, tyrannical Manette gradually destroys her lover's talent and traps him into marriage. In spite of its gloomy theme, the book gives us a fascinating picture of the Parisian art world between about 1840 and 1865. Coming out in the same year as Louis Veuillot's *Les Odeurs de Paris*, it makes as calculated an attack on Bohemia, while arguing no less forcefully than Baudelaire in favour of an aristocratic conception of the artist.

Nevertheless, as I have said, the Goncourts reveal a change of taste. They dare to speak of 'bonshommes troubadours' in Delacroix's costume-pictures! For them, Romanticism is obsolete.

The Bohemian in their novel is Anatole Bazoche, a painter without real vocation, who has been drawn to the practice of art by a desire to lead what Thackeray, again, once described as the 'easiest, merriest, dirtiest existence possible':

At bottom, it had been much less a matter of Anatole's answering the call of art than of his being attracted to the artist's way of life. The studio was his dream, the object of his schoolboy aspirations and natural appetites. What he saw were those Bohemian horizons to which distance lends enchantment: romantic poverty, freedom from rule and restraint, liberty, absence of discipline, lack of responsibility, risk, adventure, daily encounters with the unexpected, escape from the domestic round, from the endless scramble of family life, and the dullness of its Sundays, the voluptuous mystery of the female model, work without drudgery, the privilege of wearing fancy-dress the whole year through, as though always celebrating Carnival. Such were the images and enticements which the austere, exacting career of art aroused in him.[22]

In this spirit, Anatole decides to become a painter, and after a brief stay in the Classicist school, recommended by a friend of his mother's, enters of his own accord the studio of Langibout. The description of this establishment, some sixty students strong, provides a most interesting cross-section of budding professionals in the 1840's. There are no less than nineteen miniature studies of young men who play little part in the story but add much to its authenticity. The routine of the teaching-studio itself comes alive, together with its student pranks, or *blagues*, in which Langibout's, like other schools, takes great delight. The characters whose development from youth to middle age supplies the Goncourts' chief material are Anatole, Coriolis, and Garnotelle. Each is painstakingly drawn to portray a certain type and attitude. In Anatole the authors have united the most contemptible and pathetic features of the Bohemian; in Coriolis, the pride and sensitivity of the creole; in Garnotelle (type of the bourgeois artist whom Baudelaire singled out for attack), soulless industry and subservience. But Garnotelle is not important, and fellow-workers usually dismiss him with the contempt felt by the Goncourts themselves for Hippolyte Flandrin. It is Anatole, a second Pouthier, and Coriolis who engross their creators' attention.

Anatole makes his début as a practical joker. At Langibout's he is the life and soul of the company. Even the master himself, a stern, simple man, feels the attraction of his pupil's high spirits, and is willing to recognize Anatole's flair for a sketch. But praise of the sketch is always accompanied by a final scolding: '*Petit cochon*, you're bone idle!' Having allowed his enthusiasm for practical jokes to carry him, on one occasion, to lengths which incur Langibout's wrath and endanger his place in the school, Anatole suddenly decides to work. He is, in fact, not without ambition at this stage. The Goncourts, who admired Monnier's writings, doubtless remembered M. Prudhomme as an art student, and they note in Anatole a 'curious contradiction often to be met with in the world of artists': in spite of the lip-service he paid to the great Italians, and without daring to confess it, 'he liked and understood a Picot better than a Raphael'.[23] What this young man really aimed at was the comfortable existence that the Prix de Rome could ensure, an early success dispensing with the struggles and disappointments which inevitably precede real achievement.

Accordingly, having once made up his mind to succeed, Anatole attends evening classes at the École des Beaux-Arts with regularity, and in April, 1844, enters as candidate for the prize. As Langibout might have predicted had he been consulted, his pupil fails in the second competition in which the candidates have to make good the preliminary sketch. There is, in fact, some jockeying for the award, which goes to the mediocre but industrious Garnotelle; but Anatole's work is not even considered. This one reverse is sufficient to cure him of his academic ambitions; and he leaves Langibout's to set up as an artist on his own account, living in a garret and undertaking any humble job that comes along. Luckily, one piece of work brings in as much as a hundred and twenty-five francs, a sum which permits him to rent and furnish a small studio in the Rue de La Fayette. It is there that he discovers 'Bohemia'. In the Rue de La Fayette, later to become something of an artists' quarter, he entertains a crowd of friends, some of them students from Langibout's, some of them anonymous acquaintances, men and women living on their wits. Life is full of opportunities for the practical joker, and the day-to-day existence which Anatole now leads admirably suits his careless nature. While Garnotelle is slaving at his easel in the French School in Rome, the Bohemian can acquire luxuries like a piano and a canoe. Drinking and merrymaking in Paris are followed by a boating holiday at Asnières in which the canoe, 'cette barque de Bohème', plays a leading part.

Such good fortune cannot last. The winter of 1847 finds Anatole reduced to his bed, which he shares with a Polish chef turned painter. In 1848, a year unkind to artists, he has barely survived starvation when, by chance, he meets Coriolis, who was once his friend at Langibout's. Coriolis has spent the intervening period studying and painting in the East, and now takes Anatole to live with him in his Paris studio in the Rue de Vaugirard. The arrangement suits Anatole, whose second ambition, to be independent, has died a natural death. The harsh words of another character, Chassagnol, ostensibly a Bohemian like himself but in reality a kind of Vireloque who voices the Goncourts' own opinions, have convinced him of the futility of self-pity, the Bohemian's last defence. 'Let's waste no tears over *ridiculous martyrs* and crack-brained defeatists!' cries Chassagnol. 'Die of hunger, forsooth! It's the one decent example you can leave your fellow-men. . . . At least it will serve as a warning to others. . . . Upon my soul! You've done nothing to prove your talent, no one knows you from Adam, nor ever will! You've discovered nothing, invented nothing, created nothing . . . and yet, just because you're an artist, the whole world must interest itself in you, and society hang its head in shame if it doesn't deposit a four-pound loaf for you every morning with your concierge!' [24]

There are, in any case, no modern painters of any stature to emulate. What the Goncourts did not venture to print in their *Salon* appears in the tirades of Chassagnol, delivered from time to time to Anatole and Coriolis. Ingres is dismissed as nothing more than the 'nineteenth-century's inventor of colour-photography for the production of Raphaels and Peruginos'; Delacroix as a 'master still at the sketch-stage'. Courbet's name is not actually mentioned, but a reference to the 'charlatanism of the Ugly' refers obviously enough to him.[25]

Everything seems to encourage Anatole to lead a life of idleness.

Whom can one follow? What is there worth struggling for? Far better share the bread of Coriolis, to whom he can at least offer a jester's services in return. But the authors make it clear that, whatever the circumstances, Anatole would have arrived at this condition of dependence. As a painter, he has but the one talent, a gift for mimicry. And the reader's attention is skilfully drawn to this fact by the understanding which develops between Anatole and Vermillon, a monkey Coriolis has brought back from the East. The Bohemian, whose life and art have amounted to no more than a *singerie* of the real thing, finds in Vermillon his soul-mate. Anatole's tragedy, in fact, is not his dismissal at the hands of a jealous Manette, but the loss of the little animal to which he has become so deeply attached. The fate reserved for him, however, if not particularly edifying, might have been crueller: giving up art altogether, he takes a job in the Jardin des Plantes, where, 'living in', he can spend every available moment of his time in the company of the monkeys. They, almost alone among God's creatures, have not yet learnt to despise him!

V

I have just mentioned, in passing, the name of Louis Veuillot. If the authors of *Manette Salomon* seem unfairly prejudiced against the Bohemian, they only confirm what this celebrated and savage Catholic journalist writes in *Les Odeurs de Paris*:

> Around the intellectual studios of Paris there exists a tribe of parasites, ingenious as critics, impotent as artists, who chatter unceasingly and create nothing. . . . Since it is accepted that an intellectual may be idle, that even a great artist can produce his work only if the necessary tools are to hand, these fellows, in order to keep their self-respect, describe themselves as 'lazy'. Realizing, after vain attempts, that they will never produce a statue, picture, book, or poem, that they will never be able to offer the world anything but advice, the poor devils lose even their ability to do that. They become jealous, gloomy, eccentric, and the taste, true and subtle, they once possessed deserts them altogether. They lose the will to work and, feeling no longer capable of serious study, regard it as something shameful that cheapens genius. On the other hand, they can't bring themselves to vacate the peristyle of this temple of art they'll never enter. They go on prowling round it, catcalling those who do get in, and admiring others among them, who, pretending to force the doors, have suffered as yet

only the initial refusals. In their own company they adopt the splendid title of 'rebels', as the lustful eunuch makes a show of virtue before the sultanas' charms. Finally, poverty finishes them off. They become beggars, or drift into cynicism and madness and die in hospital. When this happens, an outcry goes up against society from the midst of the tribe. But society is not much disturbed at this: to tell the truth, it exhibits a most reprehensible indifference. Such is *Bohemia*![26]

The distinction Murger had attempted to draw between a Bohemia *heroic* and a Bohemia *contemptible* seems soon to have been forgotten. By 1867, Bohemianism had come to signify a state of invariable idleness and mediocrity. And, as a way of life, it was no longer associated with any particular area of the city, such as the Latin Quarter. In 1868, Guillemot found Bohemia 'swarming' along the boulevards from the Rue Montmartre to the Rue de la Paix. It was to be encountered in the alleyways of the Faubourg Montmartre, in the Rue des Martyrs, in the neighbourhood of Notre-Dame-de-Lorette, 'territories of the idle, the debauched, and the useless'; to a lesser extent, also, in the Place de la Bourse, the neighbourhood of the Tuileries and Champs Élysées. On the Left Bank, 'its former headquarters', says Guillemot, Bohemia has now become the greatest rarity.[27]

Once more, the conception of the artist was changing. A reaction had set in, not just against the literary affectations of the Romantic school (which would have transformed artists and critics at once into unquestioning admirers of Courbet: and that, we know, it did not do), but against the whole idea of the artist as an aristocrat. Baudelaire and the Goncourts were fighting a losing battle. Moreover, while they show where their sympathy lies, Baudelaire accepts as inevitable the isolation and neglect of Delacroix, and the Goncourts demonstrate that, even freed from Manette's evil influence, the aristocratic Coriolis is really too sensitive and refined to achieve success in the *métier* he has chosen. Though these acute observers believed implicitly in the superiority of the artist, they were at last forced to admit that perhaps it was not given to the most fastidious natures to create the most powerful works of art. Thus, in the *Curiosités esthétiques*, Daumier looms large behind Delacroix; and, in *Manette Salomon*, the peasant-born landscape-painter Crescent has only to make a brief appearance to reveal the limitations of Coriolis.

An intelligent critic of the period came to the same conclusion.

Though Théophile Silvestre was as enthusiastic as Baudelaire in his admiration of Delacroix, and at the same time aware of Courbet's splendid powers (the peak of the artist's achievement was reached about 1869), some remarks he let drop in his studies of Millet and Chenavard (1868) show which way the tide was turning. In the former we read: 'It is not the aim of a great artist to make some dramatic voyage to the moon or the stars, but to plod bravely and steadily along a chosen path, never losing his sincerity in the face of nature, his fellow-men, or himself'; in the latter, while paying tribute to the intelligence of Chenavard, so nearly akin to Delacroix's, he concludes: 'From always searching, questioning, arguing, mocking, and denying, he came finally to dislike everything and everybody, himself included. Seeing him deep in their library's largest volumes, a monk from the monastery of Minerva directed his attention to this profound truth: "The more knowledge we acquire, my dear Sir, the more confused we become." ' [28]

After all, it is no use denying that artists are also artisans. Heroic labour must accompany heroic intuition. Craftsmanship brings the picture into existence; and, though a great deal may be dictated by the spirit, the painter speaks first and last with the brush. Of this truth the landscapists proper, the men of Fontainebleau, reminded people less noisily and (in the end) more effectively than Courbet. Such 'boors' rarely entered a carpeted salon or literary café and were quite unpractised in dancing to the writer's tune. 'Here the artist is master', notes Taine, in 1861, on visiting a favourite painting-ground some sixty kilometres from Paris. 'Here is the beautiful forest he knows so well, all the comradeship, and all the aesthetic discussion he requires.' [29]

One representative of the Barbizon school had played already a small but impressive part in *Manette Salomon*: twelve years later, another made his humorous début in Anatole France's *Le Chat Maigre* (1879). Recently arrived from Fontainebleau, Potrel shares the Paris studio of Labanne, a sculptor, till his own becomes vacant again. Potrel is a peasant, a muscular fellow, who paints silently all day as though he were still in the Forest. Labanne, the talkative, tries to draw him out with such bait as: 'Since the absolute is unattainable, no artist can achieve absolute beauty.' But Potrel never commits himself to any answer other than a pipe-muffled: 'Possibly!' It is true that something reminiscent of Bohemia pervades *Le Chat Maigre*; yet the conception of the artist here has changed out of all recognition. Impressionism, the discovery of Primitive and Japanese art, the emergence of the Sunday-painter—Remi is the first of such painters in fiction—have finally succeeded in obliterating all memory of the sentimental Charles Munster, the heroic Bridau, the exotic Albertus, countless Chattertons in painting-smocks, and those last scarecrows of Romanticism, the Bohemians themselves.

All this Sainte-Beuve might have foreseen—indeed, he very nearly lived to see it. He it was who, fifty years before, had observed so disapprovingly some of the earliest flirtations of art and literature. When he commented:

> '. . . les peintres, dont l'honneur
> Luit en tableaux sans nombre aux vieilles galeries,
> S'occupaient assez peu des hautes théories,
> Et savaient mal de l'art le côté raisonneur;
> Mais, comme dans son champ dès l'aube un moissonneur,
> En loyaux ouvriers, sur leurs toiles chéries
> Ils travaillaient penchés, *seuls et sans rêveries. . . .*',*

it is as though, in evoking the past, he had been granted a vision of the future, and actually beheld Monet solitary on the cliffs at Varengeville, and Cézanne alone with his mountain in Provence.

* 'The painters whose lustre is preserved in countless pictures in the old galleries paid little enough attention to lofty theories, and were unskilled in arguing the finer points of art; but, like a reaper out in his field since dawn, these faithful workers laboured over their beloved canvases, backs bowed, *in solitude, and entertaining no idle fancies. . . .*'

Conclusion

i

We have now passed in review some seven decades of literary-artistic collaboration in Paris. Artist and writer had drawn close together: too close, it may be thought. Yet a certain suspicion on the part of the artist was never set wholly at rest, and to the writer's admiration there existed always discernible bounds. 'Oh, you literary men,' Delacroix complained to Maxime Du Camp, 'how you damage us with your criticisms and damn us with your compliments!' [1] while Musset confided to his friend Alfred Tattet: 'Admirable fellows, these artists—as long as they're not in the same line of business as oneself!' [2]

Nevertheless, such hobnobbing tended not unnaturally to play down the importance of the practical side of the artist's vocation. He was inveigled instead into the realm of ideas; ideas, of necessity, literary. And he was lucky if he did not pick up some of the writer's own over-concern with artistic 'sensitivity' and comparative indifference to artistic performance. He could certainly have been warned by the way these mould the fictitious characters we have just examined: for Charles Munster, Albertus, Pippo, Murger's Marcel or Francis Bernier, the Goncourts' Coriolis as well as their Bazoche, though all more or less interesting as persons, are all more or less impotent as artists. The writer may have had some justification for this unflattering conception, since dedicated, industrious painters and sculptors had less time to waste on literary cliques than the doubter and the dilettante. Yet opportunities which ought to have proved more fruitful did occur—and were actually seized. Even when the artist placed no value on their services, some writers, under the spell of his personal magnetism, went on obstinately courting him: thus Delacroix commanded always a small, enthusiastic following and even Barbizon and Marlotte were ultimately invaded by journalists, who turned these quiet painters' retreats into material for the gossip-column.

The magnetism could exert its power, however, only when the painters or sculptors in question satisfied the current literary conception of the kind of man an artist ought to be. Of course, there were never lacking artists to fulfil at least some part of the writer's expectation. Gros, during and after the Empire ('he painted as Homer sang'),[3] Delacroix under the July Monarchy, Courbet in the Second Empire: each displayed, for one faction or another, the charm or *bizarrerie* demanded. In men so different from each other as Girodet and Guérin, Gavarni and Corot, there existed a common fragment of the conception *artiste* which could be understood by the writer. For, living in the most literary phase of art, these were men who expressed literary ideas as naturally as they breathed. Even Courbet translated into paint the convictions of the socialist thinkers with whom he mixed. That the physical structure of a work of art should generate ideas on its own account was a possibility hardly envisaged even by Baudelaire or by the Goncourts themselves.

Yet this is precisely the quality that distinguishes the work of Ingres, whose roots in literature, for a painter's of those times, lie remarkably shallow, and for whom, in a profession then fashionably antagonistic to the middle class, the 'épicier' presented no particular terrors.

After due allowance is made for Théophile Silvestre's loyalty to Delacroix, the fury of his attack upon Delacroix's rival is still astonishing. What was it that this highly intelligent critic found so repulsive about the painter of the 'M. Bertin' and the 'Stratonice'? No doubt, in a general way, the spectacle of his success and the relish with which the artist appeared to accept the incense offered up to him. True it is that Ingres replied rather more bluntly than was usual under interrogation, himself laying about his contemporaries with a heavy hand. But Silvestre sufficiently understood the natural acerbity of artists not to misinterpret what he had been ready, in any case, to forgive in Courbet. Whereas Courbet's wildest tirades are passed over indulgently, however, the studio-maxims of Ingres—'Let us proceed to Venice, keeping clear of Antwerp'; 'The navel is the torso's eye'—are jeered at as typical samples of a 'solemn buffoonery'.[4] Then, at last, the real cause of Silvestre's anger is disclosed: Ingres had no ideas.

Says the critic:

David put form at the service of thought. M. Ingres, with an exclusive faith in form, turns painting into the sensual, sterile contemplation of mere matter, professes complete indifference towards man's destiny and the mysteries of creation, and is content to pursue (by lines variously curved or straight) a plastic Absolute, which in his eyes, is the principle and purpose of all things.[5]

But to merit attention, Silvestre continues, a picture ought to convey 'if not some moral reflection, at least some meaning'. To do as Ingres did, to be at such pains to study the human bone-structure and muscular system and then re-draft them to suit his own caprice, resulted in something that had neither charm nor intellectual significance. This was teratology, not art. And how ironic that the painter of the 'Ideal' fell so far short of perfection in his own person!

M. Ingres [Silvestre maliciously informs the reader] is a burly, bouncing old gentleman, whose vulgarity provides a sharp contrast to the affected elegance of his pictures and to his Olympian pretensions. If he passed you in the street, you would take him for a Spanish priest dressed up as a bourgeois: a swarthy, bilious complexion; a dark, alert, suspicious, ill-humoured eye; a brow narrow and receding; short, thick hair, jet-black once and always greasy, divided by a parting down the centre of a pointed skull; large ears; veins beating vigorously at the temples; a prominent nose, inclined to be hooked and made to appear short on account of the vast space separating it from the mouth; cheeks coarse and baggy; chin and cheekbones very pronounced; jaw like a rock, and lips thin and sullen.[6]

What serious claims to immortality could be established by a painter who did not even look 'interesting'? How unacceptable he would have been as Romantic leader! And yet that was the very position another shake of the Fates' distaff might have given him: the early 'Dream of Ossian' and 'Paolo and Francesca' would have provided excellent credentials, while that last anxiety of his to complete a tracing of Giotto's 'Christ at the Tomb' shows that he never lost his youthful, Meditator's enthusiasm for the Italian Primitives.

But because he failed so signally to *look* the part created or approved by contemporary men of letters, he was in danger of being dismissed by some of the most intelligent of them as a gross, commonplace voluptuary. Hugo, indeed, wrote a complimentary ode on Ingres's self-imposed exile of 1834, when the painter, in a huff, went off to Rome: Vigny was an admirer, too, though he spread his praise rather thin. Gautier's dripped over the crust: an article of his, entitled 'M. Ingres's studio in 1843', appeared in *L'Événement* for August 2nd of that year. In it he speaks of two pictures on which Ingres was then engaged, a 'Venus Anadyomene' and a portrait of the baronne James de Rothschild. The first provokes the most adulatory fancies and comparisons; and though the portrait of Mme de Rothschild may conceivably, with the patina of centuries, become 'as fine in colour as a Titian' [7] (stranger things have happened), to state it as a probability was a line in blandishment hardly likely to commend Ingres to his enemies. They, in fact, went on regarding him as the arch-materialist of a materialistic age, a lover of flesh for its own sake, or, in a mood even more detestable, for the jewels that loaded it. Delacroix would return from a ball at the Tuileries, disgusted by the blatant *décolleté* of the Court: Ingres, whose fate it was to paint numerous Mrs Merdles, seemed ready to prostrate himself before any Bosom, sufficiently inflated, with its due marginalia of gimp and galloons.

To-day, we can appreciate how ridiculous this view of the painter is. Far from declining, Ingres's reputation has grown with the years: and much that Delacroix set down on canvas has now lost its meaning (including many of those famous 'ideas' by which Silvestre set such store), its only imperishable memorial Baudelaire's golden opinions—because they are written by Baudelaire. Ingres, about whom there was nothing to write, triumphantly survives. Vanity, irascibility, vulgarity no longer come between the spectator and the Florentine charm of 'Mlle Rivière' or the deceptive simplicity of 'La Source'. From the 'Stamaty Family' drawing to the most suffocating of the 'Turkish Bath' compositions, a stint of over forty-five years, the work of Ingres demonstrates (among other things) the value to the artist of just those stolid, bourgeois virtues which the dilettante pretended to despise or, in his folly, really did despise.

Though Ingres is the grand example of Biedermeier genius, there were others, perfect patterns of the good bourgeois, keeping their noses to the grindstone, over-modest even. Among them we can find men of the noblest character and highest gifts: a

Corot, a Daumier. The latter, we know, often wearied of the tedious campaign against the middle class in which circumstances forced him to play, pictorially, the leading rôle. In fact, he whom Baudelaire praised for his 'luminous' good sense, never really felt at home with *artistes à barbe*, and I am quite sure he would have joined unreservedly with the admirable Lecoq de Boisbaudran in stating that no artist 'need be, or without injuring himself can be, a bad citizen, nor can his conduct be excused by his work'.[8] If we pass now from tritons to minnows, we come upon the strange case of Henri Monnier. He did not figure (the reader may have been surprised to note) among the selection of artists from the *Comédie humaine* given in Section II, though as the *ex*-painter Bixiou he is one of the rare participants in its chronicles to have been transferred there direct from life. The plain truth is that, after a brief period of doting upon Monnier, Balzac—like everyone else—grew uneasy, as the caricaturist seemed to lose his identity in the thing he caricatured. For in spite of that fascinating gallery of students and *grisettes*—and his deserved success on the stage—the creator of M. Prudhomme ended by abdicating in favour of his best-loved puppet. Where did this writing-master, the humbug, the Philistine, the arch-bourgeois end, and the man called Monnier begin? No one knew the answer then; and we are little wiser to-day. Bixiou, therefore, though he keeps the right company and frequents the right places—he took part for instance, with Léon de Lora, in the celebrated supper-party at the *Rocher de Cancale* (*Les Parents pauvres*), emerges as a character in the round only in *Les Employés*, in that domain of petty civil servants symbolized by the famous skull-scraper collar and bulging umbrella. No one could for long take Monnier seriously as an artist. What sort of skill, after all, did his mimicry amount to? 'It is as cold and clear as a glass,' said Baudelaire; 'it has no capacity for thought, but contents itself with recording momentarily, like a mirror, the passers-by.' [9] Such faithful transcripts (on silver-plate, sensitized and exposed to light) had charmed Paris, in their own way, since 1839—but bestowed no special glory on the photographer.

Ingres, Daumier, and Monnier stand out as the most notable hybrids: but there existed in practically every Romantic, however militant, his banal streak. Hugo's took the form of a wardrobe quite as frumpish as Ingres's: he seems never to have forgotten an early scolding from his mother, when he had naïvely expressed a wish to emulate the smartness of the printer Gilé—men, the General's widow had explained, are esteemed for their intelligence, not for their fine clothes.[10] Musset, less carefully brought up, launched into a garish elegance of his own devising, but with results no happier, for the Jockey-Club is said to have blackballed him on that very score.[11] Yet this vulgarian himself complained of the vulgarity of Mme Sand, not because she wore scarlet cashmere trousers and smoked *cigarritos*, but because she brought to her writing so middle-class an attitude of mind.[12] Nor did either Vigny or Delacroix dwell uninterruptedly in the clouds: the one constantly grumbled about money, the other could even regret on occasion the little comforts enjoyed by his *bête noire*, the family-man.[13] Théophile Gautier was not long in exchanging an ambrosia shared with the *Cydalise* for the mutton-chops appropriate to daily journalism. As for the Bohemians themselves, enough has been said to suggest how easily Rodolphe and Marcel dropped back into the pattern of a workaday world. Sensible men! Bravado, self-pity, a show of wit or a wildness in dress, seem to us now but feeble signs of talent. Alas, that so much energy was spent on shocking the burgher; for what shocks the burgher to-day is almost certain to bore the rest of us to-morrow. But is there any truth in the therapeutic claims of the *vie d'artiste*? Did not one stand to gain *something* from its much-vaunted alarums? There is a passage in the Goncourts' *Charles Demailly*, written nearly a century ago, which might well seem the last word on the subject:

> You can create efficiently only in silence, when the busy world around you is stilled, as it were, in sleep. Emotions disturb the gestating imagination: it needs routine and peace, a completely bourgeois condition of mind and body, the phlegm of the shopkeeper, to produce what has grandeur, excitement, pungency, and pathos. Those who spend themselves in passion and live on their nerves will never write a passionate book. It's the old story of the clever fellows who are always chattering: they'll come to no good.[14]

ii

If everything—including common sense and the briefest acquaintance with history—goes to show that the Goncourts were right, how is it that beards and shock-hair and conventionally unconventional clothing are still with us? Do we even, in the first place, owe them to Murger?

When, in 1845, Rodolphe and Marcel make their initial bow, there is little evidence that they ever sighed for velvet berets or pourpoint waistcoats. Their circumstances, as we have already noted, were identical with those of the impoverished young painter who figures in Tassaert's picture of the same year. They were never in any condition to follow fashion, conventional or unconventional. The great-coat of Schaunard, 'irremediably bald', and that of Colline, with its prodigious pockets, owed their long service to necessity. Rodolphe possessed a large-brimmed hat, such as Daumier shows us in his portrait of Théodore Rousseau and Gavarni so often caricatures, but these hats were the common property of the Quarter, and nothing further is itemized by Murger which could have distinguished his Bohemians from, say, medical students, as they appear in the original wood-block for Musset's *Mimi Pinson*. There is no suggestion that the 'official' Bohemian looked, or aspired to look, different from his fellow-men. Indeed, and unexpectedly enough, it is Marcel, painter of the little band, who is most positive in his wish to 'dress like everyone else'.[15] Many times before his final decision to leave Bohemia, he shows his respect for frock-coats and clean linen; and no doubt he ended by possessing as many and as much of these things as convention required he should. In fact, we can turn for confirmation to Fantin-Latour's 'Homage to Delacroix', a picture of 1864, in which Champfleury, that is Marcel, poses with two other writers and no less than seven painters, all spruce in best bourgeois bib and tucker.[16]

It would be going too far to say that the artist dispensed altogether with slovenly or distinctive forms of clothing. But during the years between *Hernani* and Murger's death there does seem to have been a fairly general slackening in the desire to provide sartorial shocks. To pass from some of the male figures in Joseph Guichard's 'Dream of Love' (1837: Lyons), or even from Winterhalter's portrait of a young architect (1830: Amiens), to the group of artists portrayed by Glaize at Montpellier in 1848, and still to be seen there, is like coming out of a 'bal véronèse' into the unambiguous light of day. Here it is the patron, Bruyas, in his exotic dressing-gown and morocco slippers, who outshines the artists. While there are exceptions to this quieter tendency—Courbet and Monticelli, for instance—it would really seem that, by the 1840's and 1850's, the artist was more intent on expressing his spiritual conflicts in a spiritual manner than on showing off by means of superficial eccentricities of dress. This is apparent not only in portraits of the congenitally pessimistic Chenavard, but in the brooding self-likenesses of Félon, Ricard, and Hébert (Nîmes, Dijon, Grenoble)—in turn tortured, defiant, and anxious—and, while I am speaking of such things, in a remarkable portrait of the period, artist and sitter unknown, which hangs in the Musée at Agen.

By the time we reach the 1860's, there seems little to distinguish the rebel from the most conventional of his colleagues. Except for a cap of the kind worn by students, the model's companions in Manet's famous 'Picnic on the Grass', of 1863, are as soberly turned out as the painter himself in his portrait by Fantin-Latour, of 1867, or in Fantin's later group-picture, the 'Batignolles Studio', dated 1870.[17] In 1865, Renoir exhibited his 'Cabaret de la Mère Anthony', where he is shown with Lecœur and Sisley in Murger's favourite port-of-call at Marlotte. Renoir and Sisley are irreproachably dressed, Lecœur is actually clean-shaven. On the wall behind them, amid a confused collection of graffiti, rears up a caricature of Murger himself—in a billycock hat.[18] Why, then, have we grown accustomed to look on the *Scènes de la Bohème* as a kind of artists' *Tailor and Cutter* for 1830? Largely, I suppose, because the libretto of Puccini's version of these stories is thus ante-dated, with the result that the singers are quite correctly attired in their flowing cravats, cloaks, and berets.

The beret came back into vogue, probably as a result of a reawakened respect for Rembrandt, just after 1830; and it would seem that other fashions which originally gained currency in the Gautier 'cénacles' remained vividly imprinted on the public imagination, and served to assist caricaturists in their task of building up an instantly-recognizable type. During the years when the *Scènes* were being printed in the *Corsaire*, many artists, as we have noted, were losing faith in the Romantic creed. Engrossed by new problems and the struggle to survive, they grew less and less concerned with perpetuating the fripperies of the generation which had preceded them. Yet, at the same time, we have to remember that these fripperies enjoyed such a long life, have been so often and successfully revived, that they cannot have existed, post-Gautier, entirely in the cloud-cuckoo-land of the comic papers. Puppyism and pretence, then as now, will always demand a uniform.

Murger's patient definition of the different species of Bohemian was no doubt most often skipped by the reader, hurrying on to enjoy the stories themselves. And without a study of the Preface, the reader could well imagine that every Bohemian—and every artist—conformed to a single sartorial pattern. The 'official' Bohemian painter, therefore, the special character Murger portrayed in Marcel and, to a lesser degree, in Schaunard, was confused with the eternal *rapin* of the pointed hat, the long greasy locks, and the outmoded *brandebourgs* of the Doyenné, features that enliven Grandville's block for an article entitled 'Le Chapeau pointu', towards the end of the 1830's, and in cartoons produced much later by Gavarni; and something like them can still be found as the stock-in-trade of Caran d'Ache. Having made himself responsible for a literary caricature of the artist, Murger ought not to have been surprised that his conception took graphic shape; that Rodolphe and Marcel wear the costume proper to frenzied admirers of *Chatterton* when, in truth, they had been remarkable only for their shabbiness and strong disapproval of Vigny's drama.

iii

Another question: if the devils of Bohemianism seem hard to exorcize, just how devilish are they? Is there anything in the rumoured connexion of the artist with criminal society?

In the criminal world there have always existed a wilful defiance of convention and contempt for the law-abiding citizen. Since these were also powerful elements in literary-artistic society during the period we have been considering, the reader may have looked for some reference to the artist's place in what Murger himself loosely termed 'Criminal Bohemia'.[19] In spite of the explosive atmosphere of the Latin Quarter under the July Monarchy, I believe that any such association was never more than superficial.

The Romantic and early Realist intellectual did not lack impertinence. He could be aggressively anti-social; he could boast of his contempt for private property; and he paid frequent visits to at least one prison, the debtors' gaol at Clichy. Careless of the company he kept, he might even, like Privat, split a bottle with professional thieves. But he was really more fastidious than these isolated antics suggest. Though he delighted in picturesque characters, and was therefore drawn towards the gipsy and the mountebank, he could have found nothing attractive about the average Paris blackguard of the 1840's, who had neither inherited the distinction of Goya's *picaro* nor anticipated the charm of Carco's *apache*. In the mean streets between the Palais de Justice and the cathedral of Notre-Dame (before Haussmann cleared the area) the criminal class presented an appearance scarcely seductive. Its men and women, having graduated in the gutter and learnt how to 'nourrir le poupard' or, if need be, 'chouriner' (translation superfluous), still remained as drab as peasants in their coarse smocks, caps, or *marmottes*—and as uncommunicative. Not till much later, about the first and second decades of the present century, did the inarticulate bully and his mistress arouse sentiments other than pity or indignation in the novelist. In spite of a taste for the raggle-taggle fraternity, therefore, and a lively appreciation of the night-piece provided by the less respectable quarters of the city, writer and artist had nothing in common with the clientèle of the *tapis-franc*, just as they could have had nothing in common with the elegant rascals of the *Bohème dorée*.

On certain occasions, however, the two societies of Bohemia and Crime may be said to have touched. This was when some female outcast slipped from one to the other, for it was but a short step from the Lapin Blanc to the studio. Murger's sole connexion with the world of crime is through a woman, Marie Virmal, whose 'husband' was one of a gang of petty robbers. And it is through a sentimental or philanthropic interest in the fallen woman, a Mimi or Marguerite Gautier, that we get our glimpses of the criminal world. Thus in the most elaborate picture of this world, that presented by Eugène Sue in his *Mystères de Paris*,[20] the central character, Fleur-de-Marie, is a reclaimed prostitute.

Had art and crime done more than rub shoulders and really joined hands, one would expect evidence of it in Sue's sensational tract: for the author, however artificial his plot and ingenuous his philosophy, conscientiously visited the thieves' kitchens of his day and in earlier life had himself been a student of painting under Gudin. We might, in fact, reckon on meeting an artist well to the foreground of the *Mystères*. Yet we do not. The *rapin* Cabrion is conspicuous by his absence: we are always hearing of him, but he never actually appears. When he introduced the Cabrion-Pipelet relationship, that of the mischievous artist and his long-suffering landlord, Sue was probably recalling a certain porter in the Rue du Mont Blanc whom he and Monnier had once been in the habit of teasing. Pipelet's life is rendered insupportable by the young painter's practical jokes, and Cabrion's bearded, grinning face, surmounted by a pointed hat, haunts him in constantly-recurring nightmares.

Apart from these harmless diversions, however, Cabrion's rôle in the house in the Rue du Temple was not an important one. Before Prince Rodolphe's arrival, he had lodged on the fourth floor next to a gay but virtuous *grisette* and within call of the infamous Bradamanti; but Rigolette never took him seriously, and he was neither rich nor vicious enough to arouse the interest of the more sinister cut-throats of Sue's underworld. Further, it may be surmised he would not have jumped at the opportunity to work on the Prince's model-farm for the rehabilitation of the depraved. He remains, therefore, supernumerary to the drama, and the author at length releases Pipelet from his agony by packing Cabrion off to Germany.

Though Sue's picture of the criminal world is on many counts an extremely unreliable one, the absence of the artist from its haunts of ill-fame seems to have been fair comment on the facts. In any case, it would be ludicrous to imagine that he was in the habit of plunging a knife into those who irritated him by subscribing to the *Constitutionnel*, admiring Horace Vernet, or dozing in the stalls to the soothing cadence of classical alexandrines. Irresponsible in a hundred ways, he had always on his conscience at least a duty to art: 'I find a certain satisfaction and tranquillity in the lowest depth of vice', as Restif confessed in the *Paysan perverti*, seems to have been a sentiment rare among writers and rarer still among painters and sculptors.

If we come closer to modern times, Mac Orlan's memories of a Bohemia as late as 1900–1914, when the cult of the *apache* had reached its peak, do not suggest that Picasso, Pascin, Derain, and their friends were ever mixed up with the law-breakers of Montmartre. The revolver-assault on the Lapin Agile, recounted so laconically in Mac Orlan's own *Quai des Brumes* (1927), turns out to have been a pardonable protest by thieves of the quarter against the transformation of their favoured kitchen into the Père Frédéric's Respectable Establishment for Young Writers and Artists. Thus the grouping together, in the novel, of Jean Rabe, 'young man of twenty-five *sans profession*', the casual model Nelly, the young painter Michel Kraus, and two murderers, may be taken with a pinch of salt. I think we can see an ironic twinkle in the eye of that shrewd old artist who observed to Mac Orlan, during the latter's lean years: 'Don't imagine you're wasting your time, young fellow. Out of a decade's poverty, you'll be able to build yourself a castle!' [21]

It is an embarrassment to us that the Bohemian must always build his castle of the same broken shards, quarried from the same *terrains vagues* I have re-prospected here. No doubt, the personal recollection of a particular writer, invoking his particular artist or artists, gives the castle a deceptively novel shape at times. None of these follies, however, conceals more than the single, simple truth: that, at some stage or in some degree, art and life have always proved, and are likely to go on proving, incompatible. The long legend of the artist and all the purple passages of Bohemian literature, strung together, yield just this. What we make of the irritant itself or of the ugly pearl it fosters will depend upon our willingness to recognize a double character in both, that, along with much that is cheap, goes more that is tragic.

Perhaps the familiar, shop-soiled displays of self-pity and bravado, which still continue, may teach us something after all: if mediocrity thinks it suffers in throwing off its daubs, at what real cost, unglimpsed but terrible, must masterpieces be created! 'Beware of picturesque men', said Nietzsche; to that, we may add: 'Learn from them, too.'

Notes

For books with titles in French, the place of publication—where not otherwise indicated—is Paris; for those titled in English, with the same qualification, it is London. If editions other than the first have been consulted, the original date of publication appears in parentheses. Unless otherwise stated, *Salons* were published in the year of the title.

INTRODUCTION

1. H. Dieckman, *Inventaire du Fonds Vandeul et inédits de Diderot*, Geneva, and Lille, 1951, pp. 230, 231.
2. E. and J. de Goncourt, *L'Art du XVIIIe siècle*, 3e série (1860–1870), 1909, pp. 237, 238 n. 2.
3. *Mémoires*, ed. M. Tourneux, 1891, vol. 2, pp. 103, 104. Soufflot was, of course, the architect.
4. *Œuvres complètes*, ed. Assézat and Tourneux, 1875–1877, vol. 10, p. 424.
5. J. Locquin, *La Peinture d'histoire en France de 1747 à 1785*, 1912, pp. 12, 13.
6. J. J. Winckelmann, *Geschichte der Kunst des Altertums*, Vienna, 1934, p. 134.
7. *Œuvres complètes*, vol. 4, p. 11. Diderot refers to a seascape by Joseph Vernet.
8. Antoine Coypel's self-portrait (with his daughter) is at Grenoble. Of Nicolas de Largillierre there is a particularly modest self-portrait at Tours, and a more dignified example at Toulouse. François Boucher's self-portrait at his easel is in the Louvre. The two most characteristic self-portraits of La Tour are at St-Quentin. Liotard, of course, spent four years in Constantinople.
9. Cochin, as part of a considerable literary production, wrote *Critiques de Salon* for 1753 and 1755.
10. It was to Topino-Lebrun that David confided his instructions for 'purifying' the French School in Rome. Gamelin is the hero of Anatole France's *Les Dieux ont soif* (1912).

I: THE MEDITATOR

1. M.-E.-J. Delécluze, *Louis David, son école et son temps*, 1855.
2. Léon Rosenthal, *Louis David*, 1906, p. 69.

3. David criticized Girodet both for his affected manner and heretical matter.
4. Delécluze, p. 78.
5. Delécluze, p. 90.
6. F. Benoît, *L'Art français sous la Révolution et l'Empire*, 1897, p. 315.
7. J.-L.-Jules David, *Le Peintre Louis David*, 1880, p. 335.
8. This was the ancient monastery of the Visitation Sainte-Marie: see A. Estignard, *Correspondance inédite de Charles Nodier*, 1796–1844, 1876, p. 22.
9. Charles Nodier, *Nouvelles*, 1840, p. 21.
10. Charles Nodier, *Romans*, 1840, p. 173.
11. Delécluze, pp. 92, 93.
12. Johann Wolfgang Goethe, *Gedenkausgabe der Werke, Briefe und Gespräche*, ed. Ernst Beutler, Zürich, 1953, vol. IV, *Der Junge Goethe*, p. 277.
13. *Le Peintre de Salzbourg, journal des émotions d'un cœur souffrant*, 1803.
14. *Romans*, p. 238.
15. *Essais d'un jeune barde*, 1804, p. 90.
16. *Ibid.*, 94.
17. Marquis de Caulaincourt, *Mémoires*, 1933, vol. 2, p. 281.
18. Delécluze, pp. 329, 330.

II: BALZAC'S ARTISTS

1. Lille.
2. Their portraits, by Pécheux and Hoin respectively, at Dijon, show them both absorbed by the *métier*.
3. In *Chien-Caillou*, 1860, p. 41.
4. Benoît, 243.
5. M. Boisson, *Les Compagnons de la Vie de Bohème*, 1929, pp. 41, 42.
6. R. Escholier, *Delacroix, peintre, graveur, écrivain*, 1926–1929, vol. 1, p. 96.
7. *La Comédie humaine*, Pléiade, 1949–1959, repr. 1955–1959, vol. 1, p. 66.
8. *Ibid.*, p. 71.
9. Escholier, vol. 2, p. 113. Did Balzac draw upon Delacroix direct, or through Gautier? The question is argued once more in Pierre Laubriet's *Un Catéchisme esthétique:* Le Chef-d'œuvre inconnu *de Balzac*, 1961. No definite answer seems likely.
10. 'We were expecting Balzac who didn't come', Delacroix wrote to Pierret from Nohant, shortly before the book's appearance, 'and

I am not put out. Such a chatterbox would have upset this easy nonchalance which I find so pleasant and soothing.' P. Burty, *Lettres de Eugène Delacroix*, 1880, vol. 1, p. 262.

11. Delacroix, *Journal*, ed. Joubin, 1932, vol. 1, p. 299; Balzac, *Le Chef-d'œuvre inconnu*, Pléiade, vol. 1, p. 400.
12. *Le Chef-d'œuvre inconnu*, p. 401; K. Badt, *Eugène Delacroix: Drawings*, Oxford, 1946, p. 54, citing J. Gigoux, *Causeries sur les artistes de mon temps*, 1885.
13. *Le Chef-d'œuvre inconnu*, p. 402.
14. *Ibid.*, p. 403.
15. *La Rabouilleuse*, Pléiade, vol. 3, p. 901.
16. Escholier, vol. 1, p. 204.
17. *Les Comédiens sans le savoir*, Pléiade, vol. 7, p. 47.
18. 1846.
19. *La Fille aux yeux d'or* (1834–1835), a story dedicated to Delacroix, Pléiade, vol. 5, p. 256.
20. *Les Parents pauvres*, Pléiade, vol. 6, p. 321.
21. *Ibid.*, pp. 322, 323.
22. *Ibid.*, p. 522.
23. *Pierre Grassou*, Pléiade, vol. 6, p. 132.

III: MUTUAL ADMIRATION

1. [Adèle Hugo] *Victor Hugo raconté par un témoin de sa vie*, 1863, vol. 2, p. 161.
2. L. Séché, *Le Cénacle de Joseph Delorme, 1827–1830*, 1912; vol. 2: *Victor Hugo et les artistes*, p. 187.
3. H. Jouin, *David d'Angers et ses relations littéraires*, 1890, p. 25.
4. Victor Hugo, *Œuvres complètes*, 1880–1889 (Hetzel-Quantin, n.d.), *Drame* I, p. 54.
5. *Ibid.*, p. 44.
6. *Les Salons de Paris. Foyers éteints*, 1858, p. 125.
7. M. Leroy, *Vie de Sainte-Beuve*, 1947, p. 55.
8. *Histoire du Romantisme* (1874), 1911, p. 227.
9. Séché, vol. 2, p. 107. References to Boulanger may be found in the *Chants du crépuscule*, XXXII; *Voix intérieures*, XIV; *Les Rayons et les ombres*, XXIX; and letters in *Alpes et Pyrénées*, 2nd ed., 1845.
10. Séché, vol. 2, p. 128.
11. *Ibid.*, p. 129. Sainte-Beuve was writing to Victor Pavie.
12. *Histoire du Romantisme*, p. 228.
13. *Portraits contemporains* (1874), 1914, p. 228.
14. *Histoire du Romantisme*, pp. 7, 8.
15. *Ibid.*, pp. 4–6.

16. *Victor Hugo raconté*, vol. 2, p. 280.
17. Leroy, *Vie de Sainte-Beuve*, p. 65.
18. Sainte-Beuve, *Œuvres*, Pléiade, 1949, vol. 1, p. 384.

IV: SHOCKING THE BURGHERS

1. Théophile Gautier, *Poésies complètes*, ed. R. Jasinski, 1932, vol. 1, p. 113; *Sonnet VII.*
2. Jean-Bernard Duseigneur, 1808–1866, exhibited regularly at the Salon between 1831 and his death; winning, in 1834, a second-class medal.
3. R. Jasinski, *Les Années romantiques de Théophile Gautier*, 1929, p. 72.
4. Sainte-Beuve, *Les Premiers Lundis*, 1894, vol. 2, p. 181.
5. *Figaro*, Aug. 30th, 1831.
6. *Les Jeunes-France* (1833), n.d. (Bibliothèque Charpentier: Fasquelle), p. xvi.
7. G. Planche, *Étude sur l'école française*, 1855, vol. 1, p. 172.
8. Th. Silvestre, *Les Artistes français*, ed. É. Faure, 1926, vol. 1, p. 158.
9. Préault's remark, however, has been variously ascribed: in *Victor Hugo raconté* (vol. 2, pp. 293, 294), for instance, to Prince Ernest of Saxe-Coburg. No doubt it was a common enough slogan. The quotation from Borel occurs in his *Champavert: contes immoraux* (1833), Brussels, 1872, p. xxxvi.
10. Stanzas LXXV and LXXVI.
11. *Journal*, vol. 1, p. 153.
12. *Contes fantastiques de Hoffmann*, 1843.
13. *Poésies complètes*, vol. 2, p. 139.
14. *Les Jeunes-France*, pp. 2, 13.
15. *Ibid.*, pp. 84, 85.
16. *Portraits et souvenirs littéraires* (1875), n.d. (Bibliothèque Charpentier), p. 25. Of the artists mentioned as taking part in the decoration of this room, Leleux was one of Nanteuil's closest friends and introduced him to the etching medium. For Nanteuil himself, see the previous chapter. Camille Rogier was a rather feeble *pasticheur* of the eighteenth-century engravers; and in P. Burty's *Camille Rogier, vignettiste*, 1887, is reproduced a Watteau-like panel by him, painted for this occasion. Alcide Lorentz, along with most of these artists, was an illustrator as well as a painter. Chassériau, of course (with Corot), being a painter only, is exceptional in this company.
17. Gérard de Nerval, *Petits Châteaux de Bohême. La Bohême galante* (1855), ed. J. Marsan, 1926, pp. 7, 8.

18. A. Houssaye, *Les Confessions*, 1885–1891, vol. 1, p. 299.
19. *La Bohême galante*, p. 6.
20. *Histoire du Romantisme*, p. 64.
21. E. Bergerat, *Théophile Gautier, Entretiens, souvenirs, et correspondance*, 1911, p. 117.
22. G. Matoré, *Théophile Gautier, La Préface de Mademoiselle de Maupin*, 1946, *Préface*, p. 1.
23. *Ibid.*, p. 32.
24. E. Delacroix, *Œuvres littéraires*, 1923, vol. 1, p. 7.
25. Matoré, *Préface*, p. 32.
26. *Les Jeunes-France*, p. 216.

V: A PHILOSOPHY OF DESPAIR

1. Alfred de Vigny, *Le Journal d'un poète*, ed. F. Baldensperger, 1935, vol. 1, pp. 64, 87.
2. Alfred de Vigny, *Correspondance*, ed. F. Baldensperger, 1933, vol. 1, pp. 244, 245.
3. Alfred de Vigny, *Stello*, ed. F. Baldensperger, 1925, p. 47.
4. *Ibid.*, pp. 77, 78.
5. *Ibid.*, p. 156.
6. *Ibid.*, p. 42.
7. *Ibid.*, p. 78.
8. *Ibid.*, p. 241.
9. *Ibid.*, p. 249.
10. *Ibid.*, p. 242.
11. *Œuvres complètes*, ed. F. Baldensperger, *Théâtre II, Notes*, p. 363.
12. *Ibid.*, p. 282.
13. *Ibid.*, pp. 335, 336.
14. *Journal*, vol. 1, pp. 333–5.
15. *Revue des Deux-Mondes*, Oct., 1835.
16. *Théâtre II*, p. 242.
17. *Journal*, vol. 1, pp. 335, 336.
18. Théophile Gautier, *Reprise de Chatterton*, Dec., 1857: *Histoire du Romantisme*, pp. 153, 154.
19. *Paris and the Parisians*, 1835, vol. 1, p. 363.
20. H. J. Hunt, *Le Socialisme et le Romantisme en France*, Oxford, 1935, p. 239.
21. *Dernière nuit de travail*, *Théâtre II*, p. 240. The anecdote concerning Berthaud and the chocolate pistol is related by Philibert Audebrand in his *Petits Mémoires du XIXe siècle*, 1892, pp. 312, 313.
22. *Chansons de Béranger*, nouv. éd. populaire, 1866, p. 457.

23. *Journal*, vol. 1, p. 444.
24. Luc-Benoist, *La Sculpture romantique*, 1928, pp. 64, 65.
25. T. Thoré ('Thoré-Bürger'), *Salons* (*1844–1848*), 1868, p. 234.
26. Luc-Benoist, p. 41.
27. 'A Théodore Rousseau': *Salons*, p. 11.
28. In the *Moniteur*, September 28th, 1863: *Histoire du Romantisme*, p. 164.

VI: ART AND LOVE

1. Alfred de Musset, *Mélanges de littérature et de critique*, 1899, p. 138.
2. *Œuvres complètes* (Bibliothèque Charpentier), 1897–1900, ed. E. Biré, vol. 6, *Contes*, pp. 360, 361.
3. *Mélanges*, p. 124.
4. *Œuvres complètes*, vol. 5, p. 270.
5. To Mme Jaubert, 1844: Maurice Allem, *Alfred de Musset*, 1947, p. 209.
6. It was Sainte-Beuve who described how Delacroix was discovered, on one occasion, copying a Gavarni in his studio. The story occurs in the first of Sainte-Beuve's *Gavarni* articles, of October 12th, 1863, which was followed by others on October 19th and 26th: *Nouveaux Lundis* (1906 ed.), vol. 6, pp. 138–212.
7. *Quelques caricaturistes français:* Baudelaire, *Œuvres*, Pléiade, 1951, vol. 2, p. 199.
8. Gavarni's *Journal intime*, quoted by the Goncourts, *Gavarni: l'homme et l'œuvre* (1868), 1879, pp. 68, 74.
9. Amaury-Duval, *L'Atelier d'Ingres: souvenirs*, 1878, p. 74.
10. Silvestre, *Les Artistes français*, vol. 2, p. 21.
11. From the English edition, *Pictures of the French*, 1841, p. 15.
12. *Ibid.*, *loc. cit.*
13. *Œuvres complètes*, 1860–1861, *Lettres parisiennes*, I, p. 240.

VII: ATTIC NIGHTS

1. M. Boisson, *Les Compagnons de la Vie de Bohème*, 1929, p. 17.
2. *L'Artiste*, vol. XL, p. 105. The pictures of Bonvin and Chaplin are here referred to.
3. Privat d'Anglemont, *Paris anecdote*, 1875, pp. 194–6.
4. *Ibid.*, p. 191.
5. *Ibid.*, pp. 191, 192.
6. P. de Kock (*et al.*), *La Grande Ville: nouveau tableau de Paris*, 1844, vol. 1, p. 340.

7. *Souvenirs littéraires*, 1882, vol. 1, pp. 345, 346.
8. J. Claretie, *Peintres et sculpteurs*, 1882, p. 31.
9. *Ibid.*, p. 42.
10. Cited by Nadar, *Journal pour rire*, April 23rd, 1852.
11. E. Moreau-Nélaton, *Bonvin raconté par lui-même*, 1927, p. 19.
12. *Corsaire*, April 29th and May 10th, 1846.
13. Champfleury, *Souvenirs et portraits de jeunesse*, 1872, p. 83.
14. A. de Fizelière, *La Vie et l'œuvre de Chintreuil*, 1874, p. xiv.
15. *Ibid.*, p. xxi.
16. Ch. de R. d'Héricault, *Murger et son coin*, 1896, p. 19.
17. In *Les Nuits d'hiver, poésies complètes, suivies d'études sur H.M. par MM. J. Janin, Th. Gautier, P.-A. Fiorentino, Arsène Houssaye, P. de Saint-Victor*, 1861, p. 274.
18. D'Héricault, p. 14.
19. Henry Murger, *Scènes de la vie de jeunesse*, 1851, p. 172.
20. *Histoire de Murger pour servir à l'histoire de la vraie Bohème par trois Buveurs d'eau*, 1862 (authors: Lelioux, Noël, and Nadar), p. 126.
21. *Ibid*, pp. 145, 152.
22. *Ibid.*, p. 155.
23. D'Héricault, p. 122.
24. *Histoire de Murger*, pp. 155, 156.
25. Henry Murger, *Le Roman de toutes les femmes*, 1856, containing the *Biographie d'un inconnu* of 1851, p. 244.
26. *Histoire de Murger*, p. 162.
27. *Les Confessions de Sylvius* in *Chien-Caillou*, p. 89.
28. P. Martino, *Le Roman réaliste sous le Second Empire*, 1913, p. 15.
29. *Histoire de Murger*, p. 171.

VIII: THE BOHEMIAN (I)

1. *Les Aventures de Mademoiselle Mariette*, 1853, p. 65.
2. Cf. Léon Beauvallet and Lemercier de Neuville, *Les Femmes de Murger;* Marcel Leconte, *Le doux Murger et les grisettes d'autrefois*; and etc., etc.
3. Henry Murger, *Scènes de la Bohème* (1851), 2nd ed., 1851, pp. 27, 28.
4. A. Karr, *Le Livre de Bord*, 2e série, 1879, p. 126.
5. A. de Fizelière, p. xiv; *Scènes de la Bohème*, p. 46.
6. *S. de la B.*, p. 229.
7. Th. Silvestre, *Les Artistes français*, vol. 2, p. 129.
8. Émile Bouvier, *La Bataille réaliste, 1844–1857*, 1914, p. 14.
9. D'Héricault, p. 29.

10. *Ibid.*, p. 40.
11. *S. de la B.*, pp. 37, 38.
12. A text of the play can be found in the *Bibliothèque dramatique*, 1849, vol. 24.
13. A. Schanne, *Les Souvenirs de Schaunard*, 1886, p. 271.
14. D'Héricault, p. 24.
15. *S. de la B.*, p. 1.
16. *Scènes de la vie de jeunesse* (1851), 1880, p. 173.
17. *Ibid.*, p. 175.
18. *Les Vacances de Camille* (1857), nouv. éd., 1858, p. 26.
19. *Ibid.*, p. 27.
20. E. and J. de Goncourt, *Journal*, 1912, vol. 1, p. 362 (January 18th, 1861).
21. A. Delvau, *H. Murger et la Bohème*, 1866, p. 126.
22. *Ibid.*, *loc. cit.*
23. *Nuits d'hiver*, 1861, p. 282.
24. *Revue fantaisiste*, 1861: *Œuvres*, Pléiade, 1951, vol. 2, p. 568.

IX: THE BOHEMIAN (II)

1. Derôme, p. 173.
2. G. Sand, *La Dernière Aldini* (1838), 1876, p. 6.
3. Th. de Banville, *Petits Études: mes souvenirs*, 1882, pp. 89, 90.
4. Balzac's *Un grand homme de province* is praised on p. 291 of the *S. de la B.*
5. *Un Prince de la Bohème*, Pléiade, vol. 6, pp. 823, 824.
6. René Dumesnil, *L'Époque réaliste et naturaliste*, 1945, p. 33.
7. *Portraits contemporains*, p. 234.
8. P. Martino, p. 287 (*Notes*).
9. Champfleury in the *Silhouette*, July 22nd, 1849.
10. Bouvier, *op. cit.*, p. 237.
11. *Histoire de Murger*, from the long passage beginning p. 249.
12. Reprinted in *Les Fleurs du mal* (1857), 1904, p. 365.
13. A. Zévaès, *Les Procès littéraires au XIXe siècle*, 1924, p. 112.
14. *Ibid.*, p. 129.
15. D'Héricault, p. 116.
16. Silvestre, *Histoire des artistes vivants*, 1856, p. 260.
17. B. Weinberg, *French Realism: the Critical Reaction, 1830–1870*, 1937; and Ch. Léger, *Courbet selon les caricatures et les images*, 1920.
18. From Courbet's own description of his 'Atelier du peintre' (discussed below) printed in full in André Fontainas, *Courbet* (*Art et esthétique*), 1921, pp. 38–40.

19. P.-J. Proudhon, *Du Principe de l'art et de sa destination sociale* (1865): *Œuvres complètes*, 1939, vol. 2, p. 186; vol. 13, p. 134; vol. 13, p. 333 (*La Pornocratie, ou les femmes dans les temps modernes*).
20. Silvestre, *Histoire des artistes vivants*, pp. 268, 269.
21. Jules Troubat, *Une Amitié à la d'Arthez*, 1900, p. 120.
22. Silvestre, *Les Artistes français*, vol. 2, p. 141. The fullest discussion of this picture is to be found in René Huyghe, Germain Bazin, and Hélène Jean Adhémar's *Courbet: L'Atelier du peintre, allégorie réelle, 1855, Monographies des peintures du Musée du Louvre*, 1944.
23. Written in 1873 (Th. de Banville, *Odes funambulesques*; *Poésies complètes*, 1912, *Commentaire*, pp. 224, 225).

X: ANTI-BOHEMIAN

1. *Le Messager des Théâtres*, April 12.
2. E. Bouvier, p. 263.
3. Th. de Banville, *Mes Souvenirs*, p. 71.
4. Baudelaire, *Œuvres*, Pléiade, vol. 2, p. 572.
5. *Les Martyrs ridicules*, 1862, p. 251.
6. Baudelaire, *Œuvres*, vol. 2, p. 571.
7. *Mon Cœur mis à nu*; *ibid.*, p. 660.
8. E. Crépet, *Charles Baudelaire, étude biographique*, 1906, p. 353; note by Jules Buisson.
9. *Œuvres*, vol. 2, p. 217.
10. *Le Musée classique*, *Œuvres*, vol. 2, p. 61.
11. *Salon de 1845*, *ibid.*, pp. 17, 18.
12. *L'Œuvre et la vie de Delacroix*, *ibid.*, vol. 2, p. 313.
13. *Ibid.*, p. 298.
14. *Ibid.*, p. 299.
15. *Salon de 1846*, *Œuvres*, vol. 2, p. 76.
16. *Œuvres*, vol. 2, p. 312.
17. *Ibid.*, p. 230.
18. *Les Artistes français*, vol. 2, p. 37.
19. H. Taine, *Notes sur Paris: vie et opinions de M. Frédéric-Thomas Graindorge*, 1867; ch. 19, 'Les Artistes'.
20. F. Fosca, *Edmond et Jules de Goncourt*, 1941, p. 100.
21. *Ibid.*, p. 103.
22. *Manette Salomon* (1867), 1915, p. 18.
23. F.-E. Picot, 1786–1868, winner of two 'seconds' in the Prix de Rome and elected to the Institut in 1856.
24. *Manette Salomon*, pp. 122, 123.

25. *Ibid.*, p. 231.
26. *Les Odeurs de Paris* (1867), *Œuvres*, 1924–1940, vol. 11, pp. 85, 86.
27. G. Guillemot, *La Bohème* (*Physionomies parisiennes*), 1868, p. 19.
28. Th. Silvestre, *Les Artistes français*, vol. 1, p. 194; vol. 2, p. 118.
29. H. Taine, *op. cit.*, p. 293.

CONCLUSION

1. M. Du Camp, *Souvenirs littéraires*, vol. 2, p. 294.
2. *A. de Musset*, *Correspondance* (*1827–1857*), ed. L. Séché, 1907, p. 25.
3. A. de Musset, *Exposition du Luxembourg au profit des blessés*: *Le Temps*, October 27th, 1830.
4. Th. Silvestre, *Les Artistes français*, vol. 2, pp. 23, 24.
5. *Ibid.*, p. 18.
6. *Ibid.*, p. 11.
7. From the article reprinted in *Fusains et eaux-fortes* (1880), 1907, p. 248.
8. Lecoq de Boisbaudran, *The Training of the Memory in Art and the Education of the Artist*, trans. L. D. Luard, 1914, p. xvi (Luard's *Note on the Author's Life*). The *Éducation de la mémoire pittoresque* first appeared in pamphlet-form in 1848.
9. *Œuvres*, vol. 2, p. 197.
10. *Victor Hugo raconté*, vol. 2, pp. 83, 84.
11. H. d'Alméras, *La Vie parisienne sous le règne de Louis-Philippe*, p. 481.
12. Juliette Adam, *Mes Sentiments et nos idées avant 1870*, 1905, p. 285.
13. *Journal*, vol. 1, p. 366.
14. E. and J. de Goncourt, *Charles Demailly* (1860), 1876, p. 131.
15. In the *Flots du Pactole*.
16. Louvre. The group consists of Cordier, Legros, Whistler, Manet, Bracquemond, Balleroy, Duranty, the artist, Champfleury, and Baudelaire.
17. Louvre. The group which includes Bazille, Renoir, and Manet, etc.
18. National Museum, Stockholm.
19. *Scènes de la Bohème*, *Préface*, p. ix.
20. *Les Mystères de Paris*, 1842–1843. See also Norah Atkinson, *Eugène Sue et le roman-feuilleton*, 1929.
21. P. Mac Orlan, *Montmartre: souvenirs*, Brussels, 1946, p. 117.

Select Bibliography

Amaury-Duval, Eugène, *L'Atelier d'Ingres: souvenirs*, 1878.

Balzac, H. de, *La Comédie humaine* (Pléiade), repr. 1955–1959: *La Maison du chat qui pelote* (1830); *Le Chef-d'œuvre inconnu* (1831); *Pierre Grassou* (1840); *Un Prince de la Bohème* (1840); *Les Parents pauvres: La Cousine Bette* (1846); *Les Comédiens sans le savoir* (1846).

Banville, Th. de, *Petits Études: mes souvenirs*, 1882.

Baudelaire, Charles, *Œuvres* (Pléiade), 1951, vol. 2: *Salon de 1846*; *Quelques caricaturistes français* (1857); *Salon de 1859*; *L'Œuvre et la vie de Delacroix* (1863); *Eugène Delacroix, ses œuvres, ses idées, ses mœurs* (1864); *Le Peintre de la vie moderne* (1860); *Les Martyrs ridicules* (1861). *Les Fleurs du mal* (1857), with pref. by Th. Gautier, 1940.

Benoît, F., *L'Art français sous la Révolution et l'Empire*, 1897.

Berger, K., *Géricault und sein Werk*, Vienna, 1952.

Bouvier, E., *La Bataille réaliste, 1844–1857*, 1914.

Burty, P., *Lettres de Eugène Delacroix*, 1880.

Cassagne, A., *La Théorie de l'art pour l'art en France chez les derniers romantiques et les premiers réalistes*, 1906.

Castex, P., *Le Conte fantastique en France de Nodier à Maupassant*, 1951.

Champfleury, *Chien-Caillou* (1847) in the 1860 collection of stories so entitled, containing *Les Confessions de Sylvius* (1849); *Les Excentriques* (1852), 1856; *Contes de Printemps. Les Aventures de Mademoiselle Mariette*, 1853; *Le Réalisme*, 1857.

Cladel, L., *Les Martyrs ridicules*, 1862.

Claretie, J., *Peintres et sculpteurs*, 1862.

David, J.-L. Jules, *Le Peintre Louis David, 1880*.

Delacroix, Eugène, *Œuvres littéraires*, 1923; *Journal*, ed. Joubin, 1932.

Delécluze, E., *Louis David, son école et son temps*, 1855.

Derôme, J., *Les Éditions originales des Romantiques, Ire partie*, 1887.

Diderot, Denis, *Œuvres complètes*, ed. J. Assézat and M. Tourneux, 1875–77: *Regrets sur ma vieille robe de chambre* (1772); *Salon de 1761*; *Salon de 1765* (1795); *Pensées détachées sur la peinture* (1798); *Lettres à Falconet*, 1766–1773. *Inventaire du Fonds Vandeul et inédits de Diderot*, ed. H. Dieckmann, Geneva and Lille, 1951.

Dimier, L., *Les Peintres français du XVIIIe siècle*, 1930.
Dumesnil, R., *L'Époque réaliste et naturaliste*, 1945.
Escholier, R., *Delacroix, peintre, graveur, écrivain*, 1926.
Estève, E., *Byron et le Romantisme français*, 1907.
Fizelière, A. de, *La Vie et l'œuvre de Chintreuil*, 1874.
Fosca, F., *Edmond et Jules de Goncourt*, 1941.
France, Anatole, *Jocaste* et *Le Chat maigre*, 1879.
Friedlaender, W., *David to Delacroix*, transl. R. Goldwater, Havard, 1952.
Gautier, Théophile, in the Bib. Charpentier (Fasquelle), *Les Jeunes-France* (1833), n.d.; *Histoire du Romantisme* (1874), 1911; *Portraits contemporains* (1874), 1914; *Portraits et souvenirs littéraires*, n.d.; *Fusains et eaux-fortes* (1880), 1907: contains *L'Atelier de M. Ingres en 1848*. In other editions: *Poésies complètes* (for *Albertus*, 1832), ed. Jasinski, 1932; *La Préface de Mademoiselle de Maupin*, ed. Matoré, 1946.
Gérard de Nerval, *Petits Châteaux de Bohème. La Bohème galante*, ed. Marsan, 1926.
Gigoux, J., *Causeries sur les artistes de mon temps*, 1885.
Goethe, J. W. von, *Gedenkausgabe der Werke, Briefe und Gespräche*, ed. E. Beutler, Zurich, 1948– . Vol. IV: *Der junge Goethe*, containing *Die Leiden des jungen Werthers* (1774).
Goncourt, E., and J. de, *L'Art du XVIIIe siècle* (1860–1870), 1909; *Charles Demailly* (1860), 1876; *Manette Salomon* (1867), 1915; *Gavarni: l'homme et l'œuvre* (1868), 1879; *Journal* (1887–1896), 1912.
Hautecœur, L., *Histoire de l'architecture classique en France*, 1945– ; vol. V: *Révolution et Empire, 1792–1815*, 1953.
Histoire de Murger pour servir à l'histoire de la vraie Bohème par trois Buveurs d'eau [Lelioux, Nadar, Noél], 1862.
Hugo, Victor, *Œuvres complètes*, Hetzel-Quantin, n.d. (1880–1889): *Odes et Ballades* (1826); *Cromwell* (1827); *Les Orientales* (1829); *Hernani* (1830); *Notre-Dame de Paris* (1831); [Adèle Hugo] *Victor Hugo raconté par un témoin de sa vie* (1863).
Hunt, H. J., *Balzac's Comédie humaine*, 1959.
Huyghe, R., Bazin, G., and Adhémar, H. J., *Courbet: L'Atelier du peintre, allégorie réelle, 1855. Monographies des peintures du Musée du Louvre*, 1944.
Jasinski, R., *Les Années romantiques de Théophile Gautier*, 1929.
Jouin, H., *David d'Angers et ses relations littéraires*, 1890.
Lardanchet, H., *Les Enfants perdus du Romantisme*, 1905.
Locquin, J., *La Peinture d'histoire en France de 1747 à 1785*, 1912.
Luc-Benoist, *La Sculpture romantique*, 1928.
Marie, A., *Célestin Nanteuil (La Vie et l'Art Romantiques)*, 1924.

Martino, P., *Le Roman réaliste sous le Second Empire*, 1913.

Meyerstein, H., *A Life of Thomas Chatterton*, 1930.

Monnier, Henry, *Scènes populaires* (1830), 1846; *Mémoires de Monsieur Joseph Prudhomme* (1857), 1892.

Murger, Henry, *La Vie de Bohème* (with Barrière), 1849; *Scènes de la Bohème*, 1851; *Scènes de la vie de jeunesse* (1851), 1880; *Le Roman de toutes les femmes*, containing the *Biographie d'un inconnu*, of 1851 (1856), 1887. *Les Nuits d'hiver*, 1861.

Musset, Alfred de, *Œuvres complètes* (Charpentier), 1897–1900: *Mélanges de littérature et de critique*, containing *Un Mot sur l'art moderne* (1833) and the *Salon de 1836*. *Œuvres complètes* (Garnier), n.d. (1907–1909): vol. V, *Nouvelles*, containing *Les Deux Maîtresses* (1837), *Le Fils du Titien* (1838), and *Frédéric et Bernerette* (1838); vol. VI, *Contes*, containing *Mimi Pinson* (1845) and *Lettres de Dupuis et Cotonet au Directeur de la 'Revue des Deux-Mondes'* (1836–1837).

Nettement, A., *Poètes et artistes contemporains*, 1862.

Nodier, Charles, *Nouvelles*, containing *Les Proscrits* of 1802, 1840; *Romans*, containing *Le Peintre de Salzburg* of 1803, 1841; *Essais d'un jeune barde*, 1804.

Novotny, F., *Painting and Sculpture in Europe, 1780–1880*, 1960.

Pingaud, L., *La Jeunesse de Charles Nodier: les Philadelphes*, 1919.

Planche, G., *Étude sur l'école française*, 1855.

Prost, B., *Octave Tassaert: notice sur sa vie, Gazette des Beaux-Arts*, vol. XXXIII, 1885. *Félix Trutat, 1824–48, Gazette des Beaux-Arts*, vol. XLI, 1899.

Restif de la Bretonne, Nicolas, *L'Œuvre*, ed. H. Bachelin, 1930–1932.

Rosenthal, L., *La Peinture romantique*, 1903.

Sainte-Beuve, Charles-Auguste, *Œuvres* (Pléiade), 1949–1951: *Hoffmann* (1829) in *Portraits littéraires*; in another ed., *Nouveaux Lundis*, articles on *Gavarni* (1863), 1906.

Sand, George, *La Dernière Aldini* (1838), 1876.

Séché, L., *Le Cénacle de Joseph Delorme*, 1827–1830, 1912; vol. II: *Victor Hugo et les artistes*.

Silvestre, Th., *Histoires des artistes vivants*, 1856; *Les Artistes français*, 1926, vol. I: *Romantiques*, containing studies of Delacroix, Rude, Barye, Decamps, Diaz, Préault, Th. Rousseau, and Millet; vol. II: *Éclectiques et Réalistes*, containing studies of Ingres, H. Vernet, Corot, Chenavard, Couture, and Courbet.

Stevenson, Norah, *Paris dans la Comédie humaine*, 1938.

Sue, Eugène, *Les Mystères de Paris* (1842–1843), 1879.

Taine, H., *Notes sur Paris: vie et opinions de M. Frédéric-Thomas Graindorge*, 1867.

Thoré, Th. (W. Bürger), *Salons, 1844–1848*, with pref. by W. Bürger, 1868.

Vigny, Alfred de, *Œuvres complètes*, ed. F. Baldensperger, 1914–1935: *Stello* (1832); *Chatterton* (1835); *Le Journal d'un poète* (1867).

Wildenstein, G., *The Paintings of J.-A.-D. Ingres*, 1954.

Winckelmann, J. J., *Geschichte der Kunst des Altertums*, Vienna, 1934.

Zévaès, A., *Les Procès littéraires au XIXe siècle*, 1924.

Index

Date Due

FEB 15 '72		MAY 05 '93			
JAN 28 '72	JUN 22 '82	MAY 5 '93			
		MAY 09 2002			
APR 27 1978	JUN 22 1982				
	DEC 17 1982				
APR 20 '78					
MAR 20 1980					
FEB 20 '80	OCT 04 1982				
	OCT 05 1982				
NOV 04 1981					
OCT 9 '81					
JUN 08 1982					

PRINTED IN U.S.A. CAT. NO. 23231